From Imperial Myth to Democracy

From Imperial Myth to Democracy

Japan's Two Constitutions, 1889–2002

Lawrence W. Beer and John M. Maki

To Bob and Sue:
What generation gap?
Jack
2/15/03

University Press of Colorado

Published by the University Press of Colorado
5589 Arapahoe Avenue, Suite 206C
Boulder, Colorado 80303

The University Press of Colorado is a cooperative publishing enterprise supported, in part, by Adams State College, Colorado State University, Fort Lewis College, Mesa State College, Metropolitan State College of Denver, University of Colorado, University of Northern Colorado, University of Southern Colorado, and Western State College of Colorado.

The paper used in this publication meets the minimum requirements of the American National Standard for Information Sciences—Permanence of Paper for Printed Library Materials. ANSI Z39.48-1992

Library of Congress Cataloging-in-Publication Data

Beer, Lawrence Ward, 1932–
  From imperial myth to democracy : Japan's two constitutions, 1889–2001 / Lawrence W. Beer & John M. Maki.
     p. cm.
Includes bibliographical references and index.
   ISBN 0-87081-674-8 (Hardcover : alk. paper) — ISBN 0-87081-686-1 (pbk : alk. paper)
   1. Constitutional history—Japan. 2. Japan—Politics and government—20th century. 3. Japan. Kempo (1889) 4. Japan. Kempo (1946) I. Maki, John M. (John McGilvrey), 1909– II. Title.
   KNX2101 .B44 2002
   342.52'029—dc21

                                                                                        2002005403

Design by Daniel Pratt

11 10 09 08 07 06 05 04 03 02   10 9 8 7 6 5 4 3 2 1

To those Japanese and Americans
who laid the constitutional foundation for Japan's democracy

Contents

Preface

A multitude of books about Japan's modern history have been written in Japanese and other languages, and many works have focused on the Allied Occupation of Japan (1945–1952). Others have focused on some aspect of Japan's subsequent postwar political, economic, or social development. Although studies of Japanese law have enjoyed remarkable growth in the past half century compared with studies of any other non-Western legal system, the broad sweep of Japan's constitutional history from the Tokugawa period to the present has been neglected, and the confluence of law, constitution, and society in myriad day-to-day contexts since 1947 awaits thorough study. This book sketches out that terrain. The dates in the title refer to the year of promulgation of the Meiji Constitution, 1889, to the year 2002, in which the 1947 Constitution continued to live in Japan's law and society.

To the great benefit of the United States, since 1945 Japan has become its ally and most important overseas trade partner. Japan ranks second in the world in economic and technological power, and in many other categories of human endeavor Japan's performance has also been impressive. A succession of U.S. presidents has publicly stated that the U.S. relationship with Japan is the cornerstone of U.S. policies in Asia. Ambassador Mike Mansfield went further, claiming, with others, that the

U.S.-Japan relationship is the world's most important bilateral relationship. Many Americans may have wondered what such statements meant. Some may have concluded that the presidents had in mind the terrific cars and electronics Japanese companies produce for the U.S. market or the fact that Japan has been a relatively quiet, orderly, and peaceful place. Since 1945, Japan has not complicated U.S. life in Asia as have Afghanistan, China, the Korean peninsula, and Vietnam. Japan has been an immensely helpful creditor nation as the U.S. national debt soared. And the presidents might also have been thinking of all the vibrant sister-city relationships, joint ventures, and student exchanges.

For Japan, only two relationships are considered critical: that with the United States under the 1960 U.S.-Japan Security Treaty, as explained herein, and that with the United Nations. The United Nations plays a larger role in Japanese foreign policy and human rights thinking than it does in U.S. policy. But at the core of the U.S. relationship with Japan is a shared commitment to principles of constitutional democracy. The two social cultures may be radically different in some respects, although often these differences have been exaggerated. A large majority of Japanese and Americans agree on such foundational principles as popular sovereignty, limited and divided government power under law, and protection of human rights.

Over the past half century the United States and other countries in the West and in Asia have developed a small but able corps of Japan specialists in a wide range of academic disciplines to complement Japan's group of U.S. specialists. Most U.S. Japanologists have not been politically active or highly visible, although Japan historians won Pulitzer Prizes in 1999 and 2000. Most Japanologists have worked quietly to create a solid basis of knowledge concerning Japan's art, philosophy, social culture, law, history, economics, and politics.

Over time, however, splits have developed within the Japanese studies community. For example, some authors stress the importance of understanding Japan's social culture and social values, whereas others tend to downplay the relevance of such factors to an understanding of, say, economic performance. In judging a country's economy and assessing data regarding other issue areas, a middle ground seems best, but some do not refrain from caricature.

Another problem is the division between Japan's admirers and its "bashers," the "Japanophiles" and the critical "revisionists." Japan has an unusual number of both, which does not serve well U.S. dialogue on Japan. With respect to Japanese constitutional law and politics, as well as related foreign policy, influential bashers have colored public discourse on Japan in the United States.

In this book we set forth a perspective that finds much to admire in the performance since 1945 of both the constitutional system and the people of Japan but also finds, as in the performance of the United States, noteworthy defects. Our primary focus is on neither the strongest points nor the defects but on describing and explaining the human and legal complexities of constitutional realities in Japan. We also give limited attention to comparisons with other constitutional systems, in particular that of the United States. We hope this approach continues to place us in the mainstream of Japanese studies. We are aware of the need for caution in allocating positive and negative judgments regarding the records of our own and other countries. In his useful analysis of Japanese studies, Duncan McCargo says, "If the mainstream perspective sometimes fails to see the darker side of Japan, the revisionist perspective often concentrates on little else" (*Contemporary Japan* [New York: St. Martin's, 2000], p. 3). Relatively few revisionists have appreciable familiarity with Japanese legal and constitutional studies, and this may affect judgments on such seminal issues as human rights and pacifism in Japan.

This is a collaborative work of two friends from the Pacific Northwest long interested in Japan's two modern constitutions. The authors read and discussed each other's writing and shared perspectives on Japan's constitutional law, but John Maki retained final responsibility for Part I (Chapters 1–3) on the Meiji Constitution and its consequences (1889–1946), and Lawrence Beer is responsible for Part II (Chapters 4–7) on the Showa Constitution and its origins (1946–2002). Their styles differ, but the content flows as intended. The Prologue and the final chapter were written jointly. This book is truly a joint venture.

The authors wish to thank Bill Hosokawa, leading historian of Japanese Americans and past Honorary Consul of Japan in Denver, for encouraging us to write this book. We also thank the many Japanese constitutional lawyers who over the decades have shared with us their knowledge, professional judgments, and friendship. For their comments and suggestions, we are also grateful to Walter F. Murphy (Princeton University), Alan Kimball (University of Oregon), and the two anonymous Japan specialists who reviewed the manuscript for the University Press of Colorado.

As our prior publications indicate, we recognize the duty of scholars to provide professional colleagues with ample footnotes in their technical writings, but this is a book of modest length intended for a general readership. We believe our readers will be best served not by footnotes but by brief bibliographical notes for those interested in further reading on a topic touched on in the text. Macrons over vowels have not been used because they are meaningless to all but Japan specialists.

In Japan and in our text, Japanese personal names are presented in the East Asian word order, surname followed by given name. In English-language publications of Japanese authors, sometimes the family name is given first, and other times the given name comes first. With no consistent custom, in our bibliographical notes we present the authors' names as they appear in the work cited.

Prologue

PROBLEM AND APPROACH

In the century and a third between roughly 1870 and 2000, Japan experienced the most turbulent period in the thirteen centuries of its recorded history. During that period—brief as historical time is measured—Japan witnessed the simultaneous collapse of two and a half centuries of the rule of the Tokugawa family and the seven centuries of the country's feudal system; the transformation of the society into a modern nation-state; its development into a militaristic and authoritarian state that became a world military power that eventually suffered a crushing defeat in a major war; and a bloodless revolution conceived by an enlightened policy of its conqueror, which transformed it into a peaceful and democratic society that became a world economic power.

The consequences of these wrenching historical developments were far-reaching. For centuries Japan's limited external relations were dominated by its ties with Asia, especially China; but in the late nineteenth century Japan entered the world stage, where Europe and the United States were the most powerful actors. Its transition into a nation-state was based on the model of the nation-state that had developed in the Western world. Its militarism led to a temporary domination of East and Southeast Asia and to a vanquished collapse caused by a basically non-Asian coalition led by the United States. As a result, Japan became Asia's first stable democracy. Although feudal lords allowed many farm and fishing villages a good measure of autonomy and consensual rule, constitutional democracy was a form of political and governmental organization heretofore alien to both Japan and the rest of Asia. Japan also went from an agricultural society to an industrialized world economic power. Its people experienced a happy transformation from poverty to an undreamed-of level of economic well-being.

Historians and many other observers, both Japanese and others, have been fascinated by the unfolding of the Japanese experience. How did this isolated Asian society transform itself in 130 years into a major democratic actor in world affairs? The most common analyses and explanations have involved modernization and development, political, economic, legal, and social factors.

The authors of this book take an alternative approach to explication of Japan's earlier modern and present experience. They focus on the development of Japan's two modern constitutions—the Constitution of the Empire of Japan (1890) and the Constitution of Japan (1947)—and on Japan's performance under the laws, institutions, norms, and processes established and legitimized under these constitutions in the past and in 2002. The constitutional development of Japan is mirrored in its domestic and international law, politics, economic life, and society.

A CONSTITUTION AND CONSTITUTIONALISM

This book is about two constitutions, the rise and demise of one and the creation and current status of the other; so a word about the meanings of *constitution* and *constitutionalism* is in order. Americans tend to equate *constitution* with a single national (or state) document that constitutes the polity's most basic law, a law that sets forth the fundamental principles and organization of the government in such a way that it divides and limits governmental power and assures citizen rights and freedoms. They are also inclined to think the U.S. Declaration of Independence has an important kind of constitutional status. This is understandable since that Declaration, along with Abraham Lincoln's Gettysburg Address, are the inspirational statements of U.S. principle most deeply respected around the world.

In the tradition of judicial review, courts tell us what the U.S. Constitution means in deciding concrete legal disputes. They interpret the Constitution according to the wording of the text, precedents, related statutory law, their own legal and political theories, and their assessment of societal needs. Japan's judges now do much the same thing but out of a different history.

The single-document national constitution—an institution invented by the United States in its early years—has been adopted by almost all modern nation-states as an essential, respectable, and useful part of their legal and governmental systems. Now law leaders and scholars around the world can communicate with each other about constitutions in terms mutually understood to an unprecedented degree. That greater possibility for accurate communication on fundamental matters of governance and law is itself an advance in civilization.

Of 188 UN member states, all but a few have single-document constitutions. Notable exceptions are New Zealand, Israel, the United Kingdom (where a combination of laws, principles, customs, and conventions make up the constitution), and three Islamic states—Libya, Oman, and Saudi Arabia—that call the Quran their basic governing document. Most current constitutions were written after World War II when non-Western nations gained independence from colonialist Western powers. Over 130 constitutions have been ratified since 1970.

That said, there is more to a constitution than one document and its official interpretation, as this book attempts to illustrate. And more is required of a nation than a single-document constitution to warrant characterizing it as constitutionalist. Constitutionalism implies division and limitation of government power under law and in furtherance of the central public values of a nation. Not all constitutions restrict power (for example, the emperor's formal power under the Meiji Constitution). Even the most beautifully written constitution does not establish that a state honors its provisions or even takes them as seriously as do Japan and the United States. Moreover, a strong democratic majority may oppose constitutionalist restraints on government power and, as history shows, may support slavery, discrimination, repression, or unequal voting rights; the relationship between constitutionalism and democracy is sometimes tenuous. Yet these limitations need not imply that a written constitution is meaningless within a political and social system.

As we trace Japan's modern constitutional development, it will be helpful to bear several factors in mind.

1. The single-document constitutions of modern Japan are important, but a nation's basic law involves more than that. A working formulation of a constitution might be the principles, institutions, and processes for organizing, exercising, and limiting governmental and community power on behalf of a country's primary public values in a promulgated and reasonably predictable manner. (Currently, human rights and renunciation of war are among Japan's dominant values.)

2. A constitution need not be written down in one document, or in many for that matter, to be effective. For example, what might be called the Tokugawa Constitution, discussed later, was clear and "living" but was not written down in an easily identifiable place or places.

3. Of non-Western nations, Japan has had the longest experience as a modern, independent nation-state, since the beginning of the twentieth century when freed from Western unequal treaties. The exceptions to this independence were the occupation, from 1945 to 1952, and U.S. control of Okinawa until 1972.

4. Japan's 1947 Constitution is not "new," as some have suggested, but by world standards is fairly old, one of the twenty longest in force.

5. Japan is a thoroughly East Asian nation with a distinctive history and social culture, but these factors have not rendered its values incompatible with those of its constitution and UN human rights documents. Quite the contrary.

Perhaps the most momentous twentieth-century advance in civilization was the growth of awareness in diverse world political cultures that each person possesses by nature human rights that should be promoted and protected by law, government, and society—within each country and in international law and politics. This development, more than the welcome revolutions in science, medicine, technology, and consumer conveniences, offset in a small but meaningful way the unparalleled barbarism of that historical period.

In the twenty-first century, what is it about every human being that is so inherently valuable that it rationally justifies and motivates powerful worldwide concern and action on behalf of each person's rights as a human? The answer is neither obvious nor a matter of consensus in the world community. Seeking a balanced consensus may be the foremost task for intellectuals and leaders in the century recently begun. Any satisfactory answer seems to require some persuasive philosophical or theological grounding of belief in, and mutual respect for, each person's great dignity. Japan's constitution unequivocally requires respect for the dignity of each person and for fundamental human rights but is silent on the theoretical basis of that respect. In the nineteenth century an ancient mythology centering on the Sun Goddess and the imperial family provided the indigenous, legitimizing foundation for Japan's first modern constitution.

Part 1

The Constitution
of the Empire of Japan

1

Japan:
New Nation-State
and Its Constitution

THE TOKUGAWA FOUNDATION

The defining development in Japan's modern history is the transformation of its centuries-old feudal society into a nation-state in the second half of the nineteenth century. The transformation was not willed but was brought about by a fortuitous confluence of the collapse of Tokugawa rule, which had controlled Japan for two and a half centuries, and the successful demands of Western nation-states that Japan end its more than two centuries of isolation from the non-Asian world.

Tokugawa rule had given Japan more than two centuries of political and governmental stability that, in turn, had provided an opportunity for considerable economic and social development and change. But at the same time great scientific, technological, economic, and social changes were taking place in Europe and North America that resulted, among a vast array of other things, in the emergence of the modern nation-state. The coming together of these two developments eventually led to the creation of Japan's first written constitution.

The rule of the militarily powerful Tokugawa family extended from the opening decades of the seventeenth century to the mid-nineteenth century. The Tokugawa system was politically stable but not unchanging. Tokugawa society was changing economically and socially, with the inevitable result that the Tokugawa grasp on power was slipping. By about 1850, political challenges, long kept under control, to Tokugawa power were developing. At this juncture the Tokugawas were confronted with an external challenge they were unable to handle.

In 1853 Commodore Matthew Calbraith Perry of the United States, a very young nation-state, appeared in Japanese waters and demanded that Japan end its policy of seclusion, thus concluding the first step in the mission he had been given by U.S. president Millard Fillmore. Perry returned in 1854 and concluded the treaty that ended Japan's isolation from the Western world. Within a few years a group of European nation-states concluded similar unequal treaties with Japan that gave the Western powers legal and economic rights they did not grant to Japan in return.

The emerging opposition denounced the Tokugawa for both betraying the policy of their own ancestors and simultaneously permitting the hated "barbarians" to tread on Japan's sacred soil. Their battle cry became "Revere the Emperor; expel the barbarians!" "Revere the Emperor" was political shorthand for ending Tokugawa control over the throne, which gave their rule legitimacy. The Tokugawas were unable to resist the pressure from their domestic foes. In the late 1860s the Tokugawa regime came to an end with a negotiated agreement under which the Tokugawas would give up their monopoly over government for shared responsibility with their opponents. But the latter, interpreting the Tokugawa concession as a sign of fatal weakness, soon made it clear that there would be no sharing. The Tokugawa resorted to military force to retain some power, but after fighting sporadic and limited battles for several years they gave in.

The collapse of the long-lived regime was momentous, but it was essentially a political act. It was simply the transfer of political power from one segment of the ruling class to another. It was not a civil war or a bloody revolution, either of which would have disrupted society. In the absence of such disruption Japan was in a position to initiate its transition from a feudal to a national society.

The society the Tokugawas left behind was still feudal, but it contained elements that would serve as a firm foundation for a new and vastly different national society. These elements were held in common with the contemporary Western nation-states.

First, there was human mass or population. The population in 1870 was more than 30 million, a figure probably attained by about 1700. In terms of mere numbers this was similar to the larger Western nations at the time, such as the United States. Second, each Western nation was identified with a specific area of the earth's surface, usually referred to as the homeland. Japan's island nature gave it a naturally defined area of its own. Historically, no wars had been waged over territorial boundaries. Moreover, Japan's people were ethnically unified. Here again the country's island nature played an important role. There were no successful foreign invasions, no large waves of immigration, and relatively few indigenous Ainu.

By the late nineteenth century Japan had twelve centuries of recorded history as an ethnically separate people. Intimately woven into that history was society's high culture, created and conserved in its earlier centuries by the imperial court and later by the dominant warrior class. Poetry, prose, calligraphy and its closely allied arts, ceramics, painting, and drama constituted an enduring heritage, thereby strengthening ethnic unity.

Another invaluable characteristic of the population at the end of the Tokugawa period was a high rate of literacy, estimated to have been about 50 percent, which compared favorably with the rate of Western nations. The samurai and the imperial court nobles had schools. For commoners, schools were held in Buddhist temples (*tera koya*) to create the widespread literacy required for the smooth operation of the complex Tokugawa society. Such things as a flourishing publishing industry for popular literature and family and village records were marks of a literate society. The existing literacy rate simplified the task of training the population to acquire new ideas and technological skills and to carry out the new and innovative tasks required by nation building.

Of fundamental importance to nation building was leadership. In Japan's long history there are few charismatic leaders. The triumvirate of Oda Nobunaga, Toyotomi Hideyoshi, and Tokugawa Ieyasu—who followed each other as leaders in the late sixteenth and early seventeenth centuries—constitutes perhaps the most outstanding examples. The work of Nobunaga and Hideyoshi opened the way for Ieyasu to found the regime. But that regime was not kept in power by a succession of strong individuals. Rather, it was the political astuteness and administrative skills of a self-perpetuating body of men who operated the system.

In the crunch of the Tokugawa collapse, a group of able leaders of the anti-Tokugawa opposition not only emerged victorious but remained in position to direct successfully the early decades of the drive to nationhood. They enjoyed the enormous advantage of presiding over a society that, although feudal, was evolving invisibly toward nationhood. We have seen how the human element of the society was developing toward nationhood. Now we examine Tokugawa political, economic, and social institutions that would play vital roles in the creation of the new national society.

Of prime importance to nation building was Japan's two and a half centuries of stable government that controlled both the territory and the people. When the Tokugawa government disappeared, there was no need to create the concept or machinery of a central government. But a problem remained: how to convert an existing but outmoded feudal structure of government to a modern bureaucracy equal to the task of operating the emerging nation. As has been indicated, no bitter and bloody political struggle to control the new government took place. Thus in both government and politics Japan escaped the major difficulties that confronted nation-building efforts in the nineteenth and twentieth centuries.

Throughout the Tokugawa period Japan's economy was basically agrarian based on the principal crop—rice—which was not only the basis of the economy but also the foundation of political power. The several branches of the Tokugawa family controlled about a quarter of the land and consequently a quarter of the rice yield. The feudal lords' economic base was also rice. Status and its twin, power, were determined by the size of estates and the consequent yield of rice. The Tokugawa government retained the power to control the size of the lords' estates and the yields of rice.

Although the basis of the economy remained agrarian, it was not static. It was characterized by a broad development of commerce accompanied by steady growth in the use of money. This development, however, was controlled by the merchant class, which ranked at the bottom of the social scale and had no political power.

Well before the end of the Tokugawa period the country was operating under a society-wide economic system. Rice was produced by peasants throughout the land, the peasants were controlled by their feudal lords, and rice was priced and distributed under a society-wide system. Commerce was monopolized by merchants who developed goods for distribution throughout the country. They were also instrumental in developing and operating the emerging monetary system.

Light industry (with the use of human-powered machinery) was focused on the production of consumer goods and was dependent on the labor of artisans who ranked just above merchants on the social scale. The merchant class provided the capital and management for light industry. The artisans' skill and discipline were later duplicated by workers in industrial Japan.

Another manifestation of the economic change was the growth of cities and towns. Tokugawa Japan had three major cities. Edo (renamed Tokyo in 1868) was a small village when the Tokugawas came to power and was transformed into the seat of the Tokugawa administration—where all the feudal lords had to establish residence—a major center of economic activity, and the scene of a flourishing popular culture with a population estimated at about a million by the mid-eighteenth century. Osaka had a parallel development as the country's economic hub. Kyoto had been the imperial capital since the eighth century; it remained at the center of the country's high culture yet out of the main current of Tokugawa society.

Economic change also produced the phenomenon of "castle towns." Each feudal lord had a castle as his residence and headquarters. Because these castles were the centers of control and administration, they also became economic centers. The three major cities and the castle towns served as key areas of social change as the modernization process developed in the second half of the nineteenth century.

Another product of economic change was a network of "highways," a nationwide system of heavily traveled roads for humans and their pack animals. These roads foreshadowed a modern system of land transportation.

The highway system was closely linked to the *sankin kotai* (alternate residence) system that was a key device in the Tokugawa structure of control over the feudal lords. Briefly, each of the approximately 250 feudal lords was required to maintain in Edo a mansion befitting his rank in the feudal order, to travel to it from his domain—usually annually—for a stay of about six months, and on his return to his domain to leave members of his family behind as hostages. This system kept the lords under the eye of the Tokugawa government and drained the lords' finances. All lords were required to travel with a retinue befitting their rank.

In addition to its political utility, the system played an important economic and social role. The processions were large, and those from distant domains were on the road for some time. Thus logistical requirements such as provisions and campsites stimulated local economies along the way. The annual travel involved thousands of individuals, creating what might be termed a primitive domestic tourist industry.

Apart from the *sankin kotai* system, Tokugawa authorities exerted strict control over unofficial travel of individuals by means of travel permits and barriers or checkpoints established at regular intervals on the highways where the permits had to be produced for inspection. In one notable exception, large numbers of commoners were permitted to make pilgrimages to famous temples and shrines. Over two and a half centuries, travel—both official and unofficial—had the unplanned effect of creating a wide feeling of ethnic identity and identification with the homeland, two primary requirements for the establishment of a nation-state.

The Tokugawas came to power early in the seventeenth century through the exercise of military strength, their own and that of their associated feudal lords; but after roughly two decades the Tokugawa regime never again had to use military might to fight off contenders for power. The regime's military strength was the source of its political power, but the sword was kept in its scabbard for more than two centuries.

Tokugawa power was durable because it rapidly became institutionalized. If a constitution constitutes the basic principles by which a society is organized and governed, then Tokugawa rule was based on a constitution. It was not set forth in a single formal written document. It was uncodified but was embodied in a complex arrangement of institutions, edicts, practices, and beliefs that grew over decades and was unplanned except for its central aim: the unchallenged maintenance of Tokugawa power. It was not a social or a political contract. It served the purposes of a single class of the society—the warriors—and the most powerful warrior family, the Tokugawas.

This unwritten constitution endured because by manifesting the basic principles and practices of the society, it was a faithful reflection of the society itself; as the expression of the society and its arrangement of political power at the time, it was dealing with the society's economic and social requirements. If the Tokugawa authorities had ever produced a written constitution, the principal topics would have included:

1. The emperor: the locus of sovereignty, that is, the supreme authority to bestow the right to rule on the head of the Tokugawa family; his geographical isolation in Kyoto; his exclusion from politics and government

2. The Tokugawa shogun: the recipient from the emperor of the right to rule the country from Edo and possessor of the exclusive Tokugawa hereditary right to the office

3. The Bakufu: the bureaucracy for the Tokugawa ruling the country and governing the family and its affairs

4. The daimyo: approximately 250 feudal lords subject to Tokugawa authority and control; their division into two categories, those traditionally allied with the Tokugawa family before it came to power and the "outside lords" who might (and some did) become challengers for power; vested with control over and responsibility for the administration of their estates and the *sankin kotai* system

5. The classes (in descending rank order): warriors with the exclusive right to possess weapons and with a monopoly on government and politics; peasants as the producers of rice, the basis of the economy, but with no political role and bound to the feudal domains; artisans as producers of consumer goods but without political power or

influence; and merchants with increasing economic significance but also politically powerless; clear distinction and separation of the classes

6. The Seclusion Policy: prohibition on Japanese leaving the country for any reason; prohibition against westerners entering the country, except for a handful of rigidly controlled Dutch; limited contact with neighboring China and Korea; an absolute ban on Christianity and its missionaries; and finally, imposition of the death penalty for any discovered Japanese converts

The first five points deal with the three basic issues of any modern written constitution: the locus of sovereignty (point 1), the structure of government (points 2, 3, and 4), and the relationship between the governing and the governed (point 5).

Because it was an expression of the Tokugawa system, the unwritten constitution was destined to disappear with the collapse of the Tokugawa and their system. But it had performed a useful function. As its society's fundamental law, it paved the way for the concrete written constitution that was necessary for the new society of the emergent Japanese nation-state.

The society the Tokugawa regime left behind could still be described as feudal, but lurking just below the surface was what could be termed a proto-nation-state, one that possessed in nascent form the basic elements of a national society, as has been described, but that lacked the infrastructure of a functioning one.

DAWN OF THE NATION-STATE

When Japan's new leaders came to power, they were confronted with a task the complexity of which was matched by the simplicity with which it could be stated: to build into their society an infrastructure similar to that of the Western nation-states. The principal elements of such an infrastructure were a modern bureaucratic centralized government, a national army and navy, contemporary technology and industry (including railroads, heavy and light industries using machine power, the high-speed printing press, the telegraph, and soon the telephone), the introduction of modern science as the foundation of technology, a new system of public and private finance, and a system of education designed both to create mass literacy and to train personnel to manage and operate all elements of the new infrastructure.

The Tokugawa heritage included none of these elements, but it did provide the necessary foundation on which the infrastructure could be built. The aim here is simply to state the problem, not to describe in detail its solution.

Within a few weeks after coming to power, the new leaders revealed the road they had in mind for their society. Their plan was set forth in the Imperial Oath of Five Articles, less formally known as the Charter Oath. It was issued in the name of the nineteen-year-old Meiji Emperor, whose personal name was Mutsuhito. The oath had been drafted by relatively low-ranking members of the new leadership but was based on the views of their superiors.

The oath was too general to be a master plan, but events demonstrated that Japan was under the control of leaders who understood that power alone was not enough; the government and its nation had to be built on a broad program. Its five articles were brief:

> An assembly shall be widely convoked, and all measures shall be decided by open discussion.
>
> High and low shall be of one mind, and the national economy and finances shall be greatly strengthened.
>
> Civil and military officials together, and the common people as well, shall all achieve their aspirations, and thus the people's minds shall not be made weary.
>
> Evil practices of the past shall be abandoned, and actions shall be based on world justice.
>
> Knowledge shall be sought all over the world, and the foundations of imperial rule shall be strengthened.

The first article contained the hint of a constitution. A "widely convoked assembly" and "open discussion in deciding all matters" were concepts new and foreign in Japanese government and politics. They would have to be based on a written constitution, also something new and foreign.

The abandonment of "evil practices of the past," the strengthening of "the national economy and finances," the recognition of civil officials and the common people, the seeking of knowledge "all over the world," and the strengthening of "the foundations of imperial rule" were critical problems confronting the society as it began its transition to a nation-state. The search for knowledge all over the world was vitally important because it was the means by which Japan could create the infrastructure of a nation-state, the only models of which were in the West.

The new leaders adopted a simple and highly effective program for acquiring the requisite knowledge. First, the Japanese, from political leaders to students, went to the Western world to observe and learn. Second, the new government employed a wide range of foreign experts and technicians to introduce what was modern and to train the Japanese in its use.

The strengthening of the imperial rule was an almost casual reference to the central political concern of the anti-Tokugawa leaders. It marked the realization of the "Revere the Emperor" slogan and foreshadowed the imperial sovereignty of the constitution that would be promulgated two decades later.

About six months after the Charter Oath was issued, the *Seitaisho* was proclaimed. It has been referred to as a constitution, but the three characters that make up the term could be rendered as "Document on the System of Government," which is both a literal translation of the characters and a summary description of the *Seitaisho*'s content. Significantly, the Charter Oath's five articles were set forth as the basis for the document. The government was built around the Dajokan (Grand Council of State). It was the all-powerful executive branch of the government, for although the legislative and judicial functions were recognized, they were not independent but were mere arms of the executive. In addition, its officials, both high and low, came from the ranks of the feudal lords and their retainers. Although it underwent many modifications, the Dajokan was, in effect, the government until the cabinet system was established in 1885.

The transition from the old order of feudalism to the new order of the nation began under the Dajokan. The decade of the 1880s, plus a few years on both ends, was a time of change unparalleled in the long history of Japan. Countless books have been written, in both Japanese and foreign languages, about the Meiji transformation.

Between the issuing of the *Seitaisho* in 1868 and the initiation in 1881 of the process that led to the drafting of the Meiji Constitution, several momentous developments occurred: the abolition of the feudal domains with their ruling lords; the abolition of the four-class system, including the warrior class that had ruled Japan for seven centuries; the creation of a centralized bureaucratic government; the establishment of a national army and navy; the introduction of modern science and its related technology; the emergence of the Japanese variation of capitalism; the creation of a national legal and judicial system; the beginnings of a railroad system and a merchant marine; the development of print media (newspapers, magazines, and book publishing); and the start of integration into world trade. In addition were related matters such as new kinds of clothing and food, literature, ideas, arts—indeed, many of the surface manifestations of Western civilization.

Constitutions are the texts of the fundamental laws of politics. Japan's society had undergone changes as drastic as those just described, and by 1880 it had no constitution. The time was ripe for a written constitution. On October 12, 1881, the Meiji Emperor issued a rescript ordering that a national legislature be established in 1890. No mention was made of a constitution, but if such a legislature—without precedent in Japanese history—were to be established, it clearly required the foundation of a constitution. But a constitution was also needed for three more compelling reasons: the complexity of the emerging nation-state, the need for order and stability, and as a signal to the Western world that Japan with a constitution was becoming a nation-state and thus deserved to be treated on an equal footing with the dominant Western nation-states. In turn, this would end the unequal treaties, an objective Japan's leaders had wanted to attain since they had come to power.

The drafting process of the new constitution was designed to secure maximum secrecy and thus minimum public discussion, which had been abundant once a constitution had become a possibility. A key element in the process was the appointment of Count (later Prince) Ito Hirobumi to be in charge of the operation. He had been a significant actor in the anti-Tokugawa movement and by 1881 had become a dominant figure in both politics and government.

In an English-language memoir written in 1905, Ito gave this concise account of his work (see Bibliographic Note: Part 1).

> It was in the month of March, 1882, that His Majesty ordered me to work out a draft of a Constitution to be submitted to his approval. No time was to be lost, so I started on the 15th of the same month for an extended journey to constitutional countries to make as thorough a study as possible of the actual workings of different systems of constitutional government, of their various provisions, as well as theories and opinions actually entertained by influential persons on the actual stage itself of constitutional life. I took young men with me, who all belonged to the elite of the rising generation, to assist and cooperate with me in my studies. I sojourned about a year and a half in Europe, and having gathered the necessary materials, insofar as it was possible in so short a space of time, I returned home in September, 1883. Immediately after my return I set to work to draw up the Constitution. I was assisted in my work by my secretaries, prominent among whom were the late K. Inouye, and the Barons M. Ito and K. Kaneko, and by foreign advisers such as Professor Roessler . . . and others.

A few items were omitted from this account, including the fact that Ito did not study Western democracies or their constitutions. Also unmentioned was Professor Albert Mosse who, like Professor Roessler, was a specialist in German monarchical constitutions. Ito did not mention the secrecy with which the drafters worked or the fact that drafts of proposed constitutions that appeared in the press were ignored.

Early in 1885 the Privy Council was created as the highest advisory body to the emperor. Its first task was to review and approve the constitution as drafted. Its approval was assured, for the first president was Ito himself.

THE MEIJI CONSTITUTION

Japan's first constitution (see Appendix) was revealed to the country and the world on February 11, 1889, when the Meiji Emperor bestowed it on his subjects as a gift in an impressive ceremony before many Japanese and foreign dignitaries. The date was chosen with care to associate it with Japan's Foundation Day. According to Japanese mythology (treated officially as history until after World War II), it was on February 11 (the eleventh day of the second month, according to the old calendar) in the year corresponding to 660 B.C. that the Jimmu Emperor, the first of the long imperial line (of which the Meiji Emperor was counted as the 123rd), ascended the throne.

The constitution was the centerpiece, but it was accompanied by a battery of pronouncements and documents designed to emphasize that it was graciously bestowed on the nation by a monarch descended from heaven: the Imperial Oath at the sanctuary of the Imperial Palace, the Imperial Speech on the Promulgation of the Constitution, the Imperial House Law, the Imperial Ordinance concerning the House of Peers, the Law of the Houses (of the Imperial Diet), the Law of Election of the Members of the House of Representatives, and the Law of Finance. Except for the Law of Finance, the entire package provided the foundation for a new national government in the form of imperial myth. Thus the transition from a feudal to a national state ended.

The Imperial Oath pledged that "the ancient form of government," that is, the rule of the imperial line by "the Imperial ancestors," would be maintained and "secured from decline." It also set forth that the new fundamental law was "designed to give clearness and distinction to the instructions bequeathed by the Imperial Founder of Our House and by Our other Imperial Ancestors" so that "Our Imperial posterity may possess a guide for the course they are to follow . . . and that our subjects shall be able to enjoy a wider range of action in giving Us their support, and that the observance of our laws shall continue to the remotest ages of time."

The Imperial Speech was devoted to the role of the subjects, who were to be guided by the imperial views, to sympathize with the imperial endeavors, and to cooperate to make "manifest the glory" of the country at home and abroad and to secure "forever the stability of the work bequeathed to Us by Our Imperial Ancestors."

The preamble ordained that both "Our descendants and Our subjects are forever to conform" to it. It also stated that only an occupant of the throne could originate amendments.

The meanings of the oath, the speech, and the preamble were perfectly clear: the ideological foundation of the new document was purely Japanese, untainted by foreign influence; the people were to be willing and unquestioning subjects; and there was to be no tampering with the imperial gift that was the constitution.

The Imperial House Law's first article stated simply: "The Imperial Throne of Japan shall be succeeded to by male descendants in the male line of Imperial Ancestors." The remaining fifty-five articles covered all details relating to the imperial family and its governance.

The Imperial Ordinance Concerning the House of Peers dealt mainly with membership. Members of the imperial family; princes and marquises; counts, viscounts, and barons elected by their orders; persons specially nominated by the emperor because of "service to the nation or erudition"; and one member from each city and prefecture elected by and from the highest taxpayers and nominated by the emperor constituted a highly conservative body committed to supporting the sovereign and his constitution.

The Law of the Houses and the election law for the House of Representatives dealt with the most innovative and Western-inspired organ of the government. The constitutional role of the Imperial Diet is discussed later. The Law of Finance was of basic bureaucratic importance, dealing as it did with national finances, but it was of secondary constitutional importance.

All supporting pronouncements and documents were integral to the carefully orchestrated presentation of the new fundamental law. The total package created an absolute monarchy, a familiar form of government in Europe but conspicuously lacking the features of the democracies of the time.

CONCEPT OF IMPERIAL SOVEREIGNTY

The key to understanding Japan's first modern constitution is the concept of imperial sovereignty. That constitution was titled the Meiji Constitution, derived from the Meiji Emperor during whose reign (1867–1912) the constitution was promulgated. But the concept of imperial sovereignty grew from the long history of the role of the emperor as occupant of the imperial throne.

Japan's first written history is the *Kojiki* (Record of Ancient Matters) with a date corresponding to A.D. 712. It is a mix of myth masquerading as history and a seemingly factual account of historical developments from about A.D. 650. The historical account deals with the struggle for power among powerful clans, a struggle won by a clan identified as the imperial clan (with no family name). One of the apparent motives for compiling the *Kojiki* was to establish the legitimacy of that clan as the ruler of Japan as it was then known. The basis of that legitimacy was the clan's allegedly divine origin.

The *Kojiki*'s mythology had the islands of Japan created by the gods who plunged spears into the sea, with the soil dripping from the spear points becoming the islands. Subsequently, Amaterasu no Omikami, the Sun Goddess, produced the first emperor, Jimmu, who founded the imperial clan and came to the throne on a date corresponding to 660 B.C. Thus both the land and its rulers were descended from the gods.

During the four centuries following the writing of the *Kojiki*, the country was ruled by successive emperors and their courts. The emperors functioned as both secular rulers and high priests, their divine descent giving them the power to communicate with the divine ancestors who, through them, controlled the destiny of the people.

By roughly the beginning of the twelfth century, the imperial court lost its control of government because of the decline of its powers and the appearance of a powerful new force in the society—the warrior class. But a peculiar political development occurred: the emperor and his court, although powerless politically and with no role in the operation of the government, continued as a political institution. When powerful warrior families came to power, it would seem automatic and natural for them to get rid of the emperor and his court and to create their own ruling dynasty. That did not happen.

Throughout the next seven centuries a succession of warrior families ruled Japan, but the otherwise powerless emperor formally granted them all the right to rule. The only reasonable explanation for this odd situation lies in the power of myth, namely, the divine origin of the imperial line. In other words, it served the interests of the successive lines of shoguns, the warrior rulers, to preserve the emperor as the divine source of the supreme power to bestow legitimate authority to rule on those who enjoyed political supremacy.

The single imperial dynasty was in striking contrast to the succession of imperial dynasties in China, which developed the theory of the mandate of heaven to explain and justify the transfer of power from one line of emperors to another. Dissimilarity also existed with the divine right of kings that appeared in Europe some centuries later under which a Supreme Being, a spirit far removed from direct human experience, was the source of the right to rule. In Japan, the source was a god in human form.

It was only natural that the drafters and their European advisers built their constitution on the foundation of imperial sovereignty. The tiny group of drafters held their position because their roots were in the old warrior class, they were active in the anti-Tokugawa coalition, and they were on the victorious side of the political infighting during the 1870s. Those circumstances meant they had been in the "Revere the Emperor" camp and consequently were predisposed to base both their newly won power and the new constitution on the imperial institution. And their European advisers were academics who specialized in autocratic monarchical constitutions in vogue at the time.

The first article of the Meiji Constitution read: "The Empire of Japan shall be reigned over and governed by a line of Emperors unbroken for ages eternal." In his authoritative commentary on the constitution issued shortly after its promulgation, Ito underlined the importance of the article:

> At the outset, this Article states the great principle of the Constitution of the country, and declares that the Empire of Japan shall, to the end of time, identify itself with the Imperial dynasty unbroken in lineage, and that the principle has never changed in the past, and will never change in the future to all eternity. It is intended to make clear forever the relations that shall exist between the Emperor and His subjects. By "reigned over and governed" it is meant that the Emperor on His Throne combines in Himself the sovereignty of the State and the government of the country and His subjects.

Article 3 stated baldly that the emperor is "sacred and inviolable." Ito declared that not only would no irreverence be displayed for the emperor's person but that he should not "be made topic of derogatory comment nor one of discussion." This foreshadowed the awe and reverence that later surrounded the emperor.

Article 4 brought the emperor into the real world of politics. It stated that he was "the head of the Empire, combining in Himself the rights of sovereignty and exercises them, according to the provisions of the present Constitution." The final phrase contains a hint of limitation, but it should be remembered that any limitation was self-limitation, for the constitution was the emperor's gracious gift to his subjects.

The remaining key articles of Chapter I made clear that the emperor possessed both the legislative and the executive power (which included the judicial power). Also, the constitution specified that the emperor was the supreme commander of the army and navy and had the power to declare war, make peace, and conclude treaties.

Thus Chapter I made clear that imperial sovereignty included both legislative and executive powers, with judicial power falling under the latter. There was no separation of powers or checks and balances, only a single unitary power with three faces—executive, legislative, and judicial. Later, in the 1920s, a tentative and short-lived gesture was made toward democracy, but the basic constitutional framework remained unchanged.

THE THREE EMPERORS OF THE MEIJI CONSTITUTIONAL ERA

Here we examine the role of the imperial throne and its occupants under the life of the Meiji Constitution from 1889 to 1947. Under that constitution three emperors reigned: Mutsuhito, the Meiji Emperor, from 1867 to 1912; Yoshihito, the Taisho Emperor, from 1912 to 1925; and Hirohito, the Showa Emperor, from 1925 through 1947 (when his role was completely changed under the new constitution). (Mutsuhito, Yoshihito, and Hirohito were their personal names; Meiji, Taisho, and Showa were their reign names, bestowed on them after their deaths.)

Under the Meiji Constitution the role of the emperor was clear, understood, accepted, and unchallenged by the Japanese people. At the same time, it was unclear, misunderstood, unaccepted, and challenged by the outside world. In Japan it was based on centuries of history and in the first half of the twentieth century became the central element of the country's ideology, which ended in ultranationalism. In the outside world Hirohito personified on the world scene his country's ultranationalism and aggression.

At the dawn of the twenty-first century it is difficult, if not impossible, to determine which view is "correct"—the Japanese or the foreign; that is, which is closer to being the judgment of history. What follows is an untried avenue of approach.

Initially, it may be useful to note what the three emperors were not. None was a king, an emperor (as the term is understood in the West), a president, a dictator, a charismatic figure, a politician, a chief executive, or a megalomaniac. None was a Caesar, a Napoleon, a Roosevelt, a Churchill, a Stalin, or a Mao Zedong. These statements about what the emperors were not are based on what is known about the three men, their positions, and their careers.

On the other hand, the three emperors were constitutional monarchs, descendants of a long line of allegedly divine ancestors, the high priests of a national religion, the objects (especially Hirohito) of the awe and reverence of their subjects, politically powerless, and isolated from any meaningful contact with their country's daily life.

Adding to the difficulty of understanding the imperial system, it was never seriously studied. On the Japanese side, as has been shown in Ito's comments, no serious discussion occurred beyond the narrow limits of the emperor's constitutional position. Official censorship and private ultranationalistic acts of terrorism made it both difficult and perilous to depart from rigid orthodoxy. In view of the Japanese situation, it is not surprising that there were no foreign studies of either the imperial system or the three occupants of the throne.

The Meiji Emperor's reign was undoubtedly the second most eventful in Japan's long history, behind only that of Hirohito, his grandson. In his forty-five-year reign (1867–1912) the Meiji Emperor witnessed the fall of the Tokugawas, Japan's emergence as a nation-state, the promulgation of his country's first written constitution, victories in the first war with China (1894–1895) and the war with Imperial Russia (1904–1905), and Japan's liberation from the unequal treaty system. He is said to have taken great personal interest in matters of state, both great and small. Although his name is associated with all the great developments during his reign, his role seems largely that of an interested observer.

The Taisho Emperor (1912–1925) proved mentally incompetent. His only mark on history is the use of his reign name in the phrase *Taisho democracy*, briefly discussed later.

The reign of the Showa Emperor was by far the longest in years and the most momentous of the historical line of his 123 predecessors on the imperial throne. During his sixty-four-year reign he was the constitutional monarch of a world power, the god-in-human-form of his country's state religion, and the nominal commander in chief of the armed forces that for a few brief years created one of the world's (and Asia's) great empires. Then his unconditional surrender marked Japan's only lost war and the end of the empire. He renounced his mythical divinity and approved the constitutional revision that ended the Meiji Constitution and created the present democratic constitution. He escaped indictment as a war criminal and watched his people enjoy unprecedented economic well-being and escape involvement in war. His autobiography would have been one of the most fascinating of the twentieth century. It remained unwritten probably because of the secrecy of the imperial court around him and possibly because of his lack of literary skill.

At the end of World War II the Allies talked at length of charging and trying Hirohito as a war criminal. This was never done for reasons that have not been established beyond doubt, although it has been argued that the U.S. government or General MacArthur shielded him.

If he had been charged, it would have been interesting to learn the arguments of the defense. For instance, an emperor was constitutionally the possessor of the right of sovereignty and was the head of state. But Ito, the principal drafter of and authoritative commentator on the constitution, had made clear that an emperor would act only on the advice of his ministers of state, making him in effect a rubber stamp. In addition, an emperor occupied the throne only by virtue of birth—he was not elected or appointed and was not in office by personal choice or motivation. Thus such an argument might have concluded that the emperor was only a figurehead. In other words, could the emperor be held criminally responsible for sanctioning decisions made by others and in which he had no meaningful input? We shall never know if such an argument could have been made.

It is highly unlikely that a defense on those lines offered while the heat of the recent war burned bright would have staved off a verdict of guilty. But even so, evidence might have been produced that would have contributed to an understanding of the imperial institution and of Hirohito in particular.

If an accurate understanding is ever to be achieved of the role of the imperial throne and its three occupants under the Meiji Constitution, the Imperial Household Agency must open its archives and release the documents that would shed light on precisely how the emperor was involved in the government. As has been pointed out, we know that constitutionally the emperor was an absolute monarch. But unanswered are such questions as, was he ever actively involved in the development of high-level government policy? What was presented to him for imperial sanction? The final draft? If so, did an emperor ever suggest changes that were adopted, or was he simply expected to place the imperial seal on the document before him?

To regard the imperial system as the ideology of the Japanese nation-state during the span of the Meiji Constitution may dissipate the obfuscation of regarding it as emperor worship, which was not altogether erroneous but was not a completely satisfactory explanation of the phenomenon. The phrase implied that there was something mystic and unique about it, which is how the chauvinists wanted foreigners to view it. But it also removed the phenomenon from the sphere of standard Western political understanding.

To define the imperial system as ideology places the imperial institution in the familiar territory of ideologies such as democracy, socialism, Marxism, Maoism, Nazism, and fascism. To varying degrees, the imperial system shared several characteristics with other ideologies: it was an expression of the society's fundamental values, the members of the society were ready to die in a war in its defense, it feared other ideologies and regarded itself as superior to them, and it did not tolerate the introduction of rival ideologies. In general, it should be regarded as a manifestation of a general twentieth-century political phenomenon, not as a mystical and uniquely Japanese peculiarity. But again, if future historians of early-twentieth-century Japan are ever to write a detailed and trustworthy account of the imperial institution, they must be given access to the archives of the Imperial Household Agency.

ROLE OF THE GOVERNED

Chapter II of the constitution, "Rights and Duties of the People," dealt with the role of the people under the new constitution. The title was symbolic of the broad changes that accompanied Japan's transition from feudal to modern. Individual rights were a new and foreign concept. The idea of duty, if not the specific duties mentioned in this chapter, was central to the centuries-old feudal system. Here again was modernization's familiar theme: Western form, Japanese spirit.

The list of rights was impressive: no arrest, detention, or punishment unless under law; no entry and search of homes without consent; the right to secrecy of correspondence; the rights of petition and property; and freedom of religion, writing, public meetings, publication, and association. One fundamental difficulty, however, was that the rights were listed, not guaranteed by the constitution.

That crippling limitation on rights was simple but fundamental. All rights, except that of property, were qualified by phrases such as *according to law* and other phrases typical of civil law nations: "within the limits of law," "except in cases provided for in the law," and "within limits not prejudicial to peace and order and not antagonistic to their duties as subjects." This placed law above the constitution by providing that laws duly enacted by constitutional procedures could suspend enumerated rights. Although this procedure was not out of line with some European constitutional law of the time, it proved central to the subsequent development of Japan's authoritarianism.

The restrictions on the newly bestowed rights were consistent with the principle of imperial sovereignty. Laws enacted by the Imperial Diet were simply the manifestation of the legislative face of imperial sovereignty. Rights bestowed by the sovereign could be withdrawn by the sovereign.

Ito enthusiastically praised subjects' rights, but not as basic principles of government. Such rights were simply part of the gracious gift that was the constitution. But they were a sign, as was the constitution itself, that Japan had a fundamental law that was a modern constitution—one worthy of being considered on the same level as those of the advanced Euro-American nations. The lack of a guarantee of fundamental rights was to be expected. Japan had no history of such rights. The crisis of the Tokugawa collapse was not centered on the issue of rights. The secrecy surrounding the drafting process had prevented any public debate on the guarantee of rights and simultaneously had allowed the drafters to handle the issue precisely as they did.

Only two duties were listed in the constitution: that of all able-bodied males to serve in the armed forces and the duty to pay taxes. In his commentary, Ito declared it was the duty of all males "to protect the existence, the independence and the glory of the country" with the aim that "the martial spirit of the country shall be maintained and secured from decline." Universal male conscription was not commonly included in contemporary constitutions, but its presence in Japan's fundamental law was an essential element in the later development of war as an instrument of national policy, the concrete manifestation of Japan's militarism.

Ito termed paying taxes "the pure duty" of imperial subjects because they "ought to pay taxes, in order that the expenditures necessitated by the nature and object of the state may be met." That was true of all states, but in Japan it had special resonance, for the emperor was the state. For the emperor's subjects, Ito declared, paying taxes was not "a business question of exchange of services between the government and the people."

WEAK LEGISLATURE, POWERFUL MINISTERS, PASSIVE ADVISERS

If the recognition, not the guarantee, of rights was an innovation for Japan under the new constitution, it was matched by the Imperial Diet, the "assembly widely convoked" by the Charter Oath. The drafters were careful to provide that this Western governmental institution would not become a disruptive (in their eyes) influence in the new political order. It was created as a bicameral body: an upper House of Peers and a lower House of Representatives.

The constitution decreed that the House of Peers would be composed of members of the imperial family, of the orders of nobility, and of persons appointed by the emperor. The Imperial Ordinance Concerning the House of Peers provided the details: membership consisted of adult members of the imperial family; princes and marquises; counts, viscounts, and barons elected by their orders; and persons appointed by the emperor because of their meritorious service to the state or their erudition. Thus entry into the upper house was gained by birth or meritorious service to the state (which included erudition), not by election. There was no set number of members.

Thus the House of Peers was clearly designed to be a conservative body. In the words of Ito, it was created "to restrain the undue influence of political parties, to check the evil tendencies of irresponsible discussions, to secure the stability of the Constitution, to be an instrument for maintaining harmony between the governing and the governed." He did not point out that the governed were to have no voice in maintaining harmony.

The constitution provided that the members of the House of Representatives were to be elected by the people. The law regarding the election of members of the lower house, however, provided that "the people" was limited to members of the economic elite. Voters and candidates had to be males and had to pay at least ¥15 in direct-national taxes, a considerable sum at the time. This assured that lower-house members were also likely to be conservative.

Ito made clear that the Imperial Diet was to have only a limited role in governing the country. He defined it as only "a good representative body of the people." More specifically, he wrote: "It takes part in legislation, but has no share in the sovereign power; it has power to deliberate on laws, but none to determine them. The right of consent of the Imperial Diet has to be exercised within the limits allowed by the provisions of the Constitution and is by no means an unlimited one."

Article 64 of the constitution assured that the Diet would be powerless to control the government by depriving it of control over the purse strings: "Those expenses already fixed by the Constitution upon the powers appertaining to the Emperor, and such as may have arisen by the effect of law, or that appertain to the legal obligations of the Government, shall be neither rejected nor reduced by the Imperial Diet without the concurrence of the Government." In the early decades of the Meiji system, attempts were made to define *consent* to include the capacity to withhold it, but the struggle remained political, falling far short of an attempt to modify the constitutional limitations on the legislature.

Ito listed four legislative rights: to receive petitions, to question the government and demand explanations, to address the emperor, and to control the management of finances. Only the fourth hints at anything resembling a power.

Article 38 stated that the two houses had the additional right to initiate legislation, but neither it nor Ito's commentary provides any detail on the initiation process. In commenting on Article 40, which granted the houses the right to make representations to the government regarding proposed laws, Ito revealed his attitude regarding legislators' ability:

> But were a legislative assembly to proceed to draw up clause after clause according to the opinion of the majority, much delay would very often be caused in the progress of the debate thereon, while the draft itself would not be free from the defect of crudeness and lack of arrangement. It would be far wiser to rely for such work upon the skill and experience of the commissioners of the Government.

Thus both the provisions of the constitution and the comments of its principal drafter constituted effective barriers to future development of a significant role for this potentially influential body.

The judicature under Article 5 was exercised by the courts of law "according to law, in the name of the Emperor." Thus the courts were the judicial face of the unitary imperial sovereign power; they could not interfere with the functioning of the other two faces of imperial power, the all-powerful executive and the fettered legislature. As with the U.S. constitution, no constitutional provision enabled the judiciary to review the constitutionality of executive and legislative actions. In addition, administration of the judiciary was the responsibility of the Ministry of Justice, an executive agency—as in Italy, France, and Germany.

The role of the executive was set forth in Chapter IV, which had only two brief articles: one devoted to the ministers of state and the other to the Privy Council. Thus the all-powerful executive face of the imperial government was dealt with casually.

The first sentence of Article 55 read simply: "The respective Ministers of State shall give their advice to the Emperor and be responsible for it." The second sentence stated merely that the countersignature of a minister of state was required on "all Imperial Ordinances and Imperial Rescripts of whatever kind that relate to the affairs of State." The article is silent on such matters as the appointment of the minister president of state (Ito's term for the post commonly referred to as prime minister) and the ministers of state, their term of office, nomination, qualifications, and dismissal from office. These matters were covered by the general provision in Article 10 regarding the emperor's sovereign power of appointment and dismissal of all civil and military officials. There was no mention of a cabinet, but the cabinet system was established in 1885.

The constitution was also silent on the important matter of the nature of responsibility. Ito, however, went a long way toward clarifying the concept. He offered these points:

> That the Ministers are charged with the duty of giving advice to the Emperor, which is their proper function, and that they are not held responsible on His behalf; that Ministers are directly responsible to the Sovereign and indirectly to the people; that it is the Sovereign and not the people that can decide as to the responsibility of Ministers, because the Sovereign possesses the rights of sovereignty of the State; and that the responsibility of Ministers is a political one and has no relation to criminal or civil responsibility.

He also pointed out that ministers are responsible only for matters under their jurisdiction, that there is no such thing as joint responsibility, and that the minister president has no control over the ministers.

It is safe to assume that the lack of constitutional detail concerning the ministers of state and their responsibility was intended to create the widest possible latitude for the development of executive power. That is exactly what happened, as the concentration of executive power lay at the heart of the authoritarianism that came to dominate Japan.

Article 56 dealing with the Privy Council provided simply that it was to "deliberate on important matters of State, when they [the councillors] have been consulted by the Emperor." The council had been created in 1888, and its initial task was to review the draft constitution before its promulgation. It was established by imperial ordinance. The Privy Council was to consist of a president, a vice president, a secretary-general, several secretaries, and twelve or more councillors. It was to deliberate and present its opinion to the emperor on the interpretation of the constitution and laws appertaining to it, questions relating to the budget or other financial matters, drafts of constitutional amendments or laws appertaining thereto, important imperial ordinances, drafts of new laws and drafts for abolition or amendment of existing laws, foreign treaties, the planning of administrative organizations, and other important matters. Although it was the highest advisory organ to the emperor, it "should not interfere with the executive."

The only qualification for appointment mentioned in the imperial ordinance was that a candidate had to be forty or older. For such an important position in a post so close to the emperor, however, a councillor would have to be from a high social class or be greatly accomplished in the affairs of state. The council was barred from receiving petitions, representations, or other communications from the Imperial Diet or any government office or from any of the emperor's subjects. Its only official connections were to the cabinet and its ministers of state, and it was also barred from any official communication or connection with private citizens. Such limitations meant that in spite of its closeness to the emperor the Privy Council was formally and politically powerless, and its advice to the emperor was, in effect, narrowly molded by the ministers of state—the executive face of imperial sovereignty. Since all ministers of state were, by virtue of their offices, members of the council, there was little chance that it would raise objections to what ministers proposed to present to the emperor.

Thus the Meiji Constitution created an absolute monarchy, and sovereignty resided in the emperor—not as a political leader or an active head of state but as the human manifestation of the divinely descended imperial line from which flowed the ultimate authority to rule the nation. The executive, judicial, and legislative machinery of government was constitutionally designed to rule the nation under the legitimizing authority granted by the emperor.

Ito, his fellow drafters, and their European scholarly advisers did a masterful job of creating a fundamental law for the nascent nation-state. Imperial sovereignty was the historical foundation; the machinery of government was innovative, foreign-inspired, and complex. Yet the constitution brought the two successfully together. The secret of their success lay in the foundations of the two structurally very different systems, the feudal Tokugawa and the modern national system. Under the old and vanished system, a sovereign emperor had bestowed the authority to rule on the Tokugawa shogun and his Bakufu. Under the new Meiji constitutional system, the sovereign emperor bestowed the authority to rule on a succession of individuals and their supporters whose skills enabled them to lead a society in the process of transformation and development.

The Meiji Constitution as the fundamental law was the stable foundation for a Japan that in the 1890s was firmly set toward becoming a modern nation-state and a leading actor in world affairs. But the leaders who took Japan through the momentous second half of the nineteenth century had no way of knowing that their work would lead directly into the militarism and authoritarianism of the first half of the twentieth century.

THE MEIJI CONSTITUTION AND TAISHO DEMOCRACY

The development of authoritarianism under the Meiji Constitution raises the question of the road not traveled, namely, constitutional democracy. The idea of democracy flowed into Japan with the wave of Westernism following the Tokugawa collapse, leading to the movement for people's rights and the organization of the first political parties in the 1870s. As we have seen, these early tentative steps toward a possible Japanese variation on democracy had little influence on the creation of the Meiji Constitution. Nevertheless, by the 1920s political parties had developed to the point that they were able to produce the first prime ministers who were party politicians. Also in that decade, the influence of the military in the government had been temporarily dulled, and universal male suffrage had been established. These developments were perceived, both inside and outside Japan, as promising indicators of a democratic order, dubbed Taisho democracy after the reign name of the Taisho Emperor.

The promise was short-lived. It soon provoked an irresistible reaction from the armed forces. In 1922, admirals were disgruntled when the government agreed to the Naval Limitation Treaty signed in Washington, D.C. This treaty limited the expansion of the navy and placed Japan in a position inferior to the two other naval powers, Great Britain and the United States, awakening unpleasant memories of the vanished unequal treaty system. Generals, in defiance of attempts at control by the government, engineered the Manchurian Incident, which simultaneously brought Manchuria under Japanese control and initiated fourteen years of war with China. The generals were ably supported by the so-called young officers' movement, which resorted to assassination and intimidation of civilian leaders.

These actions not only ended Taisho democracy but led Japan into what has been termed "the dark valley" of militarism and authoritarianism. The young officers who used violence as a political device did not seize control of the machinery of government; they did not subvert the existing constitutional order. Far from being treasonous by attempting to overthrow the government, they argued in their trials for mutiny and assassination that they were defending the emperor and his government by eliminating those officials who were guilty of giving bad advice in violation of their constitutional duty. In their eyes the assassins were defending, not subverting, the constitutional order.

The events just outlined have been accepted as the explanation for the failure of Taisho democracy. What has been largely overlooked is that the steps toward democracy in the 1920s were doomed from the start because their unspoken challenge to the constitution's imperial sovereignty contained the seeds of democracy's destruction. Democracy, which by definition gives sovereignty to the people, was incompatible with imperial sovereignty. If the pale promise of democracy were to be realized, an accommodation of these incompatibilities would have had to be worked out. No such attempt was possible.

In 1925, when universal male suffrage was established by law—an undeniable step toward democracy—the most recent in a succession of "peace preservation" laws dating back to the 1870s, all of which imposed restrictions on political freedoms, was simultaneously passed. It provided that any attempt to alter either the national polity (or *kokutai*, as the Meiji constitutional system was dubbed) or the system of private property was a crime. The death penalty was soon added by amendment but was never imposed. The law had the sanction of imperial sovereignty because it was compatible with constitutional provisions: it was drafted by the responsible ministry of state, it was submitted to and approved by the Privy Council, it received the consent of the Imperial Diet, and it was given imperial sanction and promulgation. The law granting universal male suffrage went through the same procedures, but the Peace Preservation Law guaranteed that male suffrage would not impinge on the sacred precinct of the imperial constitutional order.

The Meiji Constitution was an insuperable barrier to the development of a democratic order in Japan's version of the modern nation-state. Imperial sovereignty, its foundation, however, provides a starting point for a speculative examination of reasons Japan failed to go beyond the tentative, illusory, ephemeral, and failed tendencies toward democracy.

As we have seen, the constitution's imperial sovereignty was absolute and omnipotent. Theoretically, then, an emperor—Hirohito, for example—was in a position to sanction the creation of a democratic system of government and politics. But there was never a chance that such a theoretical possibility could be realized.

Let us make the unrealistic assumption that the Showa Emperor became a genuine convert to the ideals, principles, and institutions of democracy after he came to the throne. How could he have reached his goal of a democratic constitution?

His first problem—political isolation—would have been insolvable. Both the constitution and so-called emperor worship placed him above politics. In the isolation of the imperial court the emperor had daily but restricted contact only with his high court officials. He had no contact with political leaders except those in power, let alone with political parties and their leaders. He had no direct access to the media. He had no meaningful contact with business or financial leaders. As the object of worship by his people, he had no contact with them. Neither Hirohito nor his father had the strength of personality, to say nothing of the charisma, that might have fueled an attempt to break through this isolation.

Then there was the daunting fact that two generations of men had come to positions of power or influence under the Meiji Constitution.

They had no experience under another system, democracy, for example. They were responsible for operating the government through their advice to their emperor and were responsible only to him. They were not likely to urge the adoption of another system or even to support a movement toward one.

Finally, there was no organized movement favoring democracy (or any other movement of foreign origin) that might have come to the banner of an emperor favoring it. No Taisho political party actively advocated democratic principles. Education on the primary and secondary levels was built on the principle of loyalty to the emperor. On the tertiary level no independent-minded teaching or research was conducted on alternative systems of government and politics; and even on Japan's system, teaching and research were tightly restricted to the accepted line supporting the Meiji constitutional order.

The Meiji Constitution and the system built on it possessed a strength and rigidity that only unseen and undreamed-of pressures could test and find wanting. War, the physical destruction and psychological trauma of crushing defeat, and a transforming military occupation by a compassionate democratic power combined to bring about a new constitutional order.

2

War
as an Instrument
of National Policy

ROAD TO MILITARISM

The conventional interpretation of modern Japanese history purports that during the reign of the Meiji Emperor (1867–1912) a profound change occurred in Japanese society: the disappearance of a centuries-old feudal society and its replacement by an emergent nation-state. Yet by the end of the twentieth century an alternative, less dramatic interpretation of the significance of the Meiji period had become possible. The break with the past was less complete than events seemed to indicate; the heritage of the past persisted and controlled the development of Japanese society until the midpoint of the twentieth century.

Although the face of Japanese society went through the startling changes of modernization, the body and soul, as formed by centuries of history, remained basically stable. Their form and expression did change in conformity with the broad shifts the society itself was experiencing. The two major elements of the past that constituted the foundation of the new Japanese nation-state were the imperial system and the almost seven centuries of domination of Japanese society by the warrior class. We have seen how the Meiji Constitution converted the historical role of the emperor into the concept of imperial sovereignty. Here we turn to the role of the self-deracinated samurai class in the collapse of the Tokugawa system.

The fall of the Tokugawas was brought about by fellow members of the warrior class. It was a political event, not a revolutionary one pitting one sociopolitical class against another. The victors in the struggle against the Tokugawas performed an unusual political act: they destroyed their own class, a deed made possible by the fact that they retained political and governmental power. The anti-Tokugawa leaders, as a group of like-minded individuals, emerged in clear control over both politics and government in the immediate post-Tokugawa period. Such control made possible the dissolution not only of their own class but of the other classes as well. The leaders retained their positions of power, although not without limited infighting among themselves. In addition, the declassed majority among the lower former warriors enjoyed new roles in the society in transition. Many former warriors found positions in the national (government) police force. Others became members of the newly created army and navy. Also, many who had occupied administrative positions both in the Tokugawa government and in the numerous clan governments underwent a relatively easy transformation into the new central bureaucratic government.

Thus Japan had a government manned from top to bottom by men predisposed to accept the expansion and utilization of military forces. This situation was supported by an imperial edict issued in 1873 establishing universal male conscription, thus extending to all males the privilege of bearing arms—a right previously limited to the warrior class. In 1877 the new national army of conscripts put down an antigovernment insurrection by the Satsuma clan, historically one of the most powerful of the non-Tokugawa families, thus gaining much prestige.

Even before the fall of the Tokugawas, two leading anti-Tokugawa clans were taught a powerful lesson in the use of force in international relations. The Satsuma clan in southern Kyushu and the Choshu clan at the western tip of the main island became disastrously involved with the naval forces of the Western powers that had been allowed to enter the country less than a decade earlier. The Satsuma had murdered an Englishman who, because of ignorance or bad judgment, had ridden on horseback through a Satsuma procession near Tokyo. The Choshu forts at the Shimonoseki Strait between the main island and Kyushu had made the bad decision to fire at foreign ships passing through the strait. In 1863, in retaliation, a British naval squadron inflicted heavy damage on the Satsuma capital; and in 1864 an allied group (British, American, French, and Dutch) did the same to the Choshu capital. Thus men who would come to power in Japan a few years later were given an object lesson in the disparity between Japanese and foreign military power. Japan, unlike China, had not been opened to the Western powers by war. But negotiations by the Western powers with the Tokugawa government had been powerfully reinforced by the show of military force. The new leaders bitterly resented the unequal treaties that had opened the country, and a major goal of the new government was to eliminate those treaties. Indeed, it was a major force behind Japan's drive to become a modern nation.

Thus Japan's new leaders, fully cognizant of the importance of weapons in their internal politics, were thrown into international politics in which military strength was a powerful instrument. It is little wonder that they were more than willing to regard the creation of a modern army and navy as a major element in the broad program of modernization they were developing.

Finally, the strategic situation in Asia in the last quarter of the nineteenth century was highly favorable to Japan's new goal of becoming a military power. Japan at the time was one of only four Asian countries that was even nominally independent; the other three were a powerless Korea, a crumbling Imperial China, and a small and isolated Thailand (then known as Siam). The rest of Asia was controlled by the Western powers as a congeries of colonies.

With a political/governmental leadership predisposed to think in military terms, intent on building the military strength of their society, aware of the weakness of their Asian neighbors, and bitterly resentful of an unequal treaty system, it is not surprising that the nascent Japanese nation-state resorted to war as an instrument of policy. This resort was aided tremendously by the fact that China was in a state of collapse. Consequently, it became the target of Japanese warfare from 1894 to 1945. China's inability to defend itself invited Japan's aggression.

Although the new Meiji Constitution did not deal with the subject of war, it contained a number of provisions that became a foundation for the militaristic state Japan became. We have seen how the Meiji Constitution was based on imperial sovereignty, which in turn led to the establishment of a unitary and authoritarian state. The constitution listed a few specific powers relating to military matters under the broad umbrella of imperial sovereignty: command of the army and navy and their peacetime organization, the declaration of war, and the making of peace. But those powers were not to be personally exercised, as we have seen, but rather constituted specific areas of the sovereign powers, the execution of which required imperial sanction. The actual administration of these powers, as the Ito commentaries made clear, was to be carried out by the appropriate ministers of state, each of whom was made responsible by imperially sanctioned law. And ministerial responsibility ran only upward to the emperor.

The ministers of war (for the army) and of the navy soon became the most influential members of the cabinet because they were responsible for the nation's security. The paramount importance of the cabinet's responsibilities was reinforced in 1871 when an imperial ordinance established that only generals and admirals in active service could become service ministers. This ordinance was dropped in 1913 but was revived in 1936. In addition, in 1907 the device of *iakujosoken* (*iaku* = high command, *joso* = report to the throne, *ken* = right) was created by military order. This right to report was not mentioned in the Meiji Constitution, but the reasoning behind it gave the device the veneer of constitutionality: namely, that the security of the nation was of prime importance, that the high command was responsible for that security, that the emperor was constitutionally the commander in chief of the armed forces, and that therefore the high command had the right to carry its advice directly to the emperor. In effect, this right assured that no civilian prime minister or his cabinet could block the plans and policies of the service ministries.

The constitution made no provision for control or supervision of the military services by the Diet. The budgetary system established by the constitution did not provide for control of the military budget. The constitutional limitations on the freedoms of expression and assembly prevented opposition to the use of war as an instrument of national policy.

The Meiji Constitution remained in force for just under six decades. In five of those decades Japan was involved in wars involving most of Asia, Russia, and the United States. None of these wars was initiated by an attack on Japan. The initial wars resulted in positive gains for Japan, which to Japanese leaders demonstrated the soundness of the policy; but ultimately it ended in crushing defeat. A review of this succession of wars is necessary to understand both the vanished Meiji Constitution and the creation of the new constitution.

Japan's use of war as an instrument of national policy was intimately bound to its transition from a premodern society to a modern nation-state. As Japan hastened its transition to a modern society in the last three decades of the nineteenth century, it strengthened its war-making capacity by developing its new army and navy based on practices of contemporary Western nation-states. And as that war-making capacity grew in the first half of the twentieth century, it hastened the country's development toward the ultranationalistic, authoritarian nation-state that was simultaneously emerging in the Western world.

But the course of Japanese militarism as it grew from the fertile soil of the Meiji period verified the wisdom of the biblical injunction: all they who take up the sword shall perish by the sword. In the half century between 1895 and 1945, Japan experienced a spectacular, varied military history, moving from a third-rate military power to the possessor of one of the world's most formidable military machines and then to the victim of a devastating defeat by a crushingly more powerful nation-state.

It is possible to set rather precise dates for both the period when war yielded positive results for Japan and the period of eventual collapse. The first period started in April 1895, when the Treaty of Shimonoseki sealed Japan's victory in the first Sino-Japanese War, and ended in early 1943 after Japanese defeats in the battles of Midway and Guadalcanal. The period of collapse began with those defeats and ended in the surrender of August 15, 1945.

THE FIRST SINO-JAPANESE WAR, 1894–1895

Japan's first war with China produced a clear-cut victory. It was an unmistakable measure of Japan's progress toward becoming a nation-state and of Imperial China's failure to keep pace. The Japanese victory was sealed by the terms of the Treaty of Shimonoseki, which was negotiated for Japan by Ito Hirobumi, the primary creator of the Meiji Constitution. The principal terms of the treaty, all in Japan's favor, included: China's recognition of Korean independence, thus simultaneously ending Korea's historical tributary relationship with China and initiating the process of Korea becoming a Japanese colony; the payment of a large cash indemnity to the victor, thus boosting Japan's progress toward industrialization; the cession to Japan of the Liaodong Peninsula, which provided access by sea to Manchuria (as China's three northeastern provinces were then known); and the acquisition of Formosa (Taiwan) as a colony.

But in winning the peninsula Japan learned a bitter lesson in late-nineteenth-century international power politics. A week after the Shimonoseki treaty was announced, the Imperial Russian government (with the concurrence of France and Germany), as "new proof" of its sincere friendship with Japan, advised the latter to renounce the newly acquired Liaodong Peninsula. Japan soon acquiesced in the form of a convention with China retroceding the peninsula in return for a substantial increase in the indemnity. Three years later Russia obtained from China a lease for that same peninsula. Japan learned an unforgettable lesson from the intervention.

The Japanese victory resulted in a gain far greater than what was won in the Treaty of Shimonoseki. When the war broke out in late summer of 1894, the leading Western powers fully expected a Chinese victory, basing that judgment on such superficial and unreliable factors as population size and geographical extent. The ease of the Japanese victory reversed

Western opinion regarding the two countries: China's weakness was confirmed, and Japan's status was raised.

In 1902, seven years after the Sino-Japanese War, Great Britain, the world's superpower at the dawn of the twentieth century, allied itself with a Japan still not completely free of the restrictions of the unequal treaty system. The treaty establishing the alliance provided (1) a mutual recognition of the two countries' special rights and interests in China and Korea; (2) mutual recognition of their respective rights to "safeguard those interests" if "threatened by the aggressive action of any other power, or by disturbances arising in either China or Korea"; (3) neutrality in the event that either became involved in hostilities with a third power in those areas; and (4) the partners joining in a common war effort in the event that other powers became involved in such hostilities. Thus the world's leading power recognized the emergence of Japan's new military power.

THE RUSSO-JAPANESE WAR, 1904-1905

Japan's second modern war was with Russia, which, unlike China, was a major actor in international politics. Japan's relations with Imperial Russia had begun during the Tokugawa era and were informal because of Japan's seclusion policy. Contact was infrequent but was also unfriendly because of that policy. Imperial Russia had been interested in opening Japan but was anticipated by Commodore Perry. Russia concluded its own unequal treaty with Japan shortly after Perry's success.

Russia's role in the Triple Intervention after the Sino-Japanese War was a clear indication of its increasing involvement in Chinese and Korean affairs. Thus Russia was on a collision course with the expansion of Japanese interests in those two areas. Russian and Japanese involvement in Korea became increasingly confrontational at the turn of the twentieth century, and tensions between the two countries were not eased by diplomacy.

For Japan, this war was far different from that fought against China a decade earlier. It lasted approximately twice as long, from late winter of 1904 to late summer of 1905; the enemy was not a nation in collapse but a major player in world affairs; and it was far more costly in terms of casualties and national resources. At the end of the war foreigners wondered whether the outcome would have been reversed if Russia had known how severely strained Japan actually was and held out for a few more months.

Nevertheless, Japan again emerged victorious. Although Imperial Russia was still a world power, in 1905 its domestic affairs were moving toward the revolution that would begin in just over a decade. The Russian armies had to fight at the end of a long and undependable line of transportation over the vast distances of Siberia. Russian industry produced inadequate supplies for the armies in the field. And again, the war was not fought on Japanese soil. The Japanese army fought well and successfully on the continent, and the Japanese navy annihilated the Russian fleet dispatched to East Asian waters.

Through the mediation of President Theodore Roosevelt the two enemies met in Portsmouth, New Hampshire, and concluded a treaty of peace that made Japan the victor. For Japan, the major spoils of war included Russian recognition of Japan's paramount position in Korea (Korea formally became a Japanese colony in 1911); Russian cession of the southern half of the island of Sakhalin, lying to the north of Japan; and Russia's turning over, with the consent of China, its lease of the Liaodong Peninsula and of the South Manchurian Railway (which connected the Chinese Eastern Railway, roughly bisecting Manchuria from west to east, and the peninsula). Japan received no indemnity, which caused dissatisfaction on Japan's home front.

Victory over Russia added immeasurably to Japan's prestige on the international scene. Japan had defeated a major Western power. One result was a strengthening of the Anglo-Japanese Alliance. Another was the initiation of forty years of tension between Japan, the new military force in the western Pacific, and the United States, the emergent power in the eastern Pacific.

Perhaps the most significant result of the Treaty of Portsmouth was that it opened the way for Japan's acquisition of Korea as a colony, a power base on the continent. By giving Japan the South Manchurian Railway the treaty also created a problem that put Japan and China on the course to a major war that eventually led to the Pacific phase of World War II.

JAPAN IN WORLD WAR I, 1914–1918

In 1914, just nine years after the Russo-Japanese War, World War I broke out. Japan lived up to its commitment under the Anglo-Japanese Alliance by becoming a member of the Allied coalition against Germany and its allies.

Japan's military involvement in the war was slight. Shortly after it declared war against Germany in August 1914, Japan defeated Germany's limited military forces in China, simultaneously eliminating it as a rival in China and gaining revenge for Germany's role in the Triple Intervention. Japan also ejected the small forces from Germany's island possessions in the western and central Pacific. Japan later received administrative control over the islands under the League of Nations mandate system, the terms of which prohibited fortification of the islands. But Japan sealed off and fortified the islands it considered of strategic importance, thus creating a minor but significant area of tension with the United States in the Pacific.

In addition, Japan undertook two other war-related actions that had a significant impact on international politics. In the spring of 1915 Japan formally presented to China what immediately became known as the Twenty-One Demands. These demands—which covered a broad range of economic, political, military, and territorial matters—went far beyond what the Western powers had wrested from China in the closing decades of the nineteenth century and would have made China a protectorate of Japan. The unlisted twenty-second demand was that China keep the demands secret from the rest of the world. Japan was obviously hoping secrecy combined with Western concentration on the war would prevent outside intervention. The Chinese government ignored the demand, taking the only means of possible defense open to it. The United States, which would not become involved in the war for two more years, and Great Britain stood in Japan's way diplomatically. The most outrageous demands were dropped, but the incident clearly revealed the extent of Japan's lust to control China.

The other action grew out of the Russian Revolution in 1917 and quickly became known as the Siberian Intervention. The Allies were concerned that the victorious revolutionaries might gain control over Russian military supplies stockpiled in eastern Siberia. They wanted the White Russian (i.e., Tsarist) military units to prevail over the revolutionaries and for thousands of Czechoslovakian prisoners of war in Russia to be aided as they escaped through Siberia to join Allied forces in Europe. The Allies agreed to send an expeditionary force into Siberia to intervene in the civil war. The force was to be small, fewer than 20,000 men principally from the United States and Japan, with the latter supplying a slight plurality. The Japanese, however, sent approximately ten times the agreed number of troops. The Japanese forces remained in Siberia for about four years. There was little fighting, but relations between the U.S. and Japanese forces were far from friendly and led to diplomatic exchanges between the two governments.

The Siberian Intervention was by far the most unsuccessful Japanese military operation prior to World War II. The operation was not a war but was still costly, with no favorable result for Japan. It was a blow to the prestige of the military. In addition, it was a source of friction with the United States and of lasting resentment in the Soviet Union.

THE WASHINGTON SETTLEMENT, 1921-1922

The Treaty of Versailles in 1919 marked the formal end of World War I. But it suffered from a serious omission. It did not deal with international issues in Asia (or the Far East, to use the standard geographical appellation of the time) that had developed during the war. In 1921 the United States took up the war's unfinished business in Asia. President Warren G. Harding invited China and Japan and seven other nations with interests in Asia to what became known as the Washington Conference.

The conference lasted approximately four months at the end of 1921 and the beginning of 1922. Its major achievements were three treaties: the Four-, Five-, and Nine-Power Pacts. The Four-Power Pact involved France, the British Empire, Japan, and the United States. The stated objectives of the pact held that (1) in the event of a controversy between any members of the pact over "any Pacific question" that could not be settled by diplomatic negotiation, the other parties to the pact would be called in to assist in reaching a solution to the controversy; and (2) the parties would join together to take appropriate action if their rights in the Pacific area were threatened "by the aggressive action of any other Party." The unstated objective was to eliminate the Anglo-Japanese Alliance, which had concerned the United States from the beginning because of the possibility that Britain might ally with Japan against the United States. No action was ever taken under this pact.

The Five-Power Pact (also known as the Naval Limitation Treaty) was signed by the five leading naval powers at the time, divided into a major group and a minor group with the British Empire, the United States, and Japan in the former and France and Italy in the latter. Because of its substantially smaller forces, the minor group was included largely as a matter of courtesy.

The principal provisions of the treaty involved the big three and concerned their capital ships: battleships and aircraft carriers. Limitations were placed on the size of such ships and on their total tonnage. But a critical provision established a 5:5:3 ratio on such tonnage: 5 for the British, 5 for the United States, and 3 for Japan. The strategic reasons for the imbalance among the big three seemed reasonable. The British navy was responsible for protecting the sea lanes of a worldwide empire. The U.S. navy was responsible for long coastlines on two oceans separated by a continent. The Japanese navy was responsible for protecting a smaller island nation thousands of miles removed from the principal bases of its two naval rivals, a technological consideration favoring Japan because of the existing limited cruising radius of the navies of its rivals.

The Japanese representatives requested a 3.5 ratio but accepted the 3 when it appeared that the treaty would be rejected if they did not. What was overlooked at the time was the impact of the unequal ratio number in Japan. The unfortunate echo of the hated unequal treaty system came at a time when Japan's nationalistic spirit was inflamed by its recent military successes, which in Japanese eyes more than merited parity with the United States and Britain.

The Five-Power Pact was motivated by the simplistic view that a mechanical limitation on naval power might serve to reduce the possibility of war. The treaty never served a useful purpose because within a decade Japan's actions indicated that it would not live up to its treaty commitments and because the world was soon on a downward path to a second and greater world war.

The Nine-Power Pact was the centerpiece of the Washington Conference. The nine powers included China, although it was the object of the treaty and was not bound to any action of its own. The contracting powers other than China agreed (1) to respect the sovereignty, independence, and territorial integrity of China; (2) to provide China with the fullest opportunity to develop and maintain for itself an effective and stable government; (3) to establish and maintain the open-door principle throughout China; and (4) to refrain from taking advantage of conditions in China to seek special rights and privileges that would abridge the rights of subjects or citizens of friendly states and from taking action inimical to the security of such states.

The four objectives were clearly designed to change drastically the role of victim China had been forced to play for three-quarters of a century so it could become a normal actor in world affairs. But unspoken in the treaty was the fact that it was also directed at Japan, the extent of whose ambitions had been clearly revealed in the treaties ending the Sino-Japanese War and the Russo-Japanese War and in the Twenty-One Demands.

The open-door principle had been injected into the chaotic international scene created inside China by the so-called scramble for concessions. In the last half of the nineteenth century some European nations and Japan concluded treaty arrangements with Imperial China that would give them special rights and privileges inside the country. Germany developed its sphere of influence in northern China, Great Britain in central China, France in southern China, and Russia in northeast China.

The United States did not get involved in the scramble for concessions, but it did retain commercial rights under its unequal treaty with China. In principle, the United States retained those rights even in areas in which other nations had wrested their own special rights from China.

The Department of State proclaimed the open-door policy in formal notes to the British and German governments in 1899 and to the French, Russian, and Japanese governments in spring of 1900. All accepted the principle, secure in the knowledge that their presence in their spheres of influence gave them an advantage over the general rights and interests of the United States. The United States based its objections to the Twenty-One Demands on the open-door principle and supported the inclusion of that policy in the Nine-Power Pact. Of even greater significance, throughout the 1930s the United States based its opposition to Japan's actions in China largely on the view that Japan was violating America's treaty-based rights in China.

THE LULL OF THE 1920s

The 1920s was the only decade in the first half of the twentieth century in which Japan did not resort to war as an instrument of national policy. The overly optimistic Washington Settlement (as it became known) seemingly reined in Japan's intentions toward China. In addition, Japan became a signatory of the Pact of Paris (also known as the Kellogg-Briand Pact, 1928), a broadly international agreement condemning war as a means of settling international disputes. These developments were part of what turned out to be fruitless efforts to prevent a recurrence of the tragic disaster of World War I. Japan's participation was the result of the temporary eclipse of the determining role of the armed services in the country's foreign policy. The civilian Foreign Ministry had determined that policy in both the Washington Settlement and the Pact of Paris.

The Washington Settlement and the Pact of Paris did not foresee developments in both Japan and China that would lead to the collapse of the settlement and the pact. Japan's limited military role in World War I had the unplanned consequence of fostering an economic boom in the country. First, the war complicated relations between the European colonial powers and their Asian colonies. One result was that Japan supplanted the colonial powers as the supplier of the colonial areas' needs. The Japanese economy, free of the disruptions of war, was also able to fill some of the needs of the participants in the war. Japanese industry rapidly expanded, resulting in jobs for many and in wealth for a few. But the end of the war in 1918 was an economic disaster for Japan because the demand for Japanese products in the colonial powers and their colonies disappeared. Thus Japan was the first of the world's economic powers to suffer in what by the end of the 1920s had become the world depression.

Japan's postwar economic difficulties mirrored historical problems since the collapse of the Tokugawa system. The leaders of Japan and the government they were creating perceived correctly that if Japan was to become a nation-state, it had to deal effectively with the daunting problem of incorporating a modern industrial component into its basically agricultural economy. It did so, aided in no small part by the realization that industry was essential to build the military power that would enable Japan to maintain its independent progress toward a national standing on a level equal to Western nations.

Between 1870 and 1930 Japan took major strides toward industrialization, but it still fell short of becoming an industrialized society. By 1930, half the population still depended on agriculture for its livelihood, and agriculture depended on human labor for its productive power. The modernization process in other sectors of Japanese society had little impact on the daily life of the peasant.

Modernization also placed a new burden on the Japanese farmer: taxes. The government had to rely on a national system of taxation, dependent significantly on a land tax, for finances. And the new taxes had to be paid in money, not in produce as in premodern days. In other words, the peasant bore a disproportionately heavy portion of the financial burden for modernization. Poverty became the peasants' lot. One onerous burden for Japanese peasants was the growth of the tenant system, which was both a result and a cause of poverty.

Population growth and the lack of basic raw materials necessary to support industry were additional sources of economic difficulty. Between 1870 and 1930 Japan's population virtually doubled, paralleling the experiences of industrializing Western societies in the nineteenth century. The Japanese problem was aggravated by the restricted land area of the island country. Further, the Japanese were not migration-prone. The acquisition of Taiwan and Korea as colonial possessions did not result in significant Japanese emigration.

From the beginning of the industrialization process, it was clear that the islands of Japan had neither the quality nor the quantity of essential raw materials for the task at hand. In 1924 the U.S. Congress passed an immigration act designed to control the rate and the nature of the decades-long flow of immigration into the country. In its final form, the law included a provision ending the immigration of all aliens ineligible for naturalization. Under existing law since 1790, all aliens except people of white and black descent were ineligible. The effect was that all Japanese (indeed, all Asian) immigration was forbidden, thus ending what had been a long and vexing problem in Japan-U.S. relations—at least as far as the United States was concerned.

The exclusion was highly resented in Japan, however, because it implied racial inferiority and echoed the hated and vanished unequal treaty system. It became a principal theme of the steadily growing anti-American agenda of the militarists and ultranationalist in the years preceding Pearl Harbor. Few Americans were aware of the impact of this domestic law on Japan's image of them and their country.

In the 1920s Japan was confronted with a complex of political and economic problems that paved the way to a massive return to war as an instrument of policy. Indeed, Japan increasingly used economic problems to justify its bellicose policies and actions. The justification took the form of what was known as the *population problem*: the population was too large to be supported by a restricted and natural resource–poor land area. The justification proved as faulty as the policies it was designed to support.

Following the Washington Settlement, China was entering a course not clearly perceived by the settlement's architects. In 1911 the Empire of China finally ended in collapse. The consequences of the collapse were far different in China from those decades earlier in Japan. Chaos ensued. The Chinese lacked new leadership, an effective central government, and a functioning economy. But there was the unequal treaty system, which meant a collection of Western governments and Japan had special economic, political, diplomatic, and military rights and privileges inside the country—which intensified the purely Chinese difficulties.

By the 1930s China was showing significant signs that it was beginning to change in ways not considered by the creators of the Washington Settlement. Generalissimo Chiang K'ai-shek had begun to build a military power base; his political party, the Kuomindong (Nationalist Party), was inching toward establishing a central government; the Communist Party of China had been born; and, of most immediate significance for Japan, an antiforeign movement had appeared that was directed in general at all the so-called treaty powers but was targeted specifically at Japan.

By 1930 Japan's interest in Manchuria had grown considerably. Under the Treaty of Portsmouth Japan stationed troops both in the leased territory and, as guards, along the South Manchurian Railway. In addition, Japan created the South Manchurian Railway Company as a semigovernmental organization not only to operate the railway but also to set in motion a broad economic program designed to provide business for the railroad and to serve the interests of the Japanese economy. The Japanese forces in Manchuria became known as the Kwantung Army. (Kwantung was the Japanese reading of the Chinese characters for "Liaotong.")

THE MANCHURIAN INCIDENT

On the evening of September 18, 1931, a small explosion occurred on the railroad just outside the city of Mukden that blew out a yard of track but failed to derail an express train. Foreign observers soon charged that the perpetrators were Japanese soldiers, a charge that was later verified. Claiming that the explosion was the work of Chinese "bandits," the Kwantung Army immediately took punitive action in the area, an obviously planned and prepared campaign that soon put it in control of all of Manchuria. The Chinese were unable to mount any effective opposition.

Japan's Foreign Ministry took the position that the Mukden Incident was a limited affair that could be handled by negotiations with the Chinese government. But the Kwantung Army disregarded the Foreign Ministry's position. The Chinese government appealed to the League of Nations for assistance. The league took the only action it could, naming a commission to investigate the affair and recommend a settlement. In its final report the commission rejected Japanese claims that the explosion was the work of the Chinese and that the Japanese had acted in self-defense, but it also set forth as a principle for settling the matter of recognition of Japanese treaty rights in Manchuria.

A few months after the Mukden Incident the Kwantung Army announced the creation of a new nation, Manchukuo, declaring that this recognized a nonexistent independence movement. "Manchukuo" was immediately dubbed a puppet state. The Japanese ambassador to the new nation was the general in command of the Kwantung Army, and Japanese "advisers" were attached to all ministries of the new government. The League of Nations held that Manchukuo was a Japanese creation but recommended that Japan and China negotiate a new treaty reconciling their mutual interests in the area.

On March 25, 1933, six months after the release of the commission's report, Japan officially rejected its findings and recommendations and announced its withdrawal from the League of Nations. Yet Japan declared that its national policy was identical to the league's, namely, "to insure the peace of the Orient and thereby contribute to the cause of peace throughout the world." This claim remained basic to the government's justification of its foreign policy until the end of World War II. Attempting to justify its attitude, Japan declared:

> China is not an organized state; . . . [and] its internal conditions
> and external relations are characterized by extreme confusion and
> complexity and by many abnormal and exceptional features; and . . .
> the general principles and usages of international law which
> govern the ordinary relations between states are found to be
> considerably modified in their operation so far as China is
> concerned.

Japan charged that the League of Nations failed to grasp the realities of the China situation and take them into account, that the report completely misunderstood Japan's intentions ("the maintenance of peace in the Orient"), that it contained "gross errors" in both facts and conclusions, that it failed to recognize that the Japanese army's actions fell "within the just limits of self-defense," and that it failed to place full responsibility on China for the situation that led to the Japanese action.

This defense of the seizure of Manchuria was important not only as a justification of the Kwantung Army's actions but also as a concise statement of Japan's approach to China in subsequent years. It could be paraphrased as: "Only Japan understands the problem of China; therefore, only Japan can solve the problem." The policy was successful in that it won domestic Japanese support, particularly since no alternative was put before the public; it failed because it did not win acceptance in the outside world.

The Manchurian Incident added significantly to the long-standing tensions between Japan and the United States over China. Early in 1932, just over three months after the Mukden explosion, Secretary of State Henry L. Stimson drafted a formal note to the Japanese and Chinese governments that contained what became known as the doctrine of non-recognition. The key passage read:

> In view of the present situation and its own rights and obligations therein, the American government deems it to be its duty to notify both the Imperial Japanese Government and the Government of the Republic of China that it cannot admit the legality of any situation de facto nor does it intend to recognize any treaty or agreement entered into by those Governments, or agents thereof, which may impair the treaty rights of the United States or its citizens in China, including those which relate to the sovereignty, the independence, or the territorial and administrative integrity of the Republic of China, or to the international policy relative to China, commonly known as the open door policy.

The doctrine remained at the core of U.S. policy toward Japan's actions in China throughout the period leading to Pearl Harbor.

The Manchurian Incident was a decisive development in Japan's resort to war as an instrument of national policy. It was the climactic moment in policy toward China since the outbreak of the first war in 1894, but it was also one of the first steps toward World War II. It created an insoluble problem in Japan's relations with China. The incident placed Japan in a position to invade North China, the step that led to the outbreak of the second Sino-Japanese War in 1937. It deepened the confrontation between Japan and the United States as the two rising powers in the Pacific area. It led to the collapse of the League of Nations, whose primary mission was to maintain international peace. Finally, the acquisition of Manchuria as a puppet state seemed to produce rich territorial and economic rewards, resulting in domestic acceptance in Japan of a continuation of the policy of war.

The military success in Manchuria was soon followed by successful unconventional ventures by the military in the Japanese domestic political scene. The first major venture occurred on May 15, 1932, less than a year after the Mukden Incident. On that day military units (gangs might be a better term) led by young officers assassinated the prime minister and attacked the residence of one of the emperor's closest advisers, as well as a major bank, a major newspaper, and power stations. They made clear at the time and later that their aim was not to take control of the government but to carry out what they callled "the Showa Restoration," that is, to remove "the bad influences" controlling the emperor. Such influences, they claimed, were responsible for such evils as the exploitative economic system and the "disgrace" of the Washington Settlement and should be replaced with advisers who could provide proper guidance for the emperor and the country.

The principals were arrested, tried, and imprisoned for their crimes. But a point of major political importance had been made: men in uniform had gone as far as assassination to express their views about serious problems confronting their country. The militarists accused the civilian leaders of failing to take appropriate action. Their own behavior showed it was dangerous to stand in the way of the military.

Four years later, on February 26, 1936, a far more serious incident took place. An army regiment, again under the leadership of lower-ranking officers, carried out a series of assassinations, attempted assassinations, and terrorist acts against banks, newspapers, and the headquarters of the national police. This action was soon put down, but only after the emperor as commander in chief of the armed forces ordered the rebels to lay down their arms.

The government—including the military leaders—took strong action, but on this occasion the minister of war issued a statement supporting the aims, if not the actions, of the rebels. He pointed out that their motives were pure because they were demanding appropriate action to solve domestic and foreign problems confronting the empire. The message of the young officers and their superiors was clear: we understand our country's problems and how to solve them; all others stand clear or else. Thus ended the brief life of Taisho democracy.

JAPAN AND WORLD WAR II, 1937–1945

The Russian Revolution in 1917 had a related and serious, if indirect, influence on Japan's domestic politics. The revolution gave Russia a new communism/Marxism that in turn fostered an international movement embodied in the Comintern (the Communist International). For Japan, these developments changed the nature of Russia as a traditional enemy. Russia now loomed as a potential ideological as well as military threat, for Marxism was incompatible with both *kokutai* and private property.

The appearance of international communism also had a significant impact on Japan's international position. In 1936 Japan and Nazi Germany entered into a treaty to cooperate in the exchange of information to combat international communism. The treaty was supported by a secret agreement that if either party should become involved in a conflict with the Soviet Union as the principal supporter of international communism, the other party would do nothing "to ease the situation" of the USSR.

In 1937 Italy joined the German-Japanese alliance, and in 1940 the three nations signed an agreement making themselves the Axis Alliance. Under this agreement Japan recognized Germany and Italy as the creators of a "New Order in Europe," and Germany and Italy recognized Japan as the creator of the "New Order in Greater East Asia." The countries agreed to assist each other "with all political, economic, and military means when one of the three contracting Powers is attacked by a Power at present not involved in the European war or in the Chinese-Japanese conflict." The other power was the United States. In the Pacific, the lineup of the opposing sides in the coming world war was established.

On the evening of July 7, 1937, a minor military skirmish of unclear origin between Japanese and Chinese troops took place at a bridge near Beijing. The Japanese forces immediately expanded the action, thus initiating an eight-year war (undeclared for the first four years).

Japan could not win this war, but China would not lose it. From the opening shots Japan demonstrated overwhelming military superiority. By 1940 Japan controlled China's underdeveloped rail system, its coastline, and the major river systems (vital for transportation because of the deficiencies of land transportation) and occupied the major cities in northern, central, and southern China. The Chinese finally found refuge in what was then the remote western city of Chongqing (Chungking), safe from Japanese armies but not from Japanese bombers. The Nationalist government did not surrender in spite of continued Japanese attempts to negotiate an end to the fighting.

Through the first four years of the war, China's will to resist was bolstered by moral, diplomatic, and limited economic support from the United States. U.S. military support could not be provided, however. First, the so-called neutrality laws of the United States, enacted during the 1930s to prevent the nation from again becoming embroiled in a foreign war, stood in the way of direct military involvement. Second, the weak state of U.S. military forces prevented direct military aid.

The war also contributed mightily to the worsening of U.S.-Japanese relations. We have seen how throughout the early decades of the twentieth century the United States had taken a stand against Japan's aggressive policy against China. America's treaty-based interests inside China had created a significant U.S. presence in the country. Since the early years of the new nation Christian missionaries had been active in China, not only in religion but also in education and medicine. Their work had led to holdings such as churches, schools, and hospitals. In addition, U.S. commercial interests in China had developed significantly by the 1930s.

Inevitably, Japanese military operations in the war had a direct and growing impact on U.S.-owned property, U.S. companies, and individual U.S. citizens. Diplomatic relations between Washington and Tokyo were characterized by clashes between the two governments' incompatible policies toward China. In the field, numerous unpleasant collisions between Japanese military operations and U.S. citizens on the scene occurred, to the latter's disadvantage.

By 1941 the undeclared war in China had already become by far the most costly war in Japan's history in terms of both human and economic resources. In addition, the population had been subjected to the government's unanswered drumbeat of ultranationalistic propaganda centering on such themes as the superiority of Japan and its people, the "holy war" in China, the refusal of the outside world to approve of that war, the necessity for the people to accept all sacrifices required by the war, and the growing encirclement of the country by the ABCD powers (America, Britain, China, and the Dutch in the East Indies). The themes were also prominent in Japanese propaganda to the outside world.

The Japanese propaganda efforts were countered in the United States not by U.S. government counteraction but by a strong groundswell of public support for the beleaguered Chinese government and people. In addition, news coverage of the war created strong pro-Chinese and anti-Japanese attitudes. There was also the sentimental U.S. attitude toward the underdog, which China definitely was. Then there were the actions of the Japanese military, ranging from the bombing of civilians in defenseless cities (before this tactic became built into what was developing into total war), the gratuitous beheading of Chinese war prisoners by sword-wielding Japanese officers, and the Rape of Nanking (also known as the Nanking Massacre), which received coverage in the world press because of eyewitness reports of foreign correspondents on the scene.

As early as 1940 it was becoming increasingly apparent that only one thing could prevent the outbreak of war between the United States and Japan: a drastic, extremely unlikely political change in Japan that would result in the abandonment of the war in China or an equally drastic and unlikely political change in the United States that would permit acceptance of the course of aggression Japan was following. The starkly opposed positions of the two countries could not be reconciled.

In 1941 the Nazis controlled Western Europe militarily, had mounted an initially highly successful campaign against the Soviet Union, and appeared to many to be on the threshold of victory. Japan dominated China and seemed poised to strike the colonies of the Western European democracies in Southeast Asia, which contained the strategic raw materials—especially oil for the navy and the army—Japan required for its war machine. The Axis powers seemed on the verge of victory in both Europe and Asia. Of the world powers, only the United States was on the sidelines, but it was clearly prepared to enter the fray on the side of the Allies.

In 1941 the United States and Japan held what turned out to be final and fruitless negotiations to reach a peaceful solution to their difficulties with each other. What followed was the attack on Pearl Harbor on December 7, 1941, and the beginning of the Pacific phase of World War II.

Pearl Harbor was a great tactical victory for Japan. It was the first blow in a tremendous military campaign that resulted in a short six months of Japan's temporary control of a vast area of the globe stretching from the Aleutian Islands in the North Pacific south to what is now Indonesia and the islands north of Australia and west to the borders of what was then British India. Had it resulted in eventual victory, the operation would have gone down in history as a masterpiece of military planning and execution. It also demonstrated that in seventy short years Japan had transformed itself from an isolated premodern feudal society into a powerful world power.

But Pearl Harbor was also a strategic error that led to the defeat and destruction of the authoritarian-militaristic nation-state Japan had become. The attack set the United States on the road to becoming the most powerful military machine the world had ever seen. In effect, responding to the Japanese Pearl Harbor victory, the United States developed land, sea, and air forces unparalleled in size and strength. One of the secrets of Japanese military success for half a century was the absence of an effective enemy. The United States, surpassing by far the military power Japan exhibited in its broad victories at and following Pearl Harbor, became an overpoweringly effective enemy.

The United States was the first nation-state to apply to the fullest extent the scientific, technological, and industrial—to say nothing of human—resources for the total war of the twentieth century. But it was aided in its efforts by being the only major combatant to escape the devastation of war.

The naval battle of Midway of June 1942 and the land and sea battles at Guadalcanal in the South Pacific, which began several months later, stopped the explosion of Japanese military might and began the three-year process of the destruction of that might. Both sides experienced many bloody and costly battles, but the overpowering U.S. offensive forces subdued the stubborn Japanese defenses.

By 1945 a steady succession of U.S. victories in the southwestern and western Pacific put U.S. long-range bombers (a major technological breakthrough) in position to begin intensively bombing Japan. The bombing was the beginning of the end, but when that end would come no one knew. The specter of invasion of the main islands remained. Both sides assumed that if the final stages of the war involved such an invasion, the cost to both sides would be staggering. The destruction of the Japanese navy; the death, destruction, and devastation caused by the bombing; the two atomic bombs; and the Soviet entry into the war in the final days combined to eliminate the necessity of an invasion.

3

Conditional Unconditional Surrender: Prelude to Constitutional Change

In the last six months of 1944, the rapidly diminishing Japanese hopes for an even remotely favorable end to the war vanished. In those six months U.S. forces won the islands of Saipan and Guam, vital as bases in the coming air war against Japan; the Tojo Cabinet, which had witnessed the great victories in the first six months after Pearl Harbor, fell; the Japanese navy had ceased to be an effective fighting force; and the U.S. offensive was well advanced toward reconquering the Philippines, a major step toward the coming invasion of Japan.

Meanwhile, on the other side of the globe, Japan's remaining Axis ally was under heavy military pressure on the western front from the Allies and on the eastern front from the Soviet Union. The Allies had recovered from the serious setbacks they had suffered at the hands of the Nazi armies in Europe and the Japanese in Asia and the Pacific, but no one could predict when the war would end.

THE EMERGING MEANING OF UNCONDITIONAL SURRENDER

In 1942, when the Allies found themselves in a decidedly unfavorable military situation, President Franklin Roosevelt and Prime Minister Winston Churchill announced that their primary war aim was to force unconditional surrender of the enemy. From the beginning, the concept was criticized even within the Allied camp. The critics charged that the concept was undefined and therefore meaningless. As long as it was undefined it could be interpreted to mean absolute defeat, with the losers completely at the mercy of the victors. Therefore, the argument ran, as a war aim it was inappropriate because the enemy could use it to spur the military on the field of battle and on the home front to generate support for the war effort. But the phrase remained undefined.

In December 1943 Japan was given its first clear signal of the meaning of the concept in the form of the Cairo Declaration, released at a conference there of Roosevelt, Churchill, and Chiang K'ai-shek. Japan would be stripped of all the territories it had taken "by violence and greed" since the first war with China. The declaration pledged that the three countries would "continue to persevere in the serious and prolonged operation to procure the unconditional surrender of Japan."

On May 7, 1945, Nazi Germany surrendered, but the war in the Pacific was continuing with no end in sight. On May 8 President Harry Truman, with the prospect of the continuing war against Japan very much a reality, issued a statement on the meaning of unconditional surrender for Japan. The statement was not addressed to the government of Japan or even to the people of Japan, although both were obviously the target.

The statement opened with a simple sentence: "Nazi Germany has been defeated." The unwritten but clear completion of that thought was "but the rest of the war will continue." The remainder of the message was presented in two parts. The first warned that the demonstrated striking power and intensity of the land, sea, and air attacks on Japan would steadily increase and "will not cease until the Japanese military and naval forces lay down their arms in *unconditional surrender*" (italics in original). Then came the five points of the meaning of the term:

It means the end of the war.

It means the termination of the influence of the military leaders who have brought Japan to the present brink of disaster.

It means provision for the return of soldiers and sailors to their families, their farms, their jobs.

It means not prolonging the present agony and suffering of the Japanese in the vain hope of victory.

Unconditional surrender does not mean the extermination or enslavement of the Japanese people.

At first glance the first meaning seems obvious. It seems to have been based on the assumption that the Japanese people would welcome the end of almost eight long years of sacrifice, death, destruction, and privation in a war that had become increasingly hopeless. The second and third meanings were later incorporated into U.S./Allied policy for the defeated enemy. The second was of long-term historical consequence and the third of short-term importance, for the word *provision* presaged the repatriation operation after the surrender that returned over 6 million military and civilian personnel to Japan from overseas.

The fourth and fifth items countered the Japanese government's propaganda directed to its own people. Especially after the setbacks in the summer of 1944 it had emphasized two strident themes: first, all loyal subjects had to endure hardship and suffering and fight to the death when the expected invasion came, and second, the beastly U.S. enemy would enslave or exterminate the Japanese people.

Truman and his advisers were undoubtedly well aware that his statement would have no direct impact on the waging of the war. It was not designed to open the road to a negotiated peace. Also, the private possession of short-wave radio receivers had been unlawful in Japan for some years, so the statement would not affect public attitudes. On the other hand, it was known that the Japanese government carefully monitored U.S. radio broadcasts, and the statement was tailored to deliver two messages to appropriate officials in the Japanese government. The first and loudest was simply that the U.S. military effort against Japan would not let up now that the Nazis had been knocked out of the war. The second made an important addition to the aim of the Cairo Declaration, namely, the elimination of the military.

Truman's statement clearly informed the Japanese government that the U.S. government was prepared to wage war until the Japanese armed forces surrendered unconditionally. But the statement also provided for the first time at least a small idea of what Japan could expect after surrender.

THE POTSDAM DECLARATION

As indicated, the Truman statement was not an overture to the Japanese government to enter negotiations to end the war, but it was the first tentative step on a ten-week journey that led to the Potsdam Declaration (see the Appendix), which stated the terms that brought the war to an end and constituted the final definition of unconditional surrender. The Potsdam Declaration was an ultimatum to Japan to end the war based on three years of work by the U.S. government on what its policy toward Japan would be after the latter's defeat.

About six months after the disaster at Pearl Harbor, when prospects of a U.S. victory in the war against Japan were dim, a small group at the

Department of State was formed to begin to develop a policy toward a defeated Japan. The late Hugh Borton, the only American who at the time was a serious scholar of Japanese history, was the working leader, although he was not in charge. As the war progressed, favorably for the United States, State Department involvement grew. Finally, in late 1944 the operation was incorporated into the State, War, Navy Coordinating Committee (known by the cumbersome acronym SWNCC, pronounced "Swenk"), created to deal with policies to cover nonmilitary problems growing out of military operations in both the European and Pacific theaters of war. Unfortunately, the history of SWNCC, and for purposes here of its Far Eastern Section, remains to be written.

As the U.S. armed forces played the major role in crushing the Japanese military forces on land, sea, and air, the State Department and the members of SWNCC dominated the development of the policies that were the foundation for both the Japanese surrender and the occupation that ensued. The war against Japan was waged by a coalition of Allied Powers, led by the military might of the United States; the surrender, occupation, and eventual peace were firmly carried out by the Allied Powers but under the policies of the United States.

The United States was propelled into leadership of the surrender and the occupation by its military defeat of Japan's land, sea, and air forces— the consequences of which were recognized at the Potsdam Conference of July 16–August 2, 1945. The conference document that embodied the terms of surrender was the Potsdam Declaration (see Appendix). It is also a key to understanding both the occupation and Japan's postwar history, including the drastic shift from the Meiji to the Showa Constitution.

The Potsdam Declaration, issued over the signatures of the president of the United States (Truman), the president of the Republic of China (Chiang K'ai-shek), and the prime minister of Great Britain (Churchill), consisted first of a warning: "The full application of our military power, backed by our resolve, *will* mean the inevitable and complete destruction of the Japanese armed forces and just as inevitably the utter devastation of the Japanese homeland." There was no mention of the atomic bomb, but the meaning of "utter destruction" was made clear a few days later. The declaration's final sentence promised "prompt and utter destruction" of Japan if the government did not proclaim "the unconditional surrender of all Japanese forces," the final definition of the Churchill/Roosevelt concept.

The terms were divided into two parts. The first was punitive: the permanent removal of the influence and authority "of those who have deceived and misled the people of Japan into embarking on world conquest," occupation of "points in Japanese territory to be designated by the Allies," limitation of Japanese sovereignty to the home islands, and "stern justice" for all war criminals. The second part dealt with what might be termed the benefits Japan could gain from surrender. Japanese forces, after being completely disarmed, could "return to their homes with the opportunity to lead peaceful and productive lives"; the Allies did not intend that the Japanese people would "be enslaved as a race or destroyed as a nation"; and the occupation would end once its objectives were attained.

Of greater significance were the political and economic terms. Politically, "The Japanese government shall remove all obstacles to the revival and strengthening of democratic tendencies among the Japanese people. Freedom of speech, of religion, and of thought, as well as respect for the fundamental human rights, shall be established." Economically, "Japan shall be permitted to maintain such industries as will sustain her economy. . . . To this end, access to, as distinguished from control of, raw materials shall be permitted. Eventual Japanese participation in world trade relations shall be permitted." Finally, it was stated that the occupation would end when its objectives had been accomplished and "there has been established in accordance with the freely expressed will of the Japanese people a peacefully inclined and responsible government."

The declaration was released on July 26, 1945, approximately the midpoint of the conference. Unlike the Truman statement of May 8, it was delivered to Japan in massive quantities. The U.S. Office of War Information featured it in its radio broadcasts directed at Japan, assuring that it would be distributed to appropriate targets in the Japanese government; and U.S. aircraft dropped millions of leaflets with the Japanese translation of the declaration, assuring that it would circulate among at least a segment of the public. After all, it was by content if not title an ultimatum to Japan's leaders to end the war.

Initially, the Potsdam Declaration did not have the intended effect. Prime Minister Suzuki Kantaro announced that his government would treat it with *mokusatsu*. The two characters mean silence (*moku*) and kill (*satsu*), but the key word is silence, so the perceived meaning is "pass over in silence" or "take no notice of" rather than "rejection."

The context for a Japanese decision was drastically altered by the dropping of the two atomic bombs on August 6 and 8 and the Soviet declaration of war also on August 8. On August 10 the chargé d'affaires of the Swiss Embassy in Tokyo transmitted to U.S. Secretary of State James F. Byrnes Japan's "qualified acceptance" of the declaration: "with the understanding that the said declaration does not comprise any demand which prejudices the prerogatives of His Majesty as a Sovereign Ruler." The qualification was ambiguous because it did not state that "prerogatives of His Majesty as a Sovereign Ruler" were based on his nation's fundamental law and were at the core of the ideology of *kokutai*, or national polity.

Byrnes in his reply also avoided the issue of the imperial prerogatives by stating that the emperor

> will be required to authorize and ensure the signature by the Government of Japan and of the Japanese Imperial Headquarters of the surrender terms necessary to carry out the provisions of the Potsdam Declaration, and shall issue his command to the Japanese military, naval and air authorities and to all the forces under their control wherever located to cease active operations and to surrender their arms and to issue such other orders as the Supreme Commander may require to give effect to the surrender terms.

Byrnes thus finally confirmed that unconditional surrender was to be imposed on the armed forces. Implicit in these words was recognition of the constitutional provision that the emperor was the commander in chief of the armed forces.

But Byrnes touched indirectly on the imperial constitutional position by also stating: "The ultimate form of government in Japan shall, in accordance with the Potsdam Declaration, be established by the freely expressed will of the Japanese people." Those words were open to interpretation by the Japanese that the freely expressed will of the imperial subjects would support retention of the imperial prerogatives.

The final struggle over the acceptance of the declaration will not be examined in depth here. Suffice it to say that the ministers of state could not agree on a single recommendation to the emperor; the minister of foreign affairs recommended acceptance, and the ministers of war and of the navy recommended rejection. The deadlock was resolved when the emperor chose to accept. He acted not as a man named Hirohito but as the sovereign monarch as set forth in the Meiji Constitution. This interpretation may be the basis for the view of some Japanese that the Potsdam Declaration was not the imposition of the will of the conqueror but an international agreement between a defeated but still sovereign Japan and its victorious enemies.

THE SURRENDER

At noon on August 16 (Japan time), 1945, the emperor announced his decision to his people in a recorded radio broadcast over the government's national network. It was the first time his voice was heard in the land.

Both the imperial voice and the message it was delivering made this a historic and highly charged moment in Japanese history.

The key sentence was "We have ordered our Government to communicate to the Governments of the United States, Britain, China and the Soviet Union that our Empire accepts the provisions of their Joint Declaration." The rescript offered the reason war had been declared in 1941: to ensure "Japan's self-preservation and the stabilization of East Asia." That characterization was a drastic condensation of the government propaganda endlessly repeated during the war. The declaration had been accepted because "the war situation has developed not necessarily to Japan's advantage," which the victors regarded as one of history's great euphemisms. Worthy of note was a warning: "Beware most strictly of any outbursts of emotion which may engender needless complication." This seems to be transparent code for "cooperate with the occupation," coming as it did from the supreme and still divine monarch.

The acceptance of the declaration instituted a brief period of what could be described as an informal and incomplete armistice. Soviet armies in Manchuria and Korea and Chinese Nationalist and Communist armies continued operations against the Japanese. The United States and its other allies ceased theirs.

The surrender was completed by the signing of the instrument of surrender on the deck of the USS *Missouri* in Tokyo Bay on September 2, 1945, by representatives of the Japanese government and formally and simultaneously by General Douglas MacArthur as Supreme Commander of the Allied Powers, Admiral Chester R. Nimitz, and representatives of the other eight powers. The document reads as if its drafters had Byrnes's statement before them. First, the two Japanese signatories were Shigemitsu Mamoru, the foreign minister, and General Umezu Yoshijiro, the chief of the Imperial General Headquarters. The instrument identified Shigemitsu, a civilian, as signing "By Command and in behalf of the Emperor of Japan and the Japanese Government" and Umezu as signing "By Command and in behalf of the Japanese Imperial Headquarters." It is reasonable to surmise that the different stipulations were a safeguard against military opponents' use of surrender of the independence of the military command to justify resistance to the occupation.

The content of the instrument of surrender can be summarized as follows: acceptance of the Potsdam Declaration; proclamation of unconditional surrender of the Imperial General Headquarters, all Japanese forces under its command, and all armed forces under Japanese command; a command to all civil, military, and naval officials to obey and enforce all proclamations, orders, and directives issued by the Supreme Commander and to remain at their posts to carry out their noncombat duties unless specifically removed by him; a command to the emperor, the Japanese government, and their successors to carry out the provisions of the Potsdam Declaration in good faith; and a command to liberate all Allied prisoners of war and civilian internees and to provide for their "protection, care, maintenance, and transportation as directed." It concluded with this statement: "The authority of the Emperor and Government to rule the State shall be subject to the Supreme Commander for the Allied Powers who will take such steps as he deems proper to effect these terms of surrender." This last stipulation recognized the continued authority of the emperor to rule the state as constitutionally provided.

With its acceptance by the emperor, the Potsdam Declaration had served its primary purpose. It had ended the war with consequent benefit to both sides. For Japan it meant an end to the death and destruction that had resulted from half a century of war as an instrument of national policy. For the Allied side it meant the end of the threat from the militaristic and authoritarian Axis enemies—Germany, Italy, and Japan. For both sides it ended the impending disaster inherent in the planned invasion of Japan. But the declaration could not be perceived as a working policy for the occupation of the defeated Japanese enemy.

U.S. INITIAL POST-SURRENDER POLICY FOR JAPAN

The Potsdam Declaration clearly told the Japanese what they could expect when the war ended, but only in general terms. The details were soon released in the form of the U.S. Initial Post-Surrender Policy for Japan (USIPPJ; see Appendix), one of the great papers in the history of U.S. foreign policy. It has never been given deserved recognition. The USIPPJ was released publicly by the White House on August 28, 1945, two weeks after the cessation of hostilities when the war's end dominated U.S. public consciousness regarding Japan and only a few days before the dramatic signing of the instrument of surrender. The occupation never caused flaming controversy in the United States, as did the U.S. role in its far more headline-generating involvement in China's tragic civil war, which entered its final stage almost simultaneously with the end of the war with Japan. Consequently, the USIPPJ never became the center of U.S. public attention.

The USIPPJ was the product of the long process of planning in the State Department and SWNCC outlined earlier. It was not only a policy paper but was later recast in the form of a military order by the U.S. Joint Chiefs of Staff and sent to General MacArthur as the basic directive for his mission as the Supreme Commander for the Allied Powers (SCAP) in the occupation of Japan. The United States had assumed the major burden of the offensive war against Japan and automatically shifted into the role of principal occupying power with the post facto acceptance of that decision by the other Allied Powers. MacArthur was the Supreme Commander "for" and not "of" the Allied Powers. The choice of the preposition was important because it made clear that he was an American general acting on behalf of the wartime allies but responsible to the U.S. government and therefore free of the authority of (and possible interference by) the other powers involved. Although the U.S. Navy had played a major role in the destruction of Japanese military power, a general, not an admiral, was chosen to command the occupation because it was to be a ground occupation requiring army, not navy, forces. The USIPPJ requires close analysis because its successful implementation sheds considerable light on both the creation of the 1947 Showa Constitution and, of even greater significance, the development of postwar Japanese society that has constituted the necessary political, social, and economic environment for that constitution.

The policy had two ultimate stated objectives:

1. To ensure that Japan will not again become a menace to the United States or to the peace and security of the world.

2. To bring about the eventual establishment of a peaceful and responsible government which will respect the rights of other states and will support the objectives of the United States as reflected in the ideals and principles of the Charter of the United Nations. The United States desires that this government should conform as closely as may be to principles of democratic self-government, but it is not the responsibility of the Allied governments to impose upon Japan any form of government not supported by the freely expressed will of the people.

These objectives faithfully reflect the punitive/benevolent dichotomy observable in the Potsdam Declaration. The first objective was backward-looking in that it was based on almost half a century of steadily growing tension in U.S.-Japanese relations that finally exploded in war and on an equally long Japanese history of economic, diplomatic, political, and, finally, military aggression against China.

The second objective was forward-looking. Its goal was to bring into being a Japan that would follow a course diametrically opposed to the one pursued in the first half of the twentieth century. It was automatic for the United States, a country proud of its democratic system, to want a new government in Japan to "conform as closely as may be to principles of democratic self-government." This goal, therefore, would also end the Meiji Constitution. Significantly, however, the policy also set forth an important self-restraint, a denial of an intention "to impose upon Japan any form of government not supported by the freely expressed will of the people."

The two objectives were to be achieved by four principal means, two backward-looking and of relatively minor importance and two forward-looking and of major import. The first two concerned the limitation of Japanese sovereignty to the principal islands (the historical limits of Japanese sovereignty) and complete disarmament and demilitarization. The meaning of disarmament was obvious. Demilitarization was described as follows: "The authority of the militarists and the influence of militarism will be totally eliminated from political, economic, and social life. Institutions expressive of the spirit of militarism will be vigorously suppressed."

The third means was political and would have a direct and vital impact on the replacement of the Meiji Constitution by a new and vastly different one: "The Japanese people shall be encouraged to develop a desire for individual liberties and respect for fundamental human rights, particularly the freedoms of religion, assembly, speech, and the press. They shall also be encouraged to form democratic and representative organizations."

The fourth means was economic. It stated the right of the Japanese people to have an "opportunity to develop for themselves an economy which will permit the peacetime requirements of the population to be met." As later developments demonstrated, this means was enormously important to Japan's economic future but was unrelated to the constitutional issue.

Part II of the USIPPJ dealt with Allied authority in Japan. It provided for an Allied military occupation under a Supreme Commander designated by the United States and for the primacy of U.S. policies if differences emerged between the United States and other Allied governments.

The key provisions of Part II concerned the relationship between the Supreme Commander and the Japanese government:

> The Supreme Commander will exercise his authority through Japanese governmental machinery and agencies, including the Emperor, to the extent that this satisfactorily furthers United States objectives. The Japanese government will be permitted under instructions to exercise the normal powers of government in matters of domestic administration. This policy, however, will be subject to the

right and duty of the Supreme Commander to require changes in governmental machinery or personnel or to act if the Emperor or other Japanese authority does not satisfactorily meet the requirements of the Supreme Commander in effectuating the surrender terms. This policy, moreover, does not commit the Supreme Commander to support the Emperor or any other Japanese governmental authority in opposition to evolutionary changes looking toward the attainment of United States objectives. The policy is to use the existing form of government in Japan, not to support it.

This formulation of the controlling character of the occupation turned out to be effective because (1) the USIPPJ contained the kind of policy later experience demonstrated was ideal for the purposes of both the U.S. government and a Japan that from the beginning was launched on a path of reconstructive transformation; (2) General MacArthur, in spite of his idiosyncrasies, turned out to be the perfect man for the job, executing his government's occupation policy with a minimum of friction with its target; and (3) the Japanese officials responsible for both running their own government and carrying out the directives of the occupation seemed, consciously or unconsciously, to be convinced that the policies of their conquerors were designed to serve the best interests of themselves and their nation.

Part III of the policy listed detailed means by which the objectives were to be achieved in the political sphere. The details included convincing the country of the responsibility of the military for the "existing and future distress of the people"; eliminating the army, navy, air force, secret police organizations, and civil aviation; removing and excluding active exponents of militarism and militant nationalism "from public office and from any other position of public or substantial private responsibility"; dissolving and prohibiting ultranationalistic or militaristic social, political, professional, and commercial societies and institutions; eliminating from the educational system "militarism and ultra-nationalism, in doctrine and practice"; and removing and excluding former military and naval officers and "all other exponents of militarism and ultra-nationalism" from public office, educational positions, and economic responsibility. Also, all persons charged with war crimes were to be arrested, tried, and, if convicted, punished. The list was impressive and was clearly designed to eliminate the militarism and authoritarianism that had flowered under the Meiji Constitution.

The list of positive political actions to be taken had far greater importance for the future. It included the immediate granting of religious freedom; the opportunity for the Japanese people to become familiar with "the history, institutions, culture, and accomplishments of the United States and other democracies"; the encouragement of political parties, with rights of assembly and public discussion; the abrogation of laws, decrees, and regulations establishing discrimination on the basis of race, nationality, creed, or political opinion; the release of political prisoners; and the reform of "judicial, legal, and police systems to conform with the policies" of the occupation to protect individual liberties and civil rights. All these actions were signposts on the road to democracy.

The economic section (Part IV) of the USIPPJ was considerably longer than the political section. The details are omitted here because the economic policy contained little of significance to constitutionalism. Suffice it to say that the principal objectives were economic demilitarization and the promotion of democratic economic forces. At the time, this was not recognized as one of the first toddling steps toward the economic miracle of the future.

The years that went into hammering out a policy for a defeated Japan were clearly well spent. It is doubtful that any victorious nation ever occupied a defeated enemy with such a solid plan. It is also clear that if the objectives of the policy were to be achieved, the result would be the transformation of Japanese society. One wonders how many of those who worked on the plan realized the enormity of the task they were creating or how many Japanese officials working with the occupation perceived the extent of the transformation that would come about if the objectives of the occupation were achieved.

This chapter deals with the development and content of U.S. policy toward a surrendered Japan, yet it does not address the problem of constitutional change. The reason is simple: constitutional change was never included in the occupation policy. However, the U.S. role in both the war against Japan and the consequent occupation was of such importance that it made the United States into Japan's collaborator in creating a new fundamental law for its recent enemy.

THE FIRST 120 DAYS

The signing of the instrument of surrender on September 2, 1945, marked the formal beginning of the occupation. By definition and in popular understanding of the term, an occupation is the act of taking possession of a country by military force. The U.S. occupation of Japan certainly fit that definition, for the overwhelming U.S. military force inflicted the defeat that resulted in the occupation. But to understand the occupation as an important historical development transcending its obviously military origins and characteristics, one must understand the role of the United

States as the occupying nation and Japan as the occupied country when the operation began in late summer of 1945.

At the beginning of the occupation Japan was in a state of crisis. All but one (Kyoto) of Japan's cities had suffered devastation from the massive U.S. bombing attacks. There was a serious shortage of food, clothing, and shelter. The economy was in chaos as a result of both the bombing and the cessation of war production. Public transportation was crippled. Family life had been disrupted by conscription for the military and war-time industry. Schools had been closed, and civilians not essential to the war effort had been evacuated (or had fled) from the cities. Both military and civilian casualties had been heavy. The crisis that had confronted Japan less than a century earlier with the collapse of the Tokugawa regime and the opening of the country to the Western powers was mild by comparison.

But Japan benefited from two postwar developments: the end of militarism and the survival of the bureaucracy. Defeat in the war had virtually eliminated the armed forces as a dominant factor in government and politics, and demobilization and disarmament ended their role in the society at large. The bureaucracy survived, and although wartime devastation made its job extremely difficult, the USIPPJ empowered it to continue to direct the country's domestic affairs—a difficult task that was performed successfully.

As a defeated and occupied nation, Japan had no conventional diplomatic relations following the surrender, but by accepting the Potsdam Declaration the Japanese government committed itself to a strange relationship with its recent enemy. The declaration provided only a general outline of what Japan could expect after surrender, but the USIPPJ provided abundant details demonstrating that the occupation was going to be far more than a military operation.

What was the structure of the occupation with which Japan had to deal? What follows is a bare-bones description of what was, in effect, a second government of Japan. At its head was the U.S. General of the Army Douglas MacArthur. From the start he was so closely identified with the occupation that for both Americans and Japanese he became the personification of the occupation; the occupation was his. But the popular image, as is sometimes the case, did not conform with the facts. Although he enjoyed the highest rank in the U.S. Army, MacArthur was still subordinate to his government and its president. His great achievement was that he successfully oversaw the implementation of his government's policy for the occupation.

MacArthur's headquarters (GHQ) had two sections as shown by his two titles, Supreme Commander for the Allied Powers (SCAP) and commander in chief, Far East (CINCFE). As SCAP he commanded the occupation, and as CINCFE he oversaw all U.S. military forces in the Far East and the western Pacific. Here we are concerned only with SCAP. In the initial stages of the occupation, however, the Far East command was involved in the occupation, for there was concern that even after the surrender armed resistance could be mounted against the occupation forces. But that concern proved groundless.

SCAP had twenty-five sections and offices, but only six will be described briefly: Public Health and Welfare, Government, Economic and Scientific, Natural Resources, Civil Information and Education, and Law. Combined, these sections covered all areas of concern to the occupation. Only the Government Section figures prominently in this book, for it became directly involved in the constitutional change.

U.S. postsurrender policy for Japan was centered on the three Ds: disarmament, demilitarization, and democracy. Disarmament—that is, demobilization of the armed forces and destruction of their war-waging capabilities—was the responsibility of GHQ, CINCFE. Demilitarization— the elimination of the ideology, indoctrination, and propaganda that were the foundation of both ultranationalism and authoritarianism—and the promotion of democracy were the responsibility of GHQ, SCAP. Specifically, the Civil Information and Education Section was responsible for demilitarization—especially in the broad field of education—through elimination of the old ideology, indoctrination, and propaganda; the Government Section was responsible for elimination of the authoritarian governmental and political systems and their replacement by democratic ones.

Although the occupation was a military operation by definition and in fact, in 1945 the U.S. armed forces were still "civilian." In 1941 those forces were tiny compared with what they became in a few short years; they were not built into the society as was, for example, the Japanese military. Consequently, few officers or men had any experience, let alone training, in the military profession. The pressure of war soon remedied that situation; it had trained men in the varied skills war demanded. It had not erased the values and qualities necessary in their prewar professions. For example, Brigadier General Courtney Whitney, the commanding officer of the Government Section, was a lawyer by profession. In early 1946 the key members of his staff were also lawyers. A sprinkling of civilians and even fewer officers who had been in the armed forces prior to Pearl Harbor were in his section.

The staff sections primarily concerned with the occupation were dealing with problems of Japan's civil society, and they were manned by officers who had been in civil professions in the United States. The result was that in form Japan was under a dual government, as it had been from roughly 1931 to 1945. The old dual government had been concerned with war as an instrument of national policy; the new dual government was, by stated policy, concerned with peace and democracy.

As the controlling member of the dual government, the occupation's initial primary task was to eliminate the old system, to push to the conclusion the military defeat the war had inflicted on Japan. The task was relatively simple. First, the armed forces had to be demobilized. Before the end of the war the navy had been eliminated as a fighting force. The air force had proved unable to defend Japan against the U.S. bombing offensive. The Potsdam Declaration and the instrument of surrender meant Japan's far-flung armies would have to be returned to Japan and to civilian life. The surrender of Japanese weapons on the Asian and western Pacific fronts and the destruction of Japan's defenses meant the end of Japan's war-making capacity.

How were the activities of the two participants in this dual government coordinated? The answer is through a bureaucratic operation called the Central Liaison Office (CLO). It richly deserves a place in the history of the occupation, but no Japanese has authored a book about it, and no one who has written about the occupation has done more than mention it. We know nothing of its origin. SCAP's 51st directive to the Japanese government, dated September 24, 1945, is addressed "Through: The Central Liaison Office, Tokyo." That is apparently the first mention of the CLO.

The CLO was placed under the jurisdiction of the Ministry of Foreign Affairs, not under the cabinet as might have been expected since the occupation was a matter of major concern to the government. But locating it under the Foreign Ministry made a lot of sense. First, the occupation was being carried out by the military force of a foreign government that had developed the basic policy for the occupation. As a natural consequence, CLO's operating staff was composed of career diplomats experienced in dealing with foreign government officials. In addition, most had a working knowledge of English, a necessary qualification given the lack of Japanese-language skill among the Americans responsible for implementing the postsurrender policy.

The CLO was neither a policy-making nor a policy-implementing agency. It could be described as the nerve center of the dual government: all official communications between the Japanese government and SCAP were channeled through CLO. It was responsible for routing SCAP directives to the proper Japanese government ministry or agency, for routing Japanese communications to the proper SCAP section, and for making English-Japanese and Japanese-English translations of important documents. It also arranged meetings and conferences between the two sides.

Although not a part of its official duties, the CLO probably served as an informal but valuable source of intelligence for the Japanese, particularly in regard to occupation personnel. Without the CLO it is hard to see how relations between the occupiers and the occupied could have escaped chaos. A detailed study of the CLO would be a major contribution to the history of the occupation.

On October 4, 1945, SCAP issued what became known as the civil liberties directive or freedom directive. It ordered the Japanese government to abrogate and suspend "all laws, decrees, orders, ordinances, and regulations" that restrict "freedom of thought, of religion, of assembly, and of speech"; that restrict "the collection and dissemination of information"; and that "operate unequally in favor or against any person by reason of race, nationality, creed, or political opinion." In addition, all political prisoners, that is, those imprisoned for violating these restrictive government acts, were to be released within a week. Also, all government agencies created to enforce these laws were to be abolished. The directive meant the end of authoritarianism and, by extension, of the restrictions on human rights embodied in the Meiji Constitution.

On December 15, 1945, SCAP ordered the abolition of State Shinto, the quasi-religion of emperor worship that was government sponsored and supported and that lay at the core of ultranationalism. The directive was careful to exclude from its terms what it called Sect Shinto, a true religion. Thus the recently guaranteed religious freedom was preserved.

Since State Shinto was a government creation built around the alleged divinity of the imperial line and since imperial sovereignty was the basis of the Meiji Constitution, its abolition raised a little-noted constitutional issue of considerable import.

NINGEN SENGEN: THE DECLARATION OF HUMANITY

On January 1, 1946, Emperor Hirohito issued an imperial rescript known as the *Ningen Sengen*, literally translated Declaration of Humanity (*Ningen* = humanity, *Sengen* = declaration). But at least in the English-speaking world it is better known as the Renunciation of Divinity. The latter title is not erroneous, but it arises from a brief passage in a fairly long statement that merits discussion both to place it in the context of modern Japanese history and, more specifically, to observe its unexpressed role in constitutional change.

As in the case of the Meiji Constitution, the date is important. It will be recalled that the Meiji Constitution was promulgated on February 11, 1889, Japan's Foundation Day. The Declaration of Humanity was issued on New Year's Day, the day in Japanese tradition of fresh renewal of daily life. As outlined earlier, the few months from the acceptance of the Potsdam Declaration to the end of the year were indeed momentous.

The Declaration of Humanity opened with a word-for-word repetition of the Meiji Emperor's Charter Oath of 1868. It then stated:

> The proclamation is evident in its significance and high in its ideals. We wish to make this oath anew and restore the country to stand on its own feet again. We have to reaffirm the principles embodied in the Charter and proceed unflinchingly toward the elimination of misguided practices of the past; and, keeping in close touch with the desires of the people, we will construct a new Japan through being thoroughly pacific, the officials and the people alike obtaining rich culture and advancing the standard of living of the people.

As "the absurd usages of the past" in the Charter Oath was code for feudalism and the power monopoly of the Tokugawa regime, "misguided practices of the past" was code for the recent militarism and authoritarianism. The vision of the new Japan as thoroughly pacific and advancing the people's standard of living was prophetic.

The declaration then listed the war's devastation, the miseries of the destitute, trade stagnation, food shortages, and unemployment as the pressing problems of the day but added that unification of the people in facing the present and striving for peace would lead to a bright future. It added that the "protracted war and defeat, popular restlessness and despondency, the spread of radical tendencies, and the loss of a sense of morality might lead to 'confusion of thoughts.'"

At this point came the declaration of humanity: "The ties between us and our people have always stood upon mutual trust and affection. They do not depend on mere legends and myths. They are not predicated on the false conception that the Emperor is divine and that the Japanese people are superior to other races and fated to rule the world."

After calling on the government and the people to exert supreme effort, the declaration concluded: "The resolution for the year should be made at the beginning of the year. We expect our people to join us in all exertions looking to the accomplishment of this great undertaking with an indomitable spirit."

Before evaluating the declaration, omissions can be pointed out. There was no mention of the cause of the recent war or of the reasons for Japan's

defeat, which had been mentioned briefly in the imperial rescript at the
end of the war. There was no mention of the occupation, of the Potsdam
Declaration, or of the abolition of State Shinto, which involved the status
of the imperial institution. There was no mention of constitutional revision, made inevitable by the renunciation of divinity. But these omissions
do not blunt the declaration's significance.

First, the declaration came approximately 120 days after the surrender. That period was significant. It was sufficient to reveal what the occupation meant to Japan. It did not mean humiliation: the government
existed to carry out basic domestic functions; the emperor remained on
the throne even though shorn of his central role in State Shinto and his
divinity, which was the source of his constitutional role as the locus of
sovereignty. Occupation policy and action indicated that no crippling
inhibition would exist on Japan's road to a peaceful economy. It meant
freedom from an oppressive system of government and politics and the
consequent building of a democratic state based on the enjoyment of
fundamental human rights.

Consequently, the time was right for a statement that carried a strong
but implicit message of the need to work with the occupation. As stated
earlier, the occupation was not mentioned; it did not have to be. All
Japanese knew it as a fact, as a "gentle" occupation with no pillage, no
victor's arrogance. As a result, the implicit message could be made explicit
by wording such as this: "We and our people now know that the occupation has contributed and can be expected to contribute to the great task
of creating a new Japan. We should continue to develop the relationship."
The history of the remaining six years of the occupation clearly reveals
that the implicit message was heard and heeded.

What was the origin of the Declaration of Humanity? Unfortunately,
no one knows for certain, and there is no guarantee that the full story will
ever be known. What follows is a brief description of what information is
available from U.S. and Japanese sources.

The most complete U.S. account is a memorandum written in late
1946 by Harold G. Henderson, then a lieutenant colonel acting as special
adviser to SCAP's Civil Information and Education Section (CIES). Before the war he had been a scholar of Japanese literature at Columbia
University, to which he returned after his service with the occupation. His
scholarly qualifications made him one of a handful of Americans with a
knowledge of Japan and its language. Henderson wrote in his memorandum that Brigadier General Ken Dyke, his superior in the CIES, suggested
that he produce a written record of his involvement in the Declaration of
Humanity.

His story, in brief summary, follows. In early October 1945 he had been approached by R. H. Blyth, an Englishman who had long resided in Japan, married a Japanese woman, and become a specialist in Henderson's field and was now in search of a job. A month later Blyth returned with the news that he had become a professor at the Peers' School and tutor to the crown prince (the present emperor). He also said he had been asked to get in touch with CIES, apparently because of his relationship with Henderson, with whom he had become friendly. When Henderson asked Blyth what the Imperial Household Ministry (which was in charge of the Peers' School) wanted him to do, he professed not to know but said household officials wanted to learn about CIES's thinking. General Dyke agreed to give Blyth a part-time appointment with the proviso that he not be given access to confidential material.

Henderson soon told Blyth that if democracy were to be achieved, something would have to be done about the alleged divine descent of the emperor. In early December Blyth announced that "the Emperor was not only willing but anxious to renounce his 'divinity' as soon as possible; that he did not believe in it himself; that he knew what evil uses had been made of the idea by the militarists; that he wished to prevent the possibility of this happening again; but that neither he nor his advisers knew how to do it. Could I make a suggestion?"

General Dyke was away, and Henderson asked for time. But he was told that "time was too short" and was asked by Blyth to offer "at least some personal and wholly unofficial suggestion." Henderson "then concocted a formula intended to be perfectly clear and yet not impossibly derogatory to the imperial dignity." He passed it to Blyth, who returned the next day with a copy of the essential part of the declaration—namely, the short section dealing with the renunciation of divinity. This passage was approved by General Dyke who undertook to get General MacArthur's approval.

Henderson's memorandum is splendid as an account of SCAP's involvement, but unfortunately for the purposes of history it has little to say about the Japanese side. For example, Blyth's account of the emperor's views on the problem does not mention how he obtained those views. Was it in a face-to-face interview? If not, who told him?

But of far greater significance is the question, Why and how did the top officials of the Imperial Household Ministry decide to issue the declaration? This was a matter of fundamental importance to the Japanese state, not simply to Hirohito or to the imperial line. It meant the acceptance of the occupation's abolition of State Shinto. It made inevitable the revision of the Meiji Constitution.

A man who was apparently an official in the Imperial Household Ministry at the time recorded his recollection of the situation almost forty years later when, he wrote, he had "lost almost all my memory." He concluded with a tantalizing sentence: "It was all due to the merit and great achievement of the Imperial Household Minister Ishiwata who relying on others always led and supervised these matters." And so, like other matters concerning the late emperor, this one also must wait for the future opening of Imperial Household archives before a complete account can be written.

DUAL GOVERNMENT: DUAL PRESSURE FOR CONSTITUTIONAL REVISION

Influential, well-founded, and well-reasoned arguments have been presented to support the view that international pressures in the early stages of the Cold War were responsible for the speed with which SCAP approached constitutional revision in early 1946. But regardless of those international pressures, inside Japan both occupier and occupied were confronted with a serious problem. After the first 120 days Japan had no fundamental law; the Meiji Constitution had become a useless piece of paper.

In its October 4 civil rights directive, the occupation nullified Chapter II of the old constitution with its impressive list of unguaranteed civil rights. No longer could civil rights be constitutionally violated by the provision placing law above possible constitutional restraints on violation. If the rights brought in by a foreign occupation were to be rooted in Japan, they would necessarily have to be based on a democratic constitution, a democratic fundamental law. Under the Meiji Constitution it was the first and fundamental code; the other five codes were tailored to fit under it. The same would be true with a new constitution. As will be seen, the other five codes were rapidly recast to fit under the new constitution. From the standpoint of the occupation, a new constitution was essential for planting democracy in the country.

The occupied, as the other element in the dual government, likewise required a new constitution. The abolition of State Shinto and the Declaration of Humanity had nullified Chapter I of the Meiji Constitution (and the governmental and political systems erected by it) by reducing the emperor from a divine being to a human being. In addition, the elimination of the military through wartime battle and peacetime directive had destroyed the military not only as a class but also as a dominant force in both government and politics. The gap had to be filled.

And so in early 1946 both national, although largely unseen at the time, and international factors were dramatically creating the necessity for constitutional revision. And the dual government characterizing the occupation was the basis for the collaboration that created the Showa Constitution.

BIBLIOGRAPHICAL NOTE (Part I)

W. G. Beasley, *The Meiji Restoration* (Stanford: Stanford University Press, 1972). The standard history in English of the restoration.

Robert J.C. Butow, *Japan's Decision to Surrender* (Stanford: Stanford University Press, 1954). The definitive work in English.

Center for Asian Cultural Studies, comp. and pub., *The Meiji Japan Through Contemporary Sources, Volume One, Basic Documents, 1854–1889* (Tokyo: 1969). Contains Ito Miyoji's official translation of the Meiji Constitution and an edited version of his translation of Ito Hirobumi's *Commentaries*.

Richard B. Finn, *Winners in Peace: MacArthur, Yoshida and Postwar Japan* (Berkeley: University of California Press, 1992). The standard one-volume history of the occupation.

Richard B. Frank, *Downfall: The End of the Imperial Japanese Empire* (New York: Random House, 1999). A definitive account of the events, military and otherwise, from early March 1945 to the surrender in September 1945.

General Headquarters, Supreme Commander for the Allied Powers, *Selected Data on the Occupation of Japan* (Tokyo: mimeo, undated, but probably 1949). Contains much factual data on the first four years of the occupation.

———, Government Section, *Political Reorientation of Japan: September 1945 to September 1948*, 2 vols. (Vol. I, *Narrative*; Vol. II, *Appendices*) (Washington, D.C.: U.S. Government Printing Office, undated, but probably 1949). Vol. I is the Government Section's history of the first three years. Vol. II contains documents relating to the surrender and the U.S. occupation policy and GHQ, SCAP's major early directives to the Japanese government.

Ito Hirobumi, *Commentaries on the Constitution of the Empire of Japan*, Ito Miyoji (trans.), (Tokyo: Igirisu Horitsu Gakko, 1889). The authoritative work; contains the official English translation of the Meiji Constitution and Ito's article-by-article commentary.

———, "Some Reminiscences on the Grant of the New Constitution," in Vol. I of Count Shigenobu Okuma (comp.), *Fifty Years of New Japan*, English version edited by Marcus B. Huish, 2 vols. (London: Smith, Elder, 1910), quotation on p. 127.

Marius B. Jansen, *The Making of Modern Japan* (Cambridge: Harvard University Press, 2000). The standard history of Japan in English from 1600 to 2000.

Kodansha (pub.), *Japan: An Illustrated Encyclopedia*, 2 vols. (Tokyo: Kodansha, 1993). A standard reference work; abbreviated version of nine-volume original.

John M. Maki (ed.), *Conflict and Tension in the Far East: Key Documents, 1894–1960* (Seattle: University of Washington Press, 1961). Contains documents relating to Japan's wars from 1895 to 1945, the Washington Settlement, the surrender, U.S. policy toward postsurrender Japan, and the peace treaties.

————, *Japanese Militarism: Its Cause and Cure* (New York: Alfred A. Knopf, 1945).

————, "United States Initial Post-Surrender Policy for Japan," in Han-Kyo Kim (ed.), *Essays on Modern Politics and History: Written in Honor of Harold M. Vinacke* (Athens: Ohio University Press, 1969), 30–56.

Miyazawa Toshiyoshi, "Characteristics of the Meiji Constitution," in Hideo Tanaka (comp.), assisted by Malcolm D.H. Smith, *The Japanese Legal System: Introductory Cases and Materials* (Tokyo: University of Tokyo Press, 1976), 630–640.

Nishiyama Matsunosuke, *Edo Culture: Daily Life and Diversions in Urban Japan, 1600–1868*, Gerald Grosmer (trans. and ed.), (University of Hawaii Press, 1997). Provides a meaningful glimpse of Japanese life in the Tokugawa period.

Takayanagi Kenzo, "A Century of Innovation: The Development of Japanese Law, 1868–1961," in Arthur Taylor von Mehen (ed.), *Law in Japan: The Legal Order in a Changing Society* (Cambridge: Harvard University Press, 1963), 5–40, esp. 5–15.

Conrad Totman, *Early Modern Japan* (Berkeley: University of California Press, 1993). The standard one-volume history in English of Tokugawa Japan.

Part 2

The Constitution of Japan

4

—— Collaborative Creation —— —— of the 1947 Constitution ——

The 1947 Constitution of Japan was written by Japanese and Americans between February 3 and November 3, 1946, and came into effect on May 3, 1947, following amendment procedures in the Meiji Constitution. A constitutional revolution had already begun in fall of 1945, however, with the abolition of authoritarian laws and agencies. Japan accepted the terms of the Potsdam Declaration (July 26, 1945): "The Japanese government shall remove all obstacles to the revival and strengthening of democratic tendencies among the Japanese people. Freedom of speech, of religion, and of thought, as well as respect for fundamental human rights shall be established." (For the complete text, see the Appendix.)

Occupying forces would be withdrawn when these objectives had been achieved and "a peacefully inclined and responsible government" had been established under the "freely expressed will" of the people (quotations from Potsdam Declaration). The office of Supreme Commander for the Allied Powers (SCAP) General Douglas MacArthur insisted in its Potsdam Directives (SCAPIN) that restraints on freedom be removed. SCAPIN 16 (September 10), 66 (September 27), and 93 (October 4, 1945) led to the dismantling of the machinery of repression. The Japanese government converted these directives into Japanese law by use of imperial ordinances. Under Imperial Ordinance No. 542 of September 20, 1945, "in accordance with acceptance of the Potsdam Declaration," 520 ordinances changed SCAP directives into Japanese law.

On January 1, 1946, the emperor publicly affirmed his ordinary humanity (*Ningen Sengen*), disavowing the core principle of the Meiji Constitution—imperial divinity—and also committing Japan to peaceful international relations (see Appendix). This eased the achievement of the Japanese government's primary goal of preserving the emperor institution in some form while also furthering the Allies' highest priority—establishing a peaceful state.

CONTRIBUTORS TO THE INITIAL DRAFT

Political leaders in Japan's first postwar government were little interested in constitutional amendment or revision. As early as September 18, 1945, however, Irie Toshio, head of the Cabinet Legislation Bureau and a major participant in the constitutional creation process in 1946, drew up a substantial list of articles of the Meiji Constitution in need of revision or deletion. The articles concerned the military, the powers of the emperor, and other issues debated in the year ahead. In October 1945 the government created an informal committee of experts under Minister of State Matsumoto Joji. Over the next three months the committee formulated proposals for minor changes in the Meiji Constitution.

In January 1946, in Washington, D.C., the State, War, Navy Coordinating Committee adopted policy guidelines, "Reform of the Japanese Government System" (SWNCC-228), for MacArthur's regime. On February 1 the Tokyo newspaper *Mainichi Shimbun* scooped others by publishing the Matsumoto Committee's secretly developed constitution proposals. At no point between October 1945 and February 1946 did the Matsumoto Committee and SCAP contact each other regarding the constitution project. Alerted by the newspaper scoop, SCAP concluded that the committee's proposals did not meet the requirements of the Potsdam Declaration and SWNCC-228. Thus SCAP reluctantly took the initiative and offered the Japanese government a document that did meet its requirements.

Other voices joined the constitutional deliberations. The Constitution Research Society (Kempo Kenkyukai), the Constitution Discussion Society (Kempo Kondankai), the Japan Federation of Bar Associations, and other groups published numerous nongovernmental proposals in late 1945 and early 1946. Four political parties submitted drafts to the Government Section (GS), SCAP's office for intergovernmental affairs. Milo Rowell of GS wrote a substantial analysis of Japanese proposals and discussed them at length with their sources.

On Monday, February 4, 1946, Brigadier General Courtney Whitney, head of GS and MacArthur's closest adviser, announced at a staff meeting in the Administrative Division of the GS that they would be acting in secret as a constitutional convention for the next week. MacArthur's Notes (handwritten, probably dictated to Whitney) would serve as one of their basic references. The Notes dealt with three points: (1) the emperor is a dynastic head of state "responsive to the basic will of the people as provided" in the constitution, (2) "war as the sovereign right of the nation is abolished" along with the right to build a defense capability, and (3) the "feudal system" and peerage are to be discontinued.

Rowell's analysis, the UN Charter, MacArthur's Notes, the draft presented by Kempo Kenkyukai, and SWNCC-228 were close at hand as nineteen Americans drafted a constitution "outline" for Japan between February 4 and February 12, 1946. On February 13 Whitney and Colonel Charles L. Kades submitted a draft document ("the GHQ [General Headquarters] Draft") to a shocked Japanese government, noting that its acceptance "would render the Emperor practically unassailable" by the many Allies who wanted him to abdicate or be tried as a war criminal. Although the Allies felt legally empowered to insist on changes in Japan's basic law to comply with the terms of surrender, the authoritative Kades maintained that during the drafting process no threats were made of retaliatory action should the Japanese disagree on nonessential points.

Why the haste in so fundamental a task as preparing a constitution? First, the likelihood that acceptable government proposals would be developed seemed slim after the appearance of the Matsumoto Committee's document. SCAP also feared interference and a possible veto of a new constitution by the Soviet Union—Stalin favored abolition of the imperial institution, for example—or other members of the Allied Powers' new policy organ, the Far Eastern Commission (FEC). The FEC included representatives of thirteen Allied nations, four of which had veto power over occupation policy: the United States, the United Kingdom, the Soviet Union, and China.

SCAP expected the April 10, 1946, lower-house election to serve as a successful referendum on a proposed new constitution. Women, as well as men ages twenty to twenty-five, would be voting for the first time under a December 1945 House of Representatives Election Law.

The draft constitution was written on the sixth floor of the Daiichi Life Insurance Building, on the same floor as the General Headquarters of the Supreme Commander for the Allied Powers. Whitney put a Steering Committee composed of three attorneys—Kades (chair), Rowell, and Commander Alfred R. Hussey—in charge of the process. According to

Kades, the initial draft was a group product: "If ever there was a group project with group thinking and group ideas, it was the drafting of the Constitution" (letter to the author, November 17, 1986). Besides MacArthur and Whitney, seventeen diverse people were divided into eight subject area subcommittees consisting of one to four members each: Legislative, Judicial, Executive, Civil Rights, Emperor, Local Government, Public Finance, and Treaties (and enabling legal provisions). Kades authored the pacifist Article 9, and Hussey drafted the Preamble. Whitney wrote Article 97 on the responsibility of all generations to hold "the fundamental human rights" inviolate. The subcommittees' informal communications were easy and frequent.

The Steering Committee reviewed and participated in the work of the subcommittees. With no GHQ reference shelf on constitutional law, Beate Sirota went about Tokyo in a jeep unobtrusively gathering about ten constitutions from public libraries, and Milton Esman borrowed from the personal library of the eminent constitutional lawyer Professor Miyazawa Toshiyoshi. Constitutions of the Weimar Republic and Scandinavian countries proved particularly useful in Japanese discussions.

The most influential American in the process of making Japan's constitution seems to have been Kades, not MacArthur, although MacArthur first suggested to the Japanese government in fall of 1945 that it consider revising the Meiji Constitution. MacArthur's support of Kades's group was essential. Sato Tatsuo of the Cabinet Legislative Bureau was the leading Japanese drafter before the Diet deliberations.

Whatever else their achievements, for their participation in this historic project the participants deserve to be named: Beate Sirota, Pieter K. Roest, Harry Emerson Wildes, Frank E. Hayes, Frank Rizzo, Guy Swope, Milton Esman, Jacob I. Miller, Osbourne Hauge, Cyrus Peake, Richard Poole, Cecil G. Tilton, George A. Nelson, and Roy Malcolm. Of the subcommittee members, Hayes (a lawyer from Lander, Wyoming), Rizzo (Whitney's successor as head of the GS), Sirota (a twenty-two-year-old graduate of Mills College who grew up in Japan), and Swope (a former congressman from Pennsylvania, auditor general and governor of Puerto Rico) seem to have been the most important, "on a par with the Steering Committee" according to Kades. All had civilian careers to which they would return. Not one was a constitutional lawyer. Except for Sirota, none had been in Tokyo for more than a few weeks. (Also noteworthy was the contribution of competent longhand note taker and drafter Ruth Ellerman. Two civilian secretaries and two translators were assigned to assist the Steering Committee and Ellerman.)

On February 22 the Japanese government responded to the Americans' first draft of February 13 with a successful counterproposal that the legislature be bicameral rather than unicameral, but the cabinet agreed to use SCAP's principles in preparing a new Japanese-language draft. At 10 A.M. on March 4, Matsumoto Joji and four other officials submitted to GS their latest draft with many changes in detail. Argument over the text between GS personnel and Matsumoto led to his angry departure at 2:30 P.M. After 6 P.M. the GS side said the final text would have to be agreed on that night. Matsumoto told the remaining Japanese to stay at the task. The only Japanese who remained until the end were Sato Tatsuo, Shirasu Jiro, and two interpreters. The cabinet was kept informed of progress. Around 8:30 P.M. an article-by-article consideration began and continued until the text of the entire draft constitution was agreed on at about 4 P.M. on March 5.

CONSTITUTIONAL REVISION PROCESS

On March 6 the Japanese government noted its compliance with the Potsdam Declaration terms and submitted to the nation the draft of a new constitution along with an authoritative imperial rescript, following amendment procedures under Article 73 of the Meiji Constitution. That same day MacArthur praised the "new and enlightened document which has my full approval." The People's National Language Movement, led by such prestigious figures as future Chief Justice Yokota Kisaburo and Judge Miyake Shotaro, successfully urged the government to use colloquial Japanese (*kogotai*) rather than the stiff formal literary style (*bungotai*) in the constitution and future laws, which has eased understanding of the legal language for the average citizen ever since. Some language had obviously been translated from English. Yet the new basic law was superior to the Meiji Constitution not only in democratic constitutionalist content but also in clarity of writing.

On April 10 the new membership of the House of Representatives was chosen in the most democratic election in Japan's history to that time. In the previous election in 1942, Prime Minister Tojo Hideki and the Imperial Rule Assistance Association chose 80 percent of the candidates, all extreme nationalists. In the 1946 election there were 2,697 candidates, ranging in age from twenty-five to eighty-seven; 38 of the 79 female candidates were elected, and 60 percent of the winners had college degrees.

The public's response to the draft constitution was very positive. In May 1946 the *Mainichi Shimbun* conducted a public-opinion survey on the constitution. A few of the findings were: 72 percent thought the renunciation of war clause was necessary (Article 9); 79 percent supported a bicameral legislature; 85 percent favored retention of the emperor institution in a reduced symbolic role, whereas 13 percent opposed retention in any form; 58 percent (78.2 percent of students) wanted the patriarchal family house system (*ie*) to be abolished; and 64.5 percent (74.4 percent of women) favored constitutional recognition of the equality of the sexes.

The cabinet formally presented the draft constitution to the Privy Council on April 17. That body approved the document on the recommendation of its investigative committee and new Prime Minister Yoshida Shigeru in early June 1946. On June 20 the emperor noted his role in implementing terms of the Potsdam Declaration by initiating the formal constitutional amendment process, and he approved constitutional revision in accordance with the will of the people. On June 25 the document went to the full House of Representatives, which then deliberated as a constitutional convention.

It was correctly assumed that the new 1946 Diet would approve the constitution with the support not only of the government but also of the opposition Socialists and others delighted by its progressive tone. On June 28 the draft was submitted to a special Diet committee of seventy-two members representing all political parties appointed by the Speaker of the House. The results of its deliberations were then sent to a subcommittee of fourteen men from all political parties (except the Communist Party), which continued the process in secret from July 25 until August 20, ironing out discrepancies between the Japanese and GS versions (for example, providing invaluable Japanese editorial services). On August 21 the special committee approved the bill and reported it to a House plenary session on August 24. The Constitution Revision Bill, with amendments, was approved by a vote of 421 to 8 (of whom 6 were Communists) on August 24 and was sent to the House of Peers.

After learned discourse and interpolations by its distinguished constitutional lawyers, particularly about the *kokutai* and the emperor system, the House of Peers approved the bill with amendments and returned it to the Diet on October 8, 1946. The amendment process approving the new Constitution of Japan (*Nihonkoku Kempo*) was completed with a pro forma review by the Privy Council and its promulgation on November 3, 1946, looking toward its effective date of May 3, 1947. In an imperial rescript Emperor Hirohito proclaimed, "I rejoice that the foundation for the construction of a new Japan has been laid according to the will of the Japanese people, and hereby sanction and promulgate the amendments of the Imperial Constitution." Since the end of the occupation in April 1952, when Japan regained sovereignty, the Japanese people have freely chosen not to amend the constitution even once.

Millions of copies of the widely welcomed document were distributed to young and old. It quickly became part of the school curriculum. In April 1947, for the first time in history, every local executive and legislative position in the prefectures, cities, towns, and villages was filled by democratic election, not central government appointment.

In the many months before and after the constitution came into effect, scores of implementing laws were passed to modify or abolish existing institutions or to create new legal principles, including the Court Organization Law, the Imperial Household Law, the Fundamental Law of Education, the Cabinet Law, the Election Law for the House of Councillors, the Petition Law, the Finance Law, the Commercial Code, and the Labor Standards Law. The Criminal Procedure Code underwent substantial democratization. The authoritarian old Home Ministry was abolished. On June 19, 1948, the Diet passed the Resolution Rescinding the Imperial Rescript on Education (1890).

Perhaps the most important American contributor to the immense task of legal reform to comply with the constitution was an exile judge from Germany, Alfred C. Oppler. As explained in Chapter 5, Japan's modern legal system has much more in common with those of Germany and France than with U.S. common law. Oppler and his Japanese colleagues spoke the same technical legal language. They were ably assisted by Thomas L. Blakemore from Oklahoma, the only American well trained in Japanese law. Before the war Blakemore had attended Tokyo Imperial University and after the war found himself working on legal reform with old friends.

DECISIONS OF JAPAN'S LEADERS ON THE CONSTITUTION

English-language studies have usually focused on the U.S. side, have often exaggerated U.S. contributions, and have concluded that the United States and its Allies "imposed" the constitution on Japan. Unfortunately, on the rare occasions when U.S. opinion makers in the mass media and the academy take notice of the Constitution of Japan, they commonly perpetuate the myth that the document was simply imposed on a helpless Japan. In Japan, such a view is associated with very conservative and rightist elements who favor constitutional revision to allow full rearmament. In the United States this interpretation of history fits well with the policy preferences of those who want Japan to shoulder a heavier burden in preserving Asian security. Such analysts have rarely thought through the geopolitical implications of their position. The seminal scholarship of Ray Moore, Donald Robinson, and others in Japan and the United States on the origins of the constitution, however, renders untenable the imposed constitution theory.

Earlier studies have neglected major Japanese contributions and the rich diversity of opinions on both sides. In the constitutional debates of 1946, the great divides were not between Americans and Japanese but between the views of individuals and groups on both sides who favored or opposed with varying degrees of passion retention of the emperor institution, an independent and powerful judiciary, equality under the law, guarantees of civil rights and civil liberties, renunciation of war and armed forces, separation of religion and the state, and recognition of social and economic constitutional rights.

Among the suggestions made on how to deal with Emperor Hirohito were abdication, abolition of the imperial institution, and trial as a war criminal. His and others' war responsibilities are still debated; extremists would exonerate not only the emperor but Japan of any wrongdoing. Continuance of the emperor institution, however, enjoyed the overwhelming support of a broad spectrum of Japanese opinion. In any case, the cabinet and House of Representatives debates changed toward progressive democracy the entire tone of Japanese discourse on the emperor (Chapter 1) and other core issues and deserve more attention. In SCAP, Whitney left matters in Kades's hands, and Kades, when consulted by the Japanese on their initiative, did not oppose amendments.

In the agonies of abject defeat and utter devastation under a flawed and failed constitutional system that allowed irresponsible authoritarian militarism to thrive, survival rather than constitutional politics riveted people's attention and energies. Once survival was assured, however, passionate nationwide expression followed of profound disillusionment and anger at the government leaders who had led the country down to hell. The prestigious and powerful were discredited; they had allied themselves with the tyrants Hitler and Mussolini. Leaders in government, education, the military, politics, religion, the mass media, and business had supported a senseless aggressive war ending not only in defeat but also in cultural collapse and national devastation.

Autumn of 1945 through 1946 was the first period in Japan's history when a high degree of freedom of expression was encouraged (except regarding the occupation). In daily political life a large majority of the Japanese people and their social leaders, then as now, shared none of the deference toward the discredited regime shown today by some in the United States and other countries and by "impositionist" Japanese politicians. By comparison, the situation was more revolutionary than that following the American Revolutionary War when the Articles of Confederation and the U.S. Constitution were created. It was widely recognized as a time for basic change in the principles, structures, and processes of government.

A leading Japanese historian of the drafting events and a key participant, Sato Tatsuo, maintained that the Americans showed respect for
Japanese preferences, refrained from applying pressure during the Diet
deliberations, and approved almost all changes recommended by the Japanese. The ideas the Americans proposed were not new to Japan but were
newly legitimized. Since the late nineteenth century, educated Japanese
had been at least as well informed of trends in Western constitutional
thought as their counterparts in North America and Europe. Until 1945,
progressive constitutional ideas had lost to ultranationalism in the Japanese political arena.

In 1946, the Americans brought an educated citizen's limited intui-
tive understanding of U.S. constitutional law, but the Japanese brought
far more professional expertise to bear on legal and issue debates. Koseki
Shoichi, a prominent scholar on the birth of the constitution, concluded:

> The energy that produced the Japanese Constitution did not by any
> means emerge solely from the power of the victor over the vanquished or
> of one nation against another. Whether that energy contributed more or
> less to the framing process, it came, essentially, only from the views of
> individuals about the constitution, and their ideas about human rights.
> Inherent in the Japanese Constitution are constitutional views and
> notions of human rights that transcend both state and race. (Koseki, 255)

Kades recalled "some thirty-odd amendments" were made by the House
of Representatives, a few against GS preferences. Without intent to be
exhaustive, here are some features of the constitution affected by Japanese
input.

- A bicameral legislature was instituted consisting of the House of
  Representatives and the House of Councillors, not a unicameral
  body as proposed by the GS.

- Popular sovereignty was recognized, with the emperor subject to
  "the will of the people with whom resides sovereign power," and all
  but ceremonial and symbolic roles for the emperor were denied;
  explicitly recognized was popular sovereignty derived from the
  proposals of Kempo Kenkyukai, published on December 16, 1945,
  not from any foreign source (Articles 1, 3, and 4).

- The emperor "shall appoint the Chief Justice of the Supreme Court
  as designated by the Cabinet" (Article 6, 2). This was designed to
  make the judiciary a branch of government equal in stature to the
  executive branch of the prime minister, whom the emperor would
  appoint "as designated by the Diet" (Article 6, 1; added by the
  House of Representatives).

- Colloquial rather than old-style literary Japanese will be used in the Constitution and other laws to help create clarity of constitutional language compared with the sometimes ambiguous Meiji Constitution (a cabinet decision).

- A suit can be filed for damages for wrongful arrest (Article 40) or for damages suffered from an illegal act by a public official (Article 17) (House of Representatives).

- Citizens were granted a right to "minimum standards of wholesome and cultured living" (Article 25) and other socioeconomic rights; they also incurred "the right and obligation to work" along with the requirement that "standards . . . [for] working conditions" (Article 27) be set by law (Democratic Socialists). In 2001 opinion polls, these provisions, rather than those on civil liberties, were most popular.

- The peerage system was abolished immediately (Article 14, 2), not gradually phased out until the current generation passed away (a contribution of the Socialists).

- A majority of cabinet members must be members of the Diet (Article 68).

- A requirement that the prime minister's cabinet appointments be confirmed by the Diet was rejected, thus strengthening the prime minister's position.

- Judgments of the Supreme Court are not subject to review by the Diet, contrary to the GS recommendation that in all but cases involving Chapter III (individual rights) the court's judgments could be overridden on a two-thirds vote of the House of Representatives.

- A provision extending equal legal rights to aliens was deleted (Kades allowed this because it was similar to the legal treatment of aliens in the United States during the 1940s).

- The Diet is allowed to hold secret sessions (Article 57).

- The autonomy of local governments was enhanced (Articles 93–95).

- A requirement for balanced budgets was eliminated.

- The required majority for constitutional amendments was raised to "two thirds or more of all members of each House" (Article 96).

- Language on the nation's purposes under Article 9, the quasi-pacifist clause, renouncing the right of belligerency and armed forces, indicated that "the threat or use of force as a means of settling international disputes" is never permissible. Self-defense may be acceptable, but that was not made explicit (House of Representatives).

A FEW MAKERS OF THE CONSTITUTION

As with the Founding Fathers of the U.S. Constitution, who also deliberated in secrecy in a much less complex situation, a stroke of serendipitous good luck was manifest in the combination of persons who founded Japan's current constitutional regime in 1946. Numerous Japanese and nineteen Americans contributed. The cases of one American and four Japanese illustrate this good fortune: Beate Sirota, Kato Shizue, Tanaka Kotaro, Ashida Hitoshi, and Kanamori Tokujiro.

Young Beate Sirota was a major drafter of Chapter III, Rights and Duties of the People, Articles 10 to 40. Particularly striking is her impact on provisions concerning women's rights long before feminism made political sense in the United States or Japan. Yet during the long March 4–5 discussions, Sirota persuaded reluctant men of both nationalities to accept guarantees of equal rights for women (Articles 14, 24, and 44), which have facilitated a revolutionary improvement in the status of Japanese women in law and society and have won her the gratitude of many Japanese to this day. In addition, she, along with her husband-to-be, 1st Lt. Joseph Gordon, used their knowledge of Japan's language and culture to affect the wording of other provisions of the constitution. Charles Kades gave her further credit:

> [Sirota and Gordon] were of such inestimable value in reconciling the two versions not only to the American side (the Steering Committee) but also to the Japanese scholars and lawyers that I seriously doubt if the Japanese would have accepted some of the more radical provisions of Chapter III but for her charm and constructive contributions in reconciling the English and Japanese versions not only of Chapter III but of the Constitution as a whole. This is not an exaggeration; at one point I recall asking the Japanese to accept as written a clause (which they wanted to omit in toto) I knew was close to Beate's heart (she had personally lobbied me on it) "for Miss Sirota's peace of mind" (or words to that effect)—and they did just that. (Letter to the author, 1986)

In the April elections for the House of Representatives, Kato Shizue, a leading Japanese feminist, was elected by one of the largest majorities of any candidate. Her husband was also elected. On July 6, in one of the memorable speeches of the Diet debates, she spoke strongly in support of the family as the foundation of society and a major arena for Japan's democratization. But she shocked many, especially among the men, by urging unequivocal constitutional recognition of the equal rights of women in matters such as marriage, property rights, legal competence, inheritance rights, and divorce. The government's Legislative Reform Commission, charged with recommending reforms in the Civil Code to implement a new constitution, took as its reform standard "time-honored manners and customs of this country." Kato considered this patently inadequate and listed some of the grossly discriminatory "customs": women were legally incompetent, unable to act in law without a husband's consent; the Civil Code allowed a man to divorce his wife for one instance of infidelity, whereas only "gross misconduct" was grounds for a woman to initiate divorce proceedings; widows with children were not allowed to remarry. These and other discriminatory laws should be abolished under the proposed terms of the Constitution Revision Bill, she said.

She called for more than equal treatment for women and children ravaged by the government's war policies. The proposed article on educational rights made no mention of the state's responsibility for the education of children without parents or guardians, she said. (Article 26 ended up guaranteeing rights to free compulsory education and equal education correspondent to ability for "all people.") The promise of freedom of thought for teachers is fine but not enough, she said. The entire pre-collegiate curriculum should be revised to get rid of the old idea that all women should be trained only to be "good wives, strong mothers." (The foundation principle for interpreting the Civil Code was subsequently changed to read "Article 1.1. All private rights shall conform to the public welfare. . . . 1.2. This Code shall be construed from the standpoint of the dignity of individuals and the essential equality of the sexes.")

Minister of Education Tanaka Kotaro of the University of Tokyo heartily agreed. A noted scholar of commercial and international law and a Roman Catholic, Tanaka was widely esteemed for his learning and his fairness in balancing Japan's traditions with universal principles. He later served as chief justice of the Supreme Court and as judge of the International Court of Justice (The Hague). He was the person who submitted to the Diet a resolution to repeal the Imperial Rescript on Education, the sacred statement of Confucian morality at the foundation of public education under the Meiji Constitution.

During the Diet debates on the constitution, Tanaka said the public school system should be reformed to promote each student's individuality and personal development based on new state foundations. Boys and girls should respect each other and be treated equally. Kato Shizue was entirely satisfied; with this spirit the dignity of Japanese womanhood could be firmly established. During the summer debates, other women and men strongly supported these views, which remain salient in 2002. Apropos of the future great constitutional debates on textbooks, Tanaka also said history teaching should be "based on fact," not myth. He added, "Much importance must be attached to the content of textbooks, in the absorption of world knowledge and information on world affairs . . . but also foreign history must be made popular . . . [and so must] foreign languages."

Ashida Hitoshi, a career diplomat who entered politics only in 1945 and served briefly as prime minister in 1948, was elected chair of the Diet's Special Committee on Revision of the Imperial Constitution and of its subcommittee, which met secretly from July 25 to August 20, 1946. Sato Isao characterized Ashida: "As Chairman, Ashida was stately; he skillfully presided over the meeting. I would say that he certainly was a fine chairman. He himself was pleased with the position and seems to have taken pride in it." In fact, Ashida believed it was the high point of his public life.

Ashida is perhaps most remembered for the "Ashida Amendment" to Article 9, which renounces war and the threat or use of force as an instrument of policy in paragraph one. He added the first clause of paragraph two: "In order to accomplish the aim of the preceding paragraph." He wished to make clear that paragraph one renounces aggressive war but not self-defense. The rest of paragraph two says Japan will never maintain "war potential." Interpretation of Article 9 has been much debated, but it remains a core provision of the constitution.

The learned Kanamori Tokujiro, minister of state, coordinated government presentations during Diet deliberations on the Constitution Revision Bill. During the debates he spoke more often than anyone else, 1,365 times. Kanamori was a liberal constitutionalist who in 1936 had been forced from office as head of the Cabinet Legislation Bureau by ultranationalists. His crime was having written a moderate book that reduced the emperor to an "organ" of the state. (In the 1920s, before constitutional lawyers succumbed to militarist pressures, scholars' mainstream interpretation of the institution of emperor was the so-called organ theory.)

Kanamori, however, had also buckled under to state censorship. For that failing he apologized in embarrassment when quotes from his earlier works were thrown at him during the constitution debates. At the same time, he reminded his critics that most elites shared his weak conformism at that time. Donald Robinson characterized Kanamori's performance as follows: "His manner was often professorial, but rarely condescending. Despite his vulnerabilities and the delicacy of his role, Diet members approached him with respect and gratitude. . . . The balance he struck between patience with the interrogations and the need to expedite the business at hand seemed acceptable and understandable to Diet members most of the time." He was "one of the heroes" of the struggle to make the government accountable.

To Kanamori and others, the central task of constitutional reformers in 1946 was to end the use of the emperor as a screen behind which leaders in government and politics hid to legitimize and gain compliance with whatever policies they adopted while remaining essentially responsible to no one. After lengthy debate and pressure from within and outside the Diet, sovereignty was placed in "the people." The more accurate translation of *kokumin* is not the people but "the nation," and as Kanamori explained to the satisfaction of many, the emperor is simply part of the nation and a symbol of the state and its cohesion. The people, however, are not subjects of the emperor as they were under the Meiji Constitution; the emperor is the subject.

The intensity and complexity of the debates over the appropriate future status of the emperor were not a measure of the historical continuity of imperial power. For roughly 1,000 years before the Meiji Period, the emperor did not possess the equivalent of state sovereignty but rather was compelled to ceremonially legitimize the regime of whomever won the conflicts among competing feudal lords. The emperor did not figure much in the daily life of Japan's real leaders or of most other Japanese.

Moreover, Meiji constitutional law deviated from time-honored traditions; it was revolutionary. For example, prior to Meiji codification a woman could become empress (two had done so during the Tokugawa period). The debates and the continued, although diminished, sensitivity of Shinto-related issues in 2002 are a tribute to the effectiveness of the state and a cooperative society in changing traditions using modern techniques of indoctrination and control. Until 1946 the young were educated to passionately believe in and be absolutely loyal to a transformed and sacralized imperial person. Nationalist controls over adult thought and action were also sophisticated. The 1947 Constitution of Japan is much more compatible with the realities of Japan's traditional kingship system than was the Meiji Constitution.

Kanamori sided with the representatives of the government and the GS who supported constitutional guarantees of civil liberties and criminal justice rights while opposing as inappropriate and unenforceable in court the proposed provisions for social and economic rights (*shakaiken*, literally, social rights), which were ultimately included (Articles 25–28). For example, Article 25, 2, reads: "In all spheres of life, the State shall use its endeavors for the promotion and extension of social welfare and security, and of public health."

When Kanamori was queried by Communist leader Nosaka Sanzo and liberal lawyer Fugita about possible improper restraints on free speech and political activities, he referred to the general provision requiring that rights be exercised "for the public welfare" (Article 12). People should feel free to criticize even the emperor and are otherwise free to express themselves as long as they do not engage in criminal acts or instigate a riot. The courts will balance the claims of free speech and the public welfare, he said. Nosaka replied that he was "almost satisfied" (Robinson, 53).

"The public welfare" (*kokyo no fukushi*) was also debated as the standard for limiting property rights, freedom of religion, and other individual rights. "The right to own or to hold property is inviolable" but "shall be defined by law, in conformity with the public welfare" (Article 29). Japanese liberals (like Kades) were uneasy about the generality of the public welfare standard (which might also be translated "communal well-being"). As Miyazawa wrote years after its adoption, public welfare in the 1947 Constitution differs significantly from similar words in wartime "in that its meaning is firmly grounded in [respect for] the individual" (Miyazawa, 205).

That Japan was in a spiritual crisis, "profound and paralyzing moral confusion" (Robinson, 62), was a matter of consensus in the Diet, and many felt regeneration would depend heavily on religious inspiration. What role should the government play? The Constitution Revision Bill proposed freedom of religion without favoring any one religion, as well as separation of religion from the state (Articles 20 and 89 of the constitution). The teaching that Japan was somehow "divine" had stopped. On December 16, 1945, government subsidies to Shinto shrines had been discontinued.

Impassioned and eloquent argument held that Japan's constitution must have Japanese (e.g., Buddhist) religious roots, just as Western constitutions are grounded in Judaeo-Christian beliefs. Could Japan's regime succeed without religious restoration? Tanaka Kotaro agreed with the diagnosis but insisted all religions be treated equally and that religion be kept separate from the government. Public schools could teach about various religions, but they must do so scientifically and without favoritism or proselytizing. Tax exemption should not be ruled out. What about local Shinto folk practices and festivals honoring local spirits? Kanamori responded that they would be constitutional as long as they were not sponsored or paid for by the government. Should the emperor be prohibited from attending religious observances as "the symbol of the state"?

The responses were fuzzy, and the activities of the emperor as a private person and as a state person became controversial during the funeral and accession ceremonies in 1989 after the death of Emperor Hirohito.

The constitutional debates within the Japanese community in 1946 were not hasty or shallow in their treatment of great issues. They were responsive but not subservient to U.S. and Far Eastern Commission pressures. They seized the moment as required by the political realities of the time. The range of viewpoints was far greater than those during the constitutional conventions of the United States and other countries over the past century. Those who contend the Constitution of Japan was simply imposed from without do not do justice to the intelligent, well-informed, and democratically committed nationalism of most of the diverse Japanese debaters laying new foundations for Japan. Those who suggest that cultural differences within languages generated substantive misunderstandings between the Japanese and American drafters may exaggerate the problem: the linguistic demands put on Japanese and American translators and authors of key drafts were indeed formidable, but not once in over fifty years has a difference in English and Japanese wording in the Constitution of 1947 led to a noteworthy problem in subsequent Japanese constitutional law.

The early contributions of the Government Section were probably a necessary catalyst for the constitution making of Japanese colleagues, most of whom were willing collaborators who reflected the concerns of the Japanese public and their deep desire to start over. In the months and years that followed, dozens of new and amended laws were passed to institutionalize and implement constitutional provisions.

THE TREATY OF PEACE WITH JAPAN

The Korean Conflict (1950–1953) and the Communist Party victory over the Nationalist Party government in the Chinese civil war (1946–1949) substantially altered the geopolitics of Northeast Asia for Japan and the United States. An occupation that had begun with purges of right-wing nationalists and encouragement of a free press and labor union movement became hostile to left-wing elements in the press and in unions and more tolerant of rehabilitated nationalists. In most practical respects, however, the Constitution of Japan took hold during the later years of the occupation.

The Allied Occupation ended with the restoration of Japan's national sovereignty on April 28, 1952. On September 8, 1951, Japan and forty-eight other nations—but not China, Russia, or Poland—signed the San Francisco Peace Treaty (formally, the Treaty of Peace with Japan), which ended their state of war. (Two hours later, Japan and the United States signed their treaty of mutual security and cooperation, the unequal features of which were not remedied until the 1960 treaty, discussed later, came into effect.) Although Japan lost all its territorial gains since 1895 in China and elsewhere (Taiwan, the Kuril Islands, other small islands, Korea, southern Sakhalin), the terms of the treaty were relatively generous, in part because of Cold War politics.

Japan agreed to pay reparations to the Allied Powers "for damage and suffering caused by it during the war" (Article 14) and to indemnify "those members of the armed forces of the Allied Powers who suffered undue hardships while prisoners of war of Japan" (Article 16). Civilian victims are not mentioned, but as noted later, litigation concerning "comfort women," slave laborers, and others continued in 2002. Also of special interest are provisions implying future Japanese membership in the United Nations (which came in 1956) and bearing upon the Article 9 no-war clause of the constitution. For example:

> Article 5. (a) Japan accepts the obligations set forth in Article 2 of the Charter of the United Nations, and in particular the obligations: (i) To settle its international disputes by peaceful means . . . (ii) to refrain in its international relations from the threat or use of force . . . (iii) to give the United Nations every assistance in any action it takes in accordance with the Charter. . . . (c) The Allied Powers for their part recognize that Japan as a sovereign nation possesses the inherent right of individual or collective self-defense referred to in Article 51 of the Charter . . . and that Japan may voluntarily enter into collective security arrangements.

One might argue that the Constitution of Japan did not come fully into effect until the restoration of sovereignty on April 28, 1952. In any case, among the central questions to be asked are, How has the 1947 Constitution of Japan fared in the legal, political, social, and economic life of the country in the past decades? How effectively are Japan's constitutional order and principles maintained in 2002? How does Japan's performance compare with that of other industrialized democracies? What are the prospects for the future of the Constitution of Japan?

BIBLIOGRAPHICAL NOTE

Lawrence W. Beer, "Constitutionalism and Rights in Japan and Korea," in Louis Henkin and Albert Rosenthal (eds.), *Constitutionalism and Rights: The Influence of the United States Constitution Abroad* (New York: Columbia University Press, 1990), 225–259. Presents a comparative East Asian perspective.

————, *Freedom of Expression in Japan: A Study in Comparative Law, Politics, and Society* (Tokyo: Kodansha International, 1984), chapter 2. Describes freedom's modern history through the occupation period.

John W. Dower, *Embracing Defeat: Japan in the Wake of World War II* (New York: W. W. Norton, 1999).

General Headquarters, Supreme Commander for the Allied Powers, Government Section, *Political Reorientation of Japan: September 1945 to September 1948*, 2 vols. (Washington, D.C.: U.S. Government Printing Office, undated, probably 1949).

Beate Sirota Gordon, *The Only Woman in the Room* (New York: Kodansha, 1997).

Charles L. Kades, "The American Role in Revising Japan's Imperial Constitution," *Political Science Quarterly* 104, no. 2 (1989): 214–248. Forty years later Kades offered authoritative reflections of the leading American participant in the drafting of the constitution.

Koseki Shoichi, *The Birth of Japan's Postwar Constitution*, Ray A. Moore (trans.), (Boulder: Westview, 1997). The book most highly recommended for the general reader.

Theodore McNelly, *The Origins of Japan's Democratic Constitution* (New York: University Press of America, 2000).

Miyazawa Toshiyoshi, *Nihonkoku Kempo* (the Constitution of Japan) (Tokyo: Nihon Hyoron Shinsha, 1963), 205.

Ray A. Moore and Donald L. Robinson (eds.), *The Constitution of Japan: A Documentary History of Its Framing and Adoption, 1945–1947* (CD-ROM) (Princeton: Princeton University Press, 1998). A monumental compilation of documents in English relevant to the creation of Japan's constitution. The electronic equivalent of 8,000 pages; helpful chronology.

————, *Partners for Democracy: Crafting the New Japanese State Under MacArthur* (New York: Oxford University Press, 2002). Excellent; best read along with the Koseki book.

Alfred C. Oppler, *Legal Reform in Occupied Japan: A Participant Looks Back* (Princeton: Princeton University Press, 1976). Memoir of a European jurist who promoted legislation implementing the constitution during the occupation.

Donald L. Robinson, "Made in America? A Study of the Origins of the Japanese Constitution," Seminar on Comparative Constitutionalism, Princeton University, April 21, 1995.

Sato Tatsuo, *Nihonkoku Kempo Seiritsushi* (The History of the Establishment of the Constitution of Japan), vols. 1 (Tokyo: Yuhikaku, 1962) and 2 (Tokyo: Yuhikaku, 1964), and, with Sato Isao, vols. 3 and 4 (Tokyo: Yuhikaku, 1994). The seminal gathering of related materials in the Japanese language.

Robert E. Ward and Sakamoto Yoshikazu (eds.), *Democratizing Japan: The Allied Occupation* (Honolulu: University of Hawaii Press, 1987). Essays by Japanese and U.S. political scientists.

5

Law, Constitution, and Reform

In 2001 Higuchi Yoichi, a leading constitutional lawyer, could appropriately maintain that the task "for us [is] to defend the Constitution in essentials as a document which has the same significance for Japanese society as the Declaration of Independence (1776) has for the United States or as the *Declaration des droits de l'homme et du citoyen* (1789) has for France" (Higuchi, vii). However distinctive in some respects, Japan's constitutional revolution after World War II was in keeping with the spirit of the emerging United Nations and with the global rethinking of basic principles of government and law of the times.

In the past half century the Constitution of Japan has been one of the world's most successful documents in legitimizing and encouraging peaceful international relations and legal, political, and social practice in pursuit of the ideals of human rights constitutionalism. In 2002 the effects of 1945–1947 are still felt: the death of militarist nationalism, the explosion of constitutionally guaranteed freedom and other human rights, and the humanization of state sovereignty in place of a divinized emperor. As of September 1945, the living Meiji Constitution had three interdependent, integral elements:

1. Extreme Shinto nationalism centered on an "Emperor state" (Tenno Kokka) or "national essence constitution" (*kokutai kempo*). These

untranslatable Japanese neologisms refer to a quasi-mystical, uniquely Japanese form of organic, absolutist monarchy requiring unquestioning obedience to the paternal emperor and his minions. The Imperial House Law, which spelled out the details of the imperial regime, was technically and practically on a par with, rather than subordinate to, the constitution.

2. Aggressive militarism in both domestic politics and international relations.

3. Refined suppression of the human rights and freedoms of the individual, especially those of the spirit, and promotion of a spirit of total self-sacrifice and absolute loyalty to an allegedly benevolent emperor.

As seen in Chapter 4, the terms of surrender in the Potsdam Declaration (July 1945) were accepted only when the emperor and his government interpreted it as assuring continuance of the emperor system in some form, their highest priority. Although some, especially in Eastern Asia, maintain that Japan's government has yet to show adequate compunction for mid-century aggression and atrocities, the country's performance since the war has given powerful witness to Japan's firm rejection of the earlier ultranationalism, authoritarianism, and militarism. The revolution begun in 1945 continues today.

JAPAN'S CIVIL LAW TRADITION

Since 1947, Japan's constitution has come alive as the law of the land through many statutes, government policies, regulations, and judicial decisions and in other implementing actions of countless public officials, attorneys, and private citizens. A nation's legal system provides important indicators of the quality of life under its constitution. Over 100 years ago, after long study and debate on the alternatives, Japan independently chose to develop its modern law according to the European civil law tradition. Very few legal traditions are now globally influential: civil law, common law, Islamic law, and Confucian legal traditions. Each has a distinctive approach to thinking about, organizing, and practicing modern law.

The civil law tradition arose from Roman law and the codes developed during and since the reign of Emperor Justinian I (483–565). Influenced by centuries of legal thought, state theory, comprehensive law codes, wars, and domestic revolutions, as well as civil wars and government efforts to centralize power and regularize trade and property, almost all modern European legal systems are in the civil law tradition—the world's most widely adopted approach to law. (In Asia, Japan, China, both Koreas,

Indonesia, Vietnam, the Philippines, East Timor, Sri Lanka, Taiwan, Thailand, Cambodia, and Laos are influenced by this tradition.) Jurists in civil law countries commonly take special cultural pride in the rationality and consistency of their law. Some harbor feelings of superiority over the legally messy common law systems. This legal chauvinism has been matched by that of many U.S. politicians, lawyers, and scholars.

Like Western countries and unlike other non-Western nations, Japan was an independent power free of unequal treaties by the early twentieth century. In part, this liberation came because Japan's law had been Westernized by 1900 and was thus intelligible and respectable to the Western powers. Today, each civil law country combines elements derived from continental Europe with legalisms emerging from its indigenous history. For example, Indonesian law is a mixture of civil law, Islamic law, and rich local customary law. Japanese, as they have for centuries, sometimes use conciliation rather than litigation to settle disputes. During the Tokugawa period, conciliation was compulsory; now its use is optional.

Since the occupation years, Japan's legal system has combined civil law and common law elements. Neither tradition is necessarily more protective of human rights than the other. In both traditions at different times and places, repression, slavery, and limits on voting rights have found homes, as has freedom. On the other hand, the fact that Japan had in place an institutionalized system of modern law and government in 1945 facilitated the country's democratization after 1945. Within an existing framework laws were added, modified, or abolished as allowed by the new constitution.

All Japanese law is organized hierarchically under what is called the Six Codes (*Roppo*): the Constitution (*Nihonkoku Kempo*), the Civil Code (*Minpo*), the Code of Civil Procedure (*Minjisoshoho*), the Criminal Code (*Keiho*), the Code of Criminal Procedure (*Keijisoshoho*), and the Commercial Code (*Shoho*), with the Constitution governing interpretation of all the other codes. These codes form a distinct level of law just below the constitution in importance and above all other statutory law. Next below the Six Codes are basic laws (*kihonho*) that cover the major agencies of government (e.g., the Diet Law [*Kokkai Ho*] and the Court Law [*Saibansho Ho*]) or set out the fundamental rules in a policy area (for example, the Basic Law on Education [*Kyoiku Kihonho*]). Every statute, regulation, local ordinance, internal administrative rule, and judicial decision in the country is expected to conform logically with the Six Codes.

No such comprehensive and internally consistent national system exists in the United States. Although federal law may trump local law in some policy areas, each state has a separate constitutional and legal system, with county and municipal subsystems. (A *code* in U.S. law is not, as in Japan, an integral part of a logically arranged set of national codes and laws that, in principle, cover all cases and situations. *Civil law* in the United States refers to law on the legal relationships of private parties or to state law as distinguished from moral law. Although *civil* as used in *Civil Code* also means law governing private relationships, not government-citizen relations, *civil law* as in *civil law tradition* refers to a long history of legal thought, institutions, and practices.)

In daily life a Japanese citizen is less likely to call a lawyer to learn about the law relevant to a given problem than to consult an abbreviated version of the *Roppo Zensho* (A Compendium of the Six Codes), over 4,000 pages of fine print. The codes are updated regularly after legislative sessions, one reason legal publishers (for example, Yuhikaku) are among the leading taxpayers. Handy smaller collections of the laws of most relevance to particular occupations or interests or stations in life (for example, students, women, human rights, taxi drivers, public servants) are easy to use. Modern law seems complicated to most laypeople in Japan, as in other countries, but nowhere is law more intricate than in the United States with its bewildering mix of federal, state, and local laws and judicial holdings. Contrary to a common misperception, the average Japanese is at least as knowledgeable about law as his American counterpart.

LEGAL EDUCATION AND THE PRACTICE OF LAW

Japan and the United States also differ in how the people who service the legal system are trained and chosen and how they see their jobs. For many years a consensus had been building that Japan had too few judges, public prosecutors, and attorneys to meet citizen needs, and in 2002 major reforms were afoot. Virtually all of Japan's judges, prosecutors, and attorneys have received the same postgraduate education at the Supreme Court's Legal Training and Research Institute (LTRI; Shiho Kenshusho), enriched by a series of three-month internships in law offices, prosecutors' offices, and both civil and criminal courts. As part of major legal reforms in 2002, this training was being reduced from two years to one year, with even more emphasis proportionately on the internships.

Entrance into the LTRI is achieved only through the extraordinarily narrow gate of the annual National Law Examinations (*Shiho shiken*); in 2000 only about 3 percent of around 30,000 examinees passed. As in other systems within the civil law tradition, judges and prosecutors hold their positions as career professionals, not as elected officials or political appointees as in the United States. In 2001 the Ministry of Justice proposed increasing the number of prosecutors from about 1,300 to 2,300, and the

Supreme Court called on the government to raise the number of judges by 500, to 2,600. In late 2001, to ease the strain on court resources, the Supreme Court and the Japan Federation of Bar Associations agreed to a new system allowing attorneys, for the first time, to serve as part-time judges. Until then, lawyers could become full-time judges but could not become part-time judges. Only about forty attorneys became judges in the 1990s.

In addition, legal scholars and opinion leaders have urged a substantial increase in the number of attorneys in response to the new challenges of globalization, deregulation, and international intellectual property law. Another driving force behind calls for more legal professionals is the excessive time taken by civil trials; the average civil trial lasted 20.5 months in 1999 (34.6 months if the court required the assistance of technical experts, as when medical issues were involved).

A large majority of LTRI students, referred to as "apprentices" (*shushusei*), choose to become attorneys rather than judges or prosecutors; but the total annual number of graduates has been small. Not until the 1990s did the annual number of LTRI admissions rise from 500 to 1,000. The goals of the LTRI are to increase the annual output of new lawyers to 3,000 by 2010 and to raise the ratio of attorneys to population from 1 per 6,300 citizens to 1 per 2,400 by 2018. This would raise the total number of attorneys from roughly 20,000 to 50,000. In comparison, France has 1 attorney per 1,640 citizens, the United Kingdom 1 per 710, Germany 1 per 740, and the United States 1 per 290 citizens.

Very few nations have U.S.-style law schools. In 2001 some Japanese law professionals recommended establishing a limited number of new institutions analogous to U.S. law schools as one way to remedy the shortage of attorneys. The law profession, however, is divided on how such law schools might best relate to the LTRI, university faculties of law (*hogakubu*), bar associations, and the commercial cram schools for those planning to take (or retake) the National Law Examination.

Each year about 50,000 men and women graduate from the ninety-three law faculties in Japan's enormous higher-education system, but only 1 percent enter the legal profession as judges, prosecutors, or attorneys. The rest are not technically attorneys and are not qualified to represent clients in court, yet in government, private, and organizational settings many develop considerable legal expertise and perform many functions for which Americans require a law degree. Also important for their role in officially finalizing contracts in law, although they are not lawyers, are notary publics (*koshonin*).

Some students of Japan have attributed this paucity of lawyers to a cultural tendency to avoid litigious behavior and stress harmony, but studies in legal sociology disprove these contentions. Humans generally find involvement with courts and lawyers uncomfortable and often need encouragement to stand up for their rights. In Japan, where one lives can seriously affect access to an attorney. About half of all lawyers live in Tokyo and Osaka, whereas some prefectures have very few practicing attorneys.

In 2001 the government submitted to parliament a major proposal to reform the Lawyers Law (*Bengoshi Ho*) and improve legal services, and thus rights protection, throughout Japan. Currently, to receive services a client enters into a contract with an individual attorney, not with a law firm. If one's attorney dies, retires, or becomes ill while a case is in litigation, the client is forced to start over with another lawyer. An attorney is usually reluctant to break long-held ties with a client by giving years of service as a judge, politician, or professor. The reform bill would allow law firms to incorporate so that a client's needs would be taken care of by other attorneys in the same firm should his or her lawyer no longer be available. Also, the bill assumes large law firms would be able to provide specialized services in rural areas through branch offices or short-term visits without taking over the practice of local attorneys.

What constitutes legal practice requiring formal qualifications as an attorney varies with a country's legal tradition and other domestic factors. The meaning of *legal practice* and *legal education* in Japan differs from U.S. definitions. In the 1970s and 1980s the United States successfully pressured Japan to amend its laws to allow foreign lawyers to "practice law" throughout Japan since New York, one of fifty states, had allowed some Japanese attorneys to operate there. Unfortunately, some foreign attorneys ended up more restricted in their practice than before because activities previously allowed as not constituting "legal practice" under Japan's definition were no longer allowed under the new law mirroring U.S. understandings.

THE DIET

The foundational principles of Japanese constitutionalism are popular sovereignty, a form of pacifism, and guaranteed human rights. The Constitution of Japan provides for a parliamentary democracy counterbalanced by a radically new and independent judiciary. Article 98 in the chapter on Supreme Law provides: "This Constitution shall be the supreme law of the nation and no law, ordinance, imperial rescript or other act of government, or part thereof, contrary to the provisions hereof, shall have legal force or validity. 2. The treaties concluded by Japan and established laws of nations shall be faithfully observed."

"Sovereign power" resides in the people of Japan (Preamble and Article 1); the emperor, like the sun flag, is a "symbol of the State and of the unity of the people" (Article 1), and "he shall not have powers related to government" (Article 4). Contrary to neonationalist claims, the relegation of the emperor to a purely ceremonial and symbolic role does not represent a serious departure from the emperor's traditional premodern status but is rather a corrective for the Meiji Constitution's disregard of the emperor's appropriate historical function. The emperor's task was to formalize the governmental leadership of whomever had won the feudal conflicts of a given time, in compliance with the orders of the victor. The emperor possessed no governmental sovereignty or centrality in the lives of the Japanese people.

Japan's parliament, the Diet (Kokkai; literally, National Assembly), is "the highest organ of state power" and "the sole lawmaking organ of the State" (Article 41), but the Supreme Court is "the court of last resort with power to determine the constitutionality of any law, order, regulation or official act" (Article 81). The Diet is composed of the House of Councillors (Sangiin; 252 members) and the more powerful House of Representatives (Shugiin; 480 members). The Diet determines the number of members in each house (Diet Law) and electoral matters (Public Offices Election Law).

Until the 1994 election law reforms under Prime Minister Hosokawa Morihiro, Japan had an unusual single-vote multimember (two to six seats) constituency system without an effective provision for periodic reapportionment based on population shifts. A seat reapportionment council, on which no Diet member may serve, is now charged by law with redistributing seats every ten years to reflect national census results and to correct disparities among election districts in the value of a vote.

Now, 480 representatives are elected under a single-member two-vote system. One vote is cast for a candidate in the voter's election district to fill 300 seats, and another is cast for a national political party. To share in the 180 seats proportionally distributed to parties in eleven electoral regions, a party must receive at least 2 percent of the popular vote. "Dual candidacy" is allowed, so candidates who lose in their home districts may win a seat if they are sufficiently high on the party's national candidate list. Representatives have a four-year term unless the House of Representatives dissolves early (Article 45), a common practice. When the House of Representatives has been dissolved, a general election must be held within forty days (Article 54).

The 252 members of the House of Councillors serve six-year terms, with half the seats (126) contested every three years (Article 46). One hundred seats are filled from national party lists in proportion to each party's national popular vote count. Upper House votes are cast for parties, not for individuals. One hundred fifty-two seats are awarded to election districts consisting of the forty-seven prefectures (*ken*) and the metropolitan areas of Tokyo (*to*), Osaka (*fu*), and Kyoto (*fu*). Each district receives a minimum of two seats, with two, four, or six additional seats awarded to the more populous prefectures. In September 2000 the Supreme Court did not find discrepancies in vote value under this system to be unconstitutional, arguing in a manner reminiscent of that supporting two Senate seats for each state in the U.S. federal system. Like France and the United Kingdom, Japan does not have a federal structure.

Japan is a colorful multiparty democracy. Since its formation in 1955, the Liberal Democratic Party (LDP; Jiyu Minshuto) has generally been the ruling party, as the least repugnant to voters of the generally unpopular political parties. As in the United States, voters tend to be less harsh in judging their own parliamentary representative than in judging Diet members from other election districts. In 2002 the LDP was part of a governing coalition with the New Komeito Party and the tiny New Conservative Party (Hoshuto). Other noteworthy parties include the Japan Communist Party (Nihon Kyosanto), the Social Democratic Party (Shakai Minshuto), the Liberal Party (Jiyuto), and the Democratic Party of Japan (Minshuto). The LDP is a loose federation of diverse factions that pull together and align with small parties as necessary to control the government and the legislative agenda. The model of numerous competing small groups seems natural in Japan's constitutional culture, rather than a strong one-party or two-party system. In keeping with its sports culture model of two competing teams, a two-party system seems to provide the only functional model for democratic U.S. party politics.

THE PRIME MINISTER AND THE CABINET

The prime minister (Sori Daijin) is chosen by the Diet. The prime minister and a majority in the cabinet (Naikaku) must be Diet members. "Executive power shall be vested in the Cabinet" (Article 65), with the prime minister as "its head." The cabinet is "collectively responsible to the Diet" (Article 66, 3). The prime minister has the authority to appoint and dismiss cabinet members. In most cases a politician has been granted the treasured first cabinet post only after winning a seat in the Diet a number of times. Generally, Japan's prime ministers have been among the least powerful of the world's premiers. Arguably, the cabinet's consensual group approach to leadership has sometimes fit well into Japan's constitutional culture.

Most laws passed by the Diet are based on legislative bills presented by the prime minister on behalf of the cabinet, but "private members bills" put forth by members of the Diet are also considered. The constitution does not provide for the Cabinet Legislative Bureau (Naikaku Hoseikyoku), but that bureau checks all legislative bills for conformity with the constitution and existing law. Too seldom noticed, this vetting of bills is one reason the constitutionality of laws is seldom successfully challenged in court. The cabinet receives guidance and research support from party policy groups and from the ministry (or ministries) most interested in the issues a legislative bill addresses. Bills ordinarily pass through a standing committee system before final debate and voting, and they become law automatically upon passage by both houses. All laws must be "signed by the competent Minister of State and countersigned by the Prime Minister" (Article 74).

Under Article 15 of the constitution, the people have "the inalienable right to choose their public officials and to dismiss them. 2. All public officials are servants of the whole community and not of any group thereof." The administrative system that serves Japan's people and their executive leaders is well-known for its stability over time, its competence, and its influence on the affairs of state. Whether the bureaucracy is the tail wagging the dog of cabinet and party leaders is debated. Cabinets change often, increasing their dependence on bureaucratic expertise. Compared with the United States, very few political appointees occupy powerful government positions.

In general, national and local civil servants share a strong ethic of public service and independent professionalism and a notably less arrogant attitude toward fellow citizens than under the former constitution. But a significant number of high-ranking civil servants "come down from heaven" (*amakudari*) and enter politics after retirement. More often than not they join their longtime partners in governance, the LDP. A strong sense of in-group identity, loyalty, and competition pervades relations between some ministries, along with awareness of the informal hierarchy (e.g., the Ministry of Finance is high and, paradoxically, the Ministry of Education is low).

In response to domestic and foreign criticism, the government embarked on a multiyear project to restructure and streamline the national government system. The new lineup of cabinet portfolios took effect in January 2001:

Prime Minister

Ministry of Justice

Ministry of Foreign Affairs

Ministry of Public Management, Home Affairs, Posts, and Telecommunications

Ministry of Finance

Ministry of Education, Culture, Sports, Science, and Technology

Ministry of Health, Labor, and Welfare

Ministry of Agriculture, Forestry, and Fisheries

Ministry of Economy, Trade, and Industry

Ministry of Land, Infrastructure, and Transport

Ministry of Environment (raised to ministry from agency status)

Chief Cabinet Secretary

National Public Safety Commission (police matters)

Defense Agency

State Minister (financial affairs)

State Minister (economic and fiscal policy and information technology policy)

State Minister (council for science and technology policy)

State Minister (administrative reform, Okinawa, and affairs related to the Northern Territories)

The net effect of this reorganization of government remains to be seen. In addition, of 163 public corporations, the government of Prime Minister Koizumi Junichoro has proposed the abolition of 17, the reorganization of 38, and the privatization of others. The jurisdictional subject matter of the affected entities is varied—for example, finance (e.g., the Housing Loan Corporation and seven others), road building and maintenance, international airport management, and gambling (e.g., the Japan Racing Association). The Japan International Cooperation Agency, the Water Resources Development Public Corporation, and others are to be reorganized into independent administrative institutions. Koizumi proposed in 2002 the establishment of a new body to oversee progress in this massive undertaking in the years ahead.

THE SUPREME COURT

Among Japanese, the most trusted and respected government institutions have been the judicial courts. In 1947, for the first time in history, Japan's judiciary became a branch of government separate from the executive, autonomously administered by the Supreme Court, equal in constitutional status to the Diet and the cabinet, and the final arbiter in all cases at law with the power of judicial review. No court-martial, administrative tribunal, or other special court is allowed (Article 76, 2). All judges are "independent in the exercise of their conscience and [are] . . . bound only by this Constitution and the law" (Article 76, 3).

In earlier times judges had the authority to decide private law disputes and criminal cases, but only one administrative court under the Justice Ministry (very rarely used) could deal with allegations of official violation of a subject's limited rights. Yet a proud tradition developed of independence in deciding individual cases with respect to the law. A key example is the 1891 Otsu case. In response to an attempt to assassinate a visiting Russian prince, the government and the public demanded the death penalty be imposed, applying the law concerning Japan's royal family rather than the ordinary homicide statute. In compliance with the latter law, the highest tribunal (the Great Court of Cassation; Daishin'in) refused to yield to public pressure and handed down a prison sentence.

Again, in the tumultuous 1930s the courts asserted their independence by standing up to prosecutors, other officials, militarists, and some media in the most important political bribery case between the wars, the Imperial Rayon Company case (commonly, the Teijin Incident). A cabinet fell, and widespread outrage at alleged corruption poisoned the political atmosphere. After a two-year trial with a record 265 court sessions, however, on December 16, 1937, the Tokyo District Court acquitted sixteen prominent politicians, bureaucrats, and businessmen charged with unfair and illegal stock sales on grounds of insufficient evidence. Presiding judge Fujii Goichiro bluntly characterized the prosecutors' case as "an attempt to scoop up the reflection of the moon from the water," drawing on a folk tale. Upon reexamination of the case record, the government decided not to appeal the decision.

The Supreme Court (Saiko Saibansho) today consists of fourteen justices and a chief justice who render final judgment on appeals from lower courts, make court rules and personnel decisions, administer all the nation's courts, and train legal professionals. The justices are selected from the ranks of career judges, career prosecutors, attorneys, and legal scholars (one), with an occasional distinguished person of other background (e.g., a diplomat or administrator). In 1994 Takahashi Hisako, former director of the Labor Ministry's Women's and Minors' Bureau, became the first woman appointed to the Supreme Court. Justices are appointed by the cabinet, almost always in accordance with the recommendations of the chief justice. Although not required by law, the chief justice, in turn, generally defers to recommendations of the procurator general and the Tokyo Bar Association or the Osaka Bar Association when openings occur in their bailiwicks. Retirement age for justices is seventy; other judges step down at sixty-five.

Few Japanese believe the U.S. practice of electing district attorneys and some judges is the best way to achieve a fair justice system. As noted earlier, Japan has a shortage of judges, and one measure under discussion for increasing their number is appointing seasoned attorneys to the lower-court bench. Although the recent restructuring of Japan's executive branch has entailed cutting back on personnel, plans for judicial reform call for expanding human resources.

For purposes of deciding most cases, the Court divides into three five-member Petty Benches (Shohotei). The Grand Bench (Daihotei) of all justices decides the relatively few cases involving constitutional issues or a possible change in prevailing legal doctrine. Each justice not fully satisfied with the majority opinion must write a dissenting or concurring opinion. The Great Court of Cassation under the Meiji Constitution issued only one opinion. Recent law school graduates serve the U.S. Supreme Court and other courts as clerks. Japan's justices are assisted in their work by research judges (*shiho chosakan*), experienced lower-court judges assigned to the Supreme Court for a few years. Unlike American judges, Japan's jurists look at the views of foreign courts to enrich their perspective on legal issues.

Under the Supreme Court are eight high courts (*koto saibansho*) located in Tokyo, Osaka, Nagoya, Hiroshima, Fukuoka, Sendai, Sapporo, and Takamatsu, with six branches in other cities. About 2,700 judges are authorized by law for a population of roughly 127 million, but their actual number is closer to 2,100—too few. Fifty district courts (*chiho saibansho*) are located in the prefectures and metropolitan areas, with 201 branches in other cities and towns; over 300 family courts (*katei saibansho*); and about 450 summary courts (*kan'i saibansho*). Nine hundred and ten judges (*saibankan; hanji*) are on the district court bench, assisted by 460 assistant judges (*hanjiho*). Graduates of the LTRI serve as assistant judges for ten years before receiving appointment as full judges. Judges not in the courts are assigned to administrative or educational activities. Most cases are decided with a single judge presiding; especially important cases are handled by a three-judge panel. Action on election law disputes begins in a high court. Trials are public (Article 82).

In assessing the status of civil liberties, equality under the law, criminal justice rights, and other constitutional issues in a nation where judicial decisions enjoy high legitimacy, as in Japan, a study of individual cases is particularly useful because judgments in law cases involving real people and concrete disputes are among the most authentic and authoritative parts of the country's historical legal narrative. That is why a fair number of judicial decisions are mentioned in remaining chapters.

On occasion, Japan's judges bluntly overturn an interpretation of another court or even of their own court in an earlier case. Precedent is important to Japan's courts but is less binding in law than in the United States. Every few weeks, large-circulation law journals carry the latest important judicial decisions and commentary (for example, *Hanrei Jiho* [The Case Reporter]) and are easily accessible to professionals and the public. To the civil law way of thinking, U.S. reliance on judges to decide the legality and constitutionality of a law may sometimes seem downright undemocratic. After all, the law was passed by a democratically elected legislature. This deference to the will of the people as expressed by the elected parliament while at the same time claiming to honor the primacy of the constitution is sometimes behind what may appear to some U.S. observers as excessive judicial restraint in matters of constitutional right.

As in other nations of the civil law tradition, Japan has no jury system. In 2002, however, after lengthy study of trial-related problems and the European and U.S. systems, Japan began to establish a fundamentally new system of lay participation in criminal trials, as recommended by an advisory council headed by the distinguished Professor Sato Koji. "Citizen judges" chosen randomly from eligible voters and screened by legal professionals to minimize bias are to enjoy the same rights as professional judges to hear and query witnesses and to decide verdicts and penalties by majority vote. No defendant will be held guilty when only judges or only citizen members of the bench vote for a conviction. The number of judges and citizen judges assigned to a first-instance trial will be proportionate to the importance of the case (for example, in terms of potential penalties) and the burden on citizens. Travel expenses and a per diem will be paid. One goal is to heighten the public's sense of its sovereignty.

Family courts seek nonlitigious settlements of domestic disputes and handle all crimes of minors under age twenty and of adults adversely affecting juveniles. A divorce case must first be brought to a family court before any formal suit can be filed in a district court. Divorce is uncommon, although divorce procedures are simple and need not involve any court. The divorce rate is 1.94 per thousand, compared with 4.33 per thousand in the United States and 0.40 in Mexico.

Usually, youth crime is handled privately with educational remedies, dismissal of the case, or probation. Laypeople and around 1,500 family court probation officers assist family court judges. In 2000 the 1949 Juvenile

Law was changed in response to heinous teenage crimes; the age of criminal accountability for serious juvenile offenses was lowered from sixteen to fourteen, and murder cases of those sixteen or older are referred to a prosecutor. Heretofore closed-door family court hearings are now opened to prosecutors, lawyers, and other judges. The controversial law will be reviewed after five years.

In addition to the courts and public and nongovernmental agencies, Japan has institutionalized a variety of alternative dispute resolution and rights protection systems. For example, thousands of unpaid, carefully screened human rights commissioners (Jinken Yogo Iin; literally, human rights protectors) promote human rights education and handle a wide range of problems at the neighborhood level. Additional thousands of volunteers serve as local administrative counselors (Gyosei Sodan Iin, average age sixty), dealing officially and often effectively with complaints against government bureaucrats. However admirable their work, their powers are now considered too limited to deal with some current problems.

In 2001 the nonpartisan Human Rights Protection Deliberation Council of the Justice Ministry recommended establishing a new independent organ to deal more firmly and comprehensively with issues discussed in Chapter 7. Among those problems are the treatment of women, the elderly, crime victims, ethnic minorities, *burakumin*, HIV victims, and resident foreigners, along with stalking, domestic violence, and school group bullying (*ijime*). Rights violations by government personnel and the mass media are other concerns of the council.

LOCAL AUTONOMY

Like many other democracies, Japan is a unitary state, not a federal system, but local government is constitutionally important. For centuries before modern times Japan had what might be termed a *federal feudal system* in which feudal lords (daimyo) had jurisdiction over many local affairs, and the Tokugawa Shogun (a politico-military national leader) held sway when national interests were involved. Hundreds of feudal domains developed their own distinctive political cultures and law and functioned much of the time with a good measure of local autonomy. The majority of Japanese were farmers or fishermen who ran their own village affairs with only occasional encounters with nobles. Under the Meiji Constitution feudal domains were replaced by prefectures, and local officials were appointed by the central government.

Now, thousands of local governments with elected governors, mayors, local assemblies, and village councils flourish alongside the regional offices of national ministries and the local courts, and they revivify traditions of local government and politics. "Local public entities" (*chiho jichi dantai*) enjoy "the right to manage their property, affairs, and administration and to enact their own regulations" (Article 94) and ordinances (*jorei*) within limits set by the Local Autonomy Law and other provisions. Local entities have limited taxing authority but are heavily dependent on national law and funds. Opposition parties unable to unseat the LDP from control of the national government have fared much better at the polls in local elections.

In regulating Japan's frequent demonstrations and parades, local public safety ordinances (*koan jorei*) have been the most important form of law. It was not national government initiative but successful experience with many local ordinances over a twenty-year period that led to the establishment of the national Information Disclosure Law in May 1999. Besides the vigor, variety, and innovation local governments offer, they provide a limited restraint on central government and have as much or more power than local governments in other centralized states such as Sweden, France, and England.

As a major step in streamlining Japan's governmental system, in 2002 reformist prime minister Koizumi proposed a reduction by mergers of the number of cities, towns, and villages from 3,200 to around 1,000 and an increase in local autonomy.

CONSTITUTIONAL LAWYERS

Japan's constitutional lawyers seem more influential in forming public opinion and are more frequently invited to serve the national community than are U.S. legal scholars. Besides their teaching and scholarly writing, constitutional lawyers comment on cases and issues in national-circulation newspapers and journals and in television and serial roundtable discussions (*zadankai*). More prominent scholars may be asked to write newspaper columns on constitutional issues spread out, say, over a month. They are also called upon to write questions for and to grade thousands of National Law Examinations, dreaded as grueling work but dutifully done. In addition, some write precollegiate and college textbooks. Of particular importance to legislative and administrative processes, they serve in various public and private advisory capacities and on deliberative bodies that formulate bills leading to new law on major issues.

Japan's constitutional lawyers differ among themselves on particulars and on theory, sometimes significantly, but they develop their own jurisprudence in dialogue with each other about current legal thinking in the United States and Europe. By contributing to public understanding of the essential principles, values, institutions, and legal processes of Japan's living constitutional culture, constitutional lawyers have been founding participants in building consensus on most aspects of the 1947 Constitution of Japan.

Regrettably, most of Japan's constitutional lawyers are little known outside Japan. Illustrative is the case of Professor Ashibe Nobuyoshi of Tokyo University, a modest and quiet man of enormous learning who was deeply committed to human rights constitutionalism. Ashibe was founding president of Japan's Association for the Study of International Human Rights Law. As professor, scholarly author, adviser, and expert witness in court, he was respected as one of Japan's most eminent constitutional lawyers. Yet he and his work had rarely appeared outside Japan or in any language except Japanese when he passed away in 1999.

Working within the framework described in this chapter, the Japanese people deserve all the credit for the success of the 1947 Constitution over the past half century. At the same time, the respectful collaboration of Americans with Japanese at the birth of the document represents one of the greatest foreign policy accomplishments in U.S. history. The power to collaborate, respectfully and effectively, is far more impressive than the military might to dominate.

The provision that continues to be most challenging to mutual understanding in the political and legal dialogue between Japan and the United States is Article 9, the "no war" clause discussed in Chapter 6.

BIBLIOGRAPHICAL NOTE

Japanese-Language Sources

Most readers may not read Japanese, but some may be interested in knowing the type of sources this book relies on. There is a vast literature in Japanese on Japan's constitutional law. Few foreign scholars are acquainted with this rich lode of Japanese scholarship, although it constitutes much of the basis for Japan's constitutional discourse. Foreign journalistic accounts of constitutional issues in Japan are few and not always reliable.

Among the most authoritative sources on Japan's constitutional law and policies are the Supreme Court's website, www.courts.go.jp; the various series of court case reporters published by the Supreme Court of Japan; *Jurisuto* (The Jurist), the most influential law journal, published twice monthly by Yuhikaku, the most important law book publisher, with occasional extra editions; *Hanrei Jiho* (The Case Reporter), published thrice monthly, the leading commercial case reporters; *Horitsu Jiho* (The Law Reporter), a progressive monthly; and *Jiyu to Seigi* (Liberty and Justice), the monthly publication of the Japan Federation of Bar Associations, to which all attorneys must belong.

Examples of specific issues containing 2001 constitutional discourse are "Seiki no tenkanten ni kempo o kangaeru" (Considering the Constitution at the Turn of the Century), *Jurisuto*, no. 1192 (January 1, 15, 2001); "Kore kara no kempogaku" (Whither Constitutional Studies), *Horitsu Jiho*, no. 900 (January 2001); "Shiho kaikaku to kokumin sanka" (Legal Reform and Citizen Participation), *Jurisuto*, special issue, no. 1198 (April 10, 2001); "Kempo Hanrei Hyakusen" (A Hundred Selected Cases in Constitutional Law; actually analyses of 227 judicial decisions), 4th ed., separate series, no. 154 (September 2000) and no. 155 (October 2000).

Besides coverage in standard textbooks for junior high school, senior high school, and university students that deal with the constitution in increasing detail at the higher levels, Japan abounds with scholarly books and articles on general and specific issues. Writings on Article 9 (the renunciation of war clause) have been most abundant, followed by discussions of individual rights and freedoms.

The monthly *Seron Chosa* (Opinion Research) presents the results of extensive survey research by public and private agencies. Major newspapers such as the *Asahi Shimbun* contain reliable factual data, public opinion reports, and analyses concerning the constitution and specific related social and economic issues. Besides journals on constitutional law, the publications of highly specialized learned societies—for example, those focused on law and society studies and criminal law—contribute to public understanding of constitutional issues.

In short, Japan has a broad and deep infrastructure in Japanese of accessible knowledge, understanding, and discourse on the Constitution of Japan that contributes to its continuing legitimacy.

Selected English-Language Publications

Nobuyoshi Ashibe, Lawrence W. Beer, and Masami Ito, "Japan: The United States Constitution and Japan's Constitutional Law," in L. W. Beer (ed.), *Constitutional Systems in Late Twentieth Century Asia* (Seattle: University of Washington Press, 1992), 128–269. A rare English-language work of two eminent Japanese scholars.

Lawrence W. Beer and Hiroshi Ito, *The Constitutional Case Law of Japan: Selected Supreme Court Decisions, 1961–1970* (Seattle: University of Washington Press, 1978). Translations.

————, *The Constitutional Case Law of Japan, 1970 Through 1990* (Seattle: University of Washington Press, 1996). Supreme Court and lower-court decisions in translation.

Gerald Curtis, *The Logic of Japanese Politics: Leaders, Institutions, and the Limits of Change* (New York: Columbia University Press, 1999). A standard text.

John Owen Haley, *Authority Without Power: Law and the Japanese Paradox* (New York: Oxford University Press, 1991). An insightful synthesis.

Dan Fenno Henderson, *Conciliation and Japanese Law, Tokugawa and Modern* (Tokyo: University of Tokyo Press, 1965). The best work on a key element of Japan's constitutional culture.

Yoichi Higuchi (ed.), *Five Decades of Constitutionalism in Japanese Society* (Tokyo: University of Tokyo Press, 2001).

Hiroshi Itoh, *The Japanese Supreme Court: Constitutional Policies* (New York: Markus Weiner, 1989).

Japanese American Society for Legal Studies, *Law in Japan: An Annual*, vols. 1–27 (1967–2001). Translations and original articles by Japanese and foreign specialists.

Percy R. Luney Jr. and Kazuyuki Takahashi (eds.), *Japanese Constitutional Law* (Tokyo: University of Tokyo Press, 1993). Essays by Japanese and U.S. specialists.

John M. Maki, *Court and Constitution in Japan: Selected Supreme Court Decisions, 1948–60* (Seattle: University of Washington Press, 1964).

————, *Japan's Commission on the Constitution: The Final Report* (Seattle: University of Washington Press, 1980).

John Henry Merryman, *The Civil Law Tradition* (Stanford: Stanford University Press, 1985). The most readable explanation of the most influential family of legal systems, of which Japan is a part, and how it differs from U.S. common law.

Richard H. Mitchell, *Justice in Japan: The Notorious Teijin Scandal* (Honolulu: University of Hawaii Press, 2002). In a major assertion of judicial independence in the late 1930s, sixteen prominent Japanese were acquitted of illegal stock sales.

————, *Political Bribery in Japan* (Honolulu: University of Hawaii Press, 1996).

Muramatsu Michio, *Local Power in the Japanese State*, B. Scheiner and J. White (trans.), (Berkeley: University of California Press, 1997).

J.A.A. Stockwin, *Governing Japan: Divided Politics in a Major Economy* (Oxford: Blackwell, 1999). A standard text with substantial coverage of constitutional questions.

6

Pacifism
and Renunciation of War

Perhaps the most remarkable provision in Japan's constitution is Article 9, the so-called no war clause; but more remarkable is Japan's compliance with the spirit of the "Peace Constitution" for over half a century. The Preamble sets the tone:

> We, the Japanese people, desire peace for all time and are deeply conscious of the high ideals controlling human relationships, and we have determined to preserve our security and existence, trusting in the justice and faith of the peace-loving peoples of the world. We desire to occupy an honored place in an international society striving for the preservation of peace. . . . We recognize that all peoples of the world have the right to live in peace, free from fear and want.

Article 9 reads:

> Aspiring sincerely to an international peace based on justice and order, the Japanese people forever renounce war as a sovereign right of the nation and the threat or use of force as a means of settling international disputes.
>
> 2. In order to accomplish the aim of the preceding paragraph, land, sea, and air forces, as well as other war potential, will never be maintained. The right of belligerency of the state will not be recognized.

Japan's arms were laid down in 1945 and have never been taken up again to settle an international dispute. Some would prefer to call it "renunciation of war," in keeping with the formal title of Chapter II of the constitution. The nature of Japan's pacifism may be historically unique. Article 9 was drafted within months of the end of the war when people strongly wanted to prevent a similar war. Indeed, General MacArthur's original notes on matters to be included in a draft constitution called for a renunciation of war even as a means of "preserving its [Japan's] own security." That thought did not make it into the constitution, perhaps fortunately, for several reasons. By the end of the occupation in 1952, the situation surrounding Japan had been drastically altered: the Cold War had developed, the People's Republic had won the civil war in China, and the Korean War was being waged next door.

Within days of the outbreak of the Korean War in 1950, MacArthur authorized the Japanese government to create a National Police Reserve (NPR), a lightly armed paramilitary force. In 1952, as a result of the end of the occupation, the NPR became the National Security Force (NSF), a stride toward becoming a regular military system. Two years later the NSF was converted into the Ground, Sea, and Air Self-Defense Forces (SDF). All three steps were bitterly opposed by many in Japan because they could again lead Japan into war, and those opposed saw these measures as violating the letter and spirit of the constitution.

Theoretically consistent philosophical or religious pacifism precludes violent personal, community, or state action—even in self-defense—in response to individual or collective violence. Pacifism requires in all circumstances that one turn the other cheek and refrain from hostile reaction, based on faith in human goodness and disciplined conviction in the face of provocation. Only peaceful resistance to evil is permissible. That does not describe Japan's official or popular pacifism, although some Japanese believe Japan should not respond militarily even to an invasion because war is such a horror.

Like all other governments, Japan's recognizes a national right of self-defense and the legitimacy of using police violence against some crimes, but Japan also denies the legitimacy of taking violent initiatives to settle international disputes (for example, to contest territorial claims). This unusual position can be termed *quasi-pacifist*. But there is more to it: a very strong and widespread popular rejection of militarism and war in response to the terrible sufferings, abject defeat, and ideological disillusionment of the Japanese people in World War II. For decades after 1945 this "psychological pacifism" permeated public debate, the mass media, and both popular and high culture.

Political parties and opinion leaders have now nearly reached a consensus on support for paragraph 1 of Article 9 but not on paragraph 2 or its proper interpretation. Article 9 forever renounces both war as a sovereign national right and the threat and use of force to settle international disputes, as well as the right of belligerency. Japan has honored these pledges in practice for over half a century. Japan's promise in paragraph 2 never to maintain "land, sea, and air forces . . . [and] other war potential," however, has been central to constitutional controversy. The 1954 law establishing the SDF (*Jieitai*) tried to avoid violating the letter of Article 9 by inventing the terms Land SDF, Maritime SDF, and Air SDF. The government takes "war potential" to mean any military capacity beyond the minimum needed for self-defense.

Perhaps an explicit recognition in Article 9 of Japan's right to self-defense would diminish domestic controversy without diluting the rest of the article. Also worth serious consideration is the addition of a third paragraph to Article 9 forever renouncing the manufacture, possession, and use of nuclear, chemical, and biological weapons of mass destruction. Might not Japan then mount a campaign to encourage others to do likewise? The cost would be minimal; any progress made would be a victory for humankind. Any movement to modify Article 9, however, might awaken fears abroad, at least among Japan's Asian war victims.

ARTICLE 9 IN THE LAW AND THE COURTS

The Supreme Court has held that under Article 9 Japan retains the natural law right to self-defense and that the Treaty of Mutual Cooperation and Security between Japan and the United States is not on its face unconstitutional. The Court has never directly decided, however, whether the Self-Defense Forces founded in 1954 are unconstitutional.

In the famous Naganuma Nike Missile Site case, the Sapporo District Court (1973) held the SDF to be unconstitutional. On appeal, however, the Sapporo High Court (1976) and the Supreme Court (1982) reversed on technical grounds, avoiding the constitutional issue. Farmers in Naganuma, Hokkaido, had challenged a government decision to build a Nike antiaircraft missile site in a forest reserve, claiming the base interfered with their water supply and flood control and also violated their Article 9 "right to peace." The appellate courts held that the farmers had lost their legal interest and thus their standing to sue when the government took steps to eliminate their water problems.

In the earlier Sunagawa decision (1959) regarding the Japan-U.S. Security Treaty, the Supreme Court maintained that extension of a runway at the U.S. Tachikawa Air Base, hotly opposed by demonstrators, was a political question for the political branches of government, not a constitutional matter for courts of law to decide. Less noticed was the 1987 Tokyo High Court decision, which the Supreme Court let stand, denying that in time of peace there was a higher public interest in the activities of the Defense Agency than in those of civilian airports or other government agencies. In the spirit of the constitution and Article 9, the court said, noise pollution is a general public concern, and noise pollution from military aircraft had violated the personal rights of citizens.

What Japan has not done under Article 9 is as instructive as what it has done. Government policy maintains that the constitution does not allow Japan the right to collective self-defense. If the United States were invaded, Japan could not come to its aid, although the United States is obligated to assist in Japan's defense. Japan has no independent military command structure. In contrast to many European countries, Japan has no national security law under which freedom of expression might be restricted during times of emergency. Neither the constitution nor other laws have provisions related to acts of war, such as declaring war or concluding peace. No article touches on declaration of martial law or military courts or preservation of military secrets (except in compliance with the Security Treaty). Government employees in general, however, are forbidden by law from revealing secrets learned in the course of their work unless affected by the recent Information Disclosure Law. Article 18 of the constitution bans "bondage of any kind," and "involuntary servitude" is prohibited except as punishment for crime; so scholars maintain that compulsory military service would be unconstitutional.

Besides Article 9, other current constitutional and legal limits on Japan's military had no place in the Meiji constitutional order or prewar government practice: the limitation of ministerial position to civilians, thus removing the once powerful military from politics (Article 66); the Diet's position as the highest organ of state power (Article 41); the cabinet's responsibility to the Diet in the exercise of executive authority (Article 66); the courts' authority to decide disputes involving the military as part of their comprehensive review powers; the ultimate control of the budget by the House of Representatives (Article 85); and the freedom of the citizenry to criticize military policy and activities with impunity (Article 21).

Since 1947, more has been written in Japanese about Article 9 than about any other constitutional provision, but in the courts human rights issues have received the most attention. The great majority of Japan's constitutional lawyers consider the SDF unconstitutional. Many pacifists would like U.S. forces to go home, but many others—including some pacifists—believe the unpredictability of Northeast Asian geopolitics would increase without a U.S. presence.

The general public considers the SDF constitutionally acceptable as long as it does not fight abroad and has a relatively modest capability. When asked in 2000 to name up to two primary functions of the SDF from that time on, about 70 percent felt the primary function was disaster relief, whereas about 41 percent cited military deterrence and 36 percent thought international peace-keeping and emergency aid abroad to be most important. Only 10.7 percent supported an increase in the size of the SDF, whereas 13.9 percent called for cutbacks and 61.7 percent thought current levels were appropriate.

Opposition political parties have been modifying long-held positions. For example, in the 1990s under Prime Minister Murayama Tomiichi, the Social Democratic Party first recognized the constitutionality of the SDF. In 2000 the Japan Communist Party changed its policy, in place since 1958, and approved use of the de facto military, the SDF, in "emergencies" while continuing to maintain the SDF is unconstitutional. The Democratic Party of Japan, the largest opposition group in parliament, reversed its policy of supporting a ban on the use of the SDF in UN peace-keeping operations.

PEACEKEEPING WITH THE UNITED NATIONS

After fierce and long debate occasioned by the Gulf War, in 1992 the Diet passed the UN Peace-Keeping Operation Cooperation Law (PKO Law). The law allows the dispatch of up to 2,000 SDF personnel abroad. Prior approval by the Diet is required, except when the purpose is humanitarian disaster relief. Apart from a postwar minesweeping operation, Japan made a generous financial contribution to the Gulf War. The Japanese, like many other people, were not sure the war was wise. (A U.S. Senate resolution approving "Operation Desert Storm" was passed by a very narrow margin.)

The debate did open a continuing discussion on how Japan might best contribute responsibly to the world community in circumstances of crisis while continuing to honor Article 9. Under the PKO Law, Japan may participate in UN peace-keeping on five conditions:

1. A cease-fire agreement must be in effect.
2. The parties in conflict must approve Japan's peace-keeping mission.
3. The peace-keeping operation must be neutral.
4. Japan's units will withdraw if any of the above conditions is not met.

5. Japanese use of weapons must be limited to the minimum necessary to prevent injury or death.

In practice, according to Reinhard Drifte, Japan's policy violated the UN's General Guidelines for Peace-Keeping Operations (October 1995) by not agreeing to defend other troop contingents under attack in its environs until 2001. In October 2001, as part of Japan's response to the September 11 bombing of the World Trade Center, a new law allowed SDF personnel to use arms not only to defend themselves but to protect those "under their care" such as refugees and wounded foreign troops.

Japan played a leading role in the UN Transitional Authority in Cambodia, sending 600 SDF members, 75 police, and 40 election monitors for one year; 2 were killed. Among other, smaller-scale involvements, Japan sent 48 SDF personnel to Mozambique in 1994 and in 2000 had 45 men in the UN Disengagement Observer Force on the Golan Heights in Israel. A law passed in 2000 allows the Maritime SDF to board foreign vessels within or beyond Japan's territorial waters as part of international economic sanctions.

In October 2001, amendments of the SDF Law during the war on terrorism allowed Japanese ships and C-130 transport planes to provide intelligence, fuel, food, and logistical aid to U.S. forces operating out of Diego Garcia in the Indian Ocean, Arabian Sea, and Persian Gulf and to bring humanitarian relief to refugees and other war victims in Afghanistan and Pakistan. Around 1,500 SDF support personnel were deployed for one year. In December the Diet further amended the SDF Law to lift the ban on monitoring cease-fires, disarming local forces, patrolling demilitarized zones, inspecting the transport of weapons, and collecting and disposing of abandoned weapons—all as participation in UN peace-keeping operations. Prior Diet approval is required for the dispatch of SDF forces for such UN activities.

On a case-by-case basis, Japan has expanded the range of its noncombatant international activities while reaffirming commitment to Article 9. Scholars involved in peace studies would find rich soil in Japan's efforts to be both pacifist and internationally responsible.

JAPAN'S MILITARY CAPACITIES

Of major powers, Japan has the lowest rate of military expenditure per capita and as a percentage of gross domestic product (GDP; 0.96 percent), yet the military budget is one of the world's largest. For many years it has been operative policy that Japan's military budget not exceed 1 percent of the GDP, but Japan's economy is the world's second-largest. Its defense capacities are not minimal. James Auer, however, a leading authority on

U.S.-Japanese military affairs, maintains that in heavily militarized East Asia those capacities are geopolitically insufficient for Japan's security without the Security Treaty with the United States.

The SDF is under the supervision of the prime minister. No independent military command structure exists as in prewar Japan. Troop levels have never reached recruitment goals. Total SDF personnel number about 236,000, with ground forces accounting for 146,000. Vessels number about 150, for a total of 365,000 tons. Japan has about 510 combat aircraft, compared with about 4,000 each in the United States, China, and Russia. The constitutionality of a particular aircraft or weapon as exclusively defensive in nature has often been debated. In 2001 such controversy centered on large tanker aircraft intended to support UN activities. Japan has no long-range combat aircraft or international missile capability.

In the spirit of Article 9, arms manufacture and trade are strictly limited, to Japan's economic loss. The U.S. military, however, benefits from Japanese technology (e.g., optics), which has both civilian and military uses ("dual use"). Under its "three no-nuclear" policy, Japan may not make or possess nuclear weapons or introduce them into the country. To their credit, every August the Japanese people and many of their leaders keep alive somber memories of the 1945 atomic bombings of Hiroshima and Nagasaki with publicly and privately sponsored commemorations. Hundreds of thousands of citizens, mostly civilians, died.

Japan consistently advocates global nuclear disarmament. In November 2001 the UN General Assembly's Disarmament and International Security Committee adopted for the eighth time Japan's proposal to eliminate all nuclear weapons. One hundred twenty-four nations voted in favor, and twenty abstained; only the United States and India opposed the resolution. (The United States also opposes ratification of the Comprehensive Test Ban Treaty.) As the world's leading donor of nonmilitary aid since 1989, Japan takes into account a potential recipient's arms manufacture and trade in weapons of mass destruction, as well as its human rights performance, environmental policies, and level of democracy.

Japan is a major contributor to the recovery of Afghanistan from prolonged warfare and the Taliban regime. A high priority of the cabinet is to provide state-of-the-art ultrasonic and infrared land mine detection equipment for the 5,000 individuals in nongovernmental organizations (NGOs) clearing mines in Afghanistan and assisting mine victims. Although some Japanese NGOs have publicly criticized the allegedly inadequate level of government aid, as Foreign Minister Tanaka Makiko said in 2002, official relief activities "would not be possible without the work done by [Japanese] nongovernmental organizations" such as Peace Winds Japan (PWJ).

The PWJ provides food and shelter for tens of thousands of Afghans. The PWJ and other NGOs receive government funds through a private entity, Japan Platform, established in 2000.

A REALISTIC MODEL?

Japan's concept and practice of quasi-pacifism are an original and valuable contribution to the world's thinking on national security and constitutionalism. Article 9 has made a considerable difference in Japan's international relations for over fifty years. Obviously, regional geopolitics affect each nation-state's options, but the operative worldwide assumption that every major power and almost all other nations need a large military force in the face of external threats is not persuasive or realistic. Many countries do not face credible external threats to their national security.

Japan's "comprehensive security" model may be the most useful current illustration. With more realism than idealism, Japan's people and many sociopolitical leaders have not felt militarily threatened by any other country. The country's security is based in part on being amiable and economically useful—even indispensable—to countries around the globe, in part on the geopolitics of Northeast Asia, in part on the SDF, in part on the Japan-U.S. Security Treaty, and in part on a constitutional law and politics of peace.

In 2002, although many Japanese see a need to amend the constitution in some way, a resounding 74 percent oppose any change to Article 9. Japan still debates how to buttress UN peace-keeping efforts logistically and militarily without violating Article 9. One issue not yet thoroughly debated is the public's willingness to have SDF members die alongside UN forces from other countries in the line of international duty to enforce peace. The two deaths during the Cambodian operations startled some into awareness of that virtually unthinkable situation. Some Japanese, although fewer than thirty years ago, still believe Article 9 requires that Japan submit in case of invasion without organized military resistance.

Sooner or later Japan and Russia will have to conclude a peace treaty formally ending World War II. When they come to the table with that serious intent, the Japanese negotiators might suggest in the spirit of Article 9 wording such as: "In accordance with Japan's constitutional renunciation of war as a means toward 'an international peace based on justice and order' and in keeping with Russia's firm commitment to international peace, the two contracting parties renounce the threat or use of force as a means of solving future disputes. They will rely on existing international adjudication or mediation agencies to settle their disputes." In a similar spirit, in the twenty-first century might Chinese leaders earn the world's respect for their statesmanship by renouncing force as a means of settling territorial disputes with its neighbors in East and Southeast Asia?

BIBLIOGRAPHICAL NOTE

James E. Auer, "Article 9: Renunciation of War," in Percy Luney and Kazuyuki Takahashi (eds.), *Japanese Constitutional Law* (Tokyo: University of Tokyo Press, 1993), 69–86.

Reinhard Drifte, *Japan's Foreign Policy for the 21st Century* (New York: St. Martin's, 1998).

John M. Maki, "Japan's Rearmament: Progress and Problems," *Western Political Quarterly* 8, no. 4 (December 1955): 545–568.

Toshihiro Yamauchi, "Constitutional Pacifism: Principle, Reality, and Perspective," in Yoichi Higuchi (ed.), *Five Decades of Constitutionalism in Japanese Society* (Tokyo: University of Tokyo Press, 2001), 27–41.

Peter J. Woolley, *Japan's Navy: Politics and Paradox, 1971–2000* (Boulder: Lynne Reinner Publishers, 2000).

Dennis Van Vranken Hickey, *The Armies of East Asia: China, Taiwan, Japan, and the Koreas* (Boulder: Lynne Reinner Publishers, 2001).

7

Human Rights and Duties Under the Constitution of Japan, 1947–2001

Some observers have contended that Japan's prosperity has been largely responsible for the stability of its democracy. (A reputable survey rated Japan the world's most stable democracy.) Granted that economic problems have not caused significant destabilization, one can also argue the other way. Japan's economic growth has been very positively affected by a firm infrastructure of constitutional government and law, with perennial democratic elections, tolerance for the wide range of views represented by numerous political parties and private organizations, and both protective and promotive attention to human rights and responsible capitalism. Often, the importance of such constitutional development has been overlooked by those preoccupied with the enormous problems attendant to a globalizing economy.

Under the 1947 Constitution of Japan, the consensual norm now goes beyond popular sovereignty—the rule of the majority and majoritarian decision making—to a guarantee of many human rights to all Japanese of whatever station. The term *human rights sovereignty* may be preferable to *popular sovereignty* to stress the primacy of human rights in the constitutional order. This paradigm shift removes the will of the democratic majority from primacy and makes everyone responsible for maintaining the human rights regime: the Diet, the cabinet, local governments, the courts, and the individual citizen. In the twenty-first century the overriding world-wide imperative of government and law is to protect and promote equal respect for the dignity and rights of each person. That ideal shines through the Constitution of Japan.

Implementing popular sovereignty by exercising democratic electoral rights is essential. Japan has enjoyed an unbroken succession of free elections under democratic law since 1946, with no more corruption of results than democratic flesh is commonly heir to elsewhere. Majoritarian democracy, however, may be friend or foe of many other human rights. The common assumption that strong national commitment to democratic elections and majoritarian decision making implies effective concern in policy and law for other human rights—such as equality rights, education rights, worker rights, criminal justice rights, and freedom of expression on controversial issues—does not square with the thinking or records of many democratic nations, in the past and at present. For example, Singapore, Malaysia, and others limit free speech while honoring some socioeconomic rights and a good measure of electoral democracy.

Substantial majorities in Japan and Germany countenanced military aggression and atrocities until 1945. Torture remains a recurrent problem under both democratically elected and authoritarian governments. The financial power of relatively few persons and corporations drives U.S. electoral processes and priorities to such a degree that the United States might better be termed a constitutional plutocracy than a constitutional democracy. At an earlier time, the U.S. free marketplace broadly supported slavery. After slavery was abolished, lynching, segregation, and denial of voting rights to African Americans followed until the 1960s. On the other hand, the accomplishments of the relatively peaceful U.S. Civil Rights Movement have been matched by few nonviolent popular movements for fundamental change in world history.

At the heart of Japan's constitutionalism is a unique linkage between human rights and the renunciation of war discussed in Chapter 6. As the Preamble says, all should enjoy "the right to live in peace, free from fear and want." The primacy of human rights is stressed in Article 97: "The fundamental human rights by this Constitution guaranteed to the people of Japan are fruits of the age-old struggle of man to be free; they have survived the many exacting tests for durability and are conferred upon this and future generations in trust, to be held for all time inviolate." They are "eternal and inviolate" rights (Article 11). Articles 11 to 13 provide general guarantees, with the injunction that rights not be "abused" and the caution that restraints are permissible only when necessary for "the public welfare." "All of the people shall be respected as individuals. Their right to life, liberty, and the pursuit of happiness shall . . . be the supreme consideration in legislation and in other governmental affairs" (Article 13) but shall carry with it correlative duties to others.

The use of the public welfare (*kokyo no fukushi*) clause as an abstract and thus suspect basis for possible government restraints on rights and freedoms has been criticized in the past, in Japan and in the United States. By themselves, however, the words *public welfare* create no presumption of improper restraint of freedom. U.S. lawyers accustomed to absolutist and individualist statements of rights, such as the First Amendment, have sometimes looked for mischief in the phrase *public welfare* and in any constitutional or legal provision that qualifies guarantees of rights with such phrases as "except as provided by law." This U.S. perspective is not common in democracies of the civil law tradition on other continents. In part, this difference is the result of contrasting traditions of legal draftsmanship in the civil law and common law worlds.

Perhaps Americans generally appreciate the importance of self-reliance whereas Japanese may place higher valuation on interdependence (in real life both are essential), but mythological rhetoric to the contrary, Americans are not at heart really "individualists"; they just tend to think they are. In general, Japanese may be more comfortable acting in quasi-familial groups, at their school or workplace, for example, but they have their share of that rare commodity, individualism. To many foreign observers Americans seem to be conformists. For example, without obedience to the market demand that one buy the latest fashions in food, music, clothes, and cars, the advertising industry and the U.S. consumer economy would collapse. Japan may be similar. Japan's constitution pursues "the public welfare," whereas the constitution of law-abiding American communitarians envisages "the general welfare" in "a more perfect union." Both constitutions honor rights and freedoms.

To knowledgeable Japanese the most important issue has been the relationship between present terminology and prewar rhetoric. The eminent scholar Miyazawa Toshiyoshi sums it up:

> There can be no objection to translating such words as *salus publica*, *bonum commune*, and *Gemeinnutz* as "*kokyo no fukushi*"; but these words have often been used in a more or less anti-individualist sense. Similarly, words used in Japan during the war . . . are not significantly different from "*kokyo no fukushi*," *considered simply as words*. Perhaps some of that wartime coloring has stuck to the phrase. . . . But [in] . . . the Constitution of Japan [it] differs significantly from those wartime expressions in that its meaning is firmly grounded in [respect for] the individual. (Miyazawa, 205)

The reader will notice that Japan's constitution contains many more rights than are found in the U.S. Constitution and amendments thereto. Some of the matters dealt with in Japan's basic document are found in U.S. federal and state statutes, but other rights are not provided for in the U.S. constitutional system, such as a right to health care. This is one reason the U.S. Declaration of Independence has been more admired and influential abroad than has the U.S. Constitution. Many ideas about rights routinely included in twenty-first-century constitutions were not available for discussion when the U.S. Constitution was written.

In Chapter 3, "Rights and Duties of the People," Articles 11 to 40 of the 1947 Constitution are commonly clustered as follows in Japan.

Equality of rights under the law: marriage rights (Article 24), a right to run for public office without discrimination (Article 44). Article 14 reads in part: "All of the people are equal under the law and there shall be no discrimination in political, economic, or social relations because of race, creed, sex, social status, or family origin. 2. Peers and peerage shall not be recognized."

Freedom of economic activities (*keizaiteki jiyu*): the rights to choose one's occupation and place of residence and to emigrate (Article 22); property rights and the right to conduct business, as long as they are compatible with "the public welfare" (Article 29).

Rights related to the quality of socioeconomic life (*shakaiken*; literally, social rights): rights to a decent life and to "minimum standards of wholesome and cultured living," to state-assured social welfare and health care (Article 25); rights to free compulsory education and to equal educational opportunity based on ability (Article 26); the right and obligation to work; workers' rights to work and "to organize and to bargain and act collectively" (Articles 27 and 28).

Rights to political participation (*sanseiken*): rights to choose and dismiss public officials and to cast secret ballots (Article 15); the right to stand for election (Article 44).

Procedural rights of each person (*jinshin no jiyu*): the right to sue the state for improper detention or other illegal treatment by a public official (Articles 17 and 40); involuntary servitude only for crime (Article 18); a right of access to the courts (Article 32); criminal justice rights such as the right to "a speedy and public trial," a prohibition on forced confessions and cruel punishment (Articles 31 and 33–39).

Rights and freedoms of the spirit (*seishinteki jiyuken*): the right to petition the state (Article 16); freedom of conscience and thought (Article 19); religious freedoms (Article 20); and the world's first constitutional provision for academic freedom (Article 23). Article 21 provides in part: "Freedom of assembly and association as well as speech, press, and all other forms of expression are guaranteed. 2. No censorship shall be maintained."

The constitution lives or dies not in the inspiring words of a document but in the details of national daily life over many years and in the behavior of both public officials and ordinary citizens. What follows is intended to indicate how well or poorly Japan implemented the rights guarantees in its constitution from 1952 to 2002, with intricacy, humane order, inconsistency, corruption, principled use and misuse of both government power and individual liberty, tragedy, occasional humor, and touches of democratic splendor. As in the United States and other constitutional democracies, the record of compliance with the letter and spirit of the constitution is mixed but predominantly positive.

"ENJOY BREATHING FREEDOM" WITH CIVIL LIBERTY

It was over lunch at Scholars House (Gakushi Kaikan) in central Tokyo, where professors and graduates of the national universities gather for business and pleasure, in 1970. Professor Miyazawa Toshiyoshi, trying to sum up for the author what difference the 1947 Constitution has made in daily life, said with a sense of lasting relief, "Every morning I enjoy breathing freedom again." Millions of Japanese with acute memories of life under militarist authoritarianism and a demigod emperor have shared the joy of freedom with the great constitutional lawyer. Today, with the passing of generational memories, most young Japanese, like Americans, take freedom for granted.

So deeply institutionalized has freedom of expression become that it is now the natural order of things: like-minded people can freely form associations that may support or oppose any policy or rival group without government interference; political leaders at every level are elected, not appointed; newspapers and magazines, television and radio stations, professors and entertainers are free to regulate themselves with only minimal government attention; each person may freely follow any religious faith or philosophy.

Japan's group-oriented sociopolitics has been expressed in frequent protest or advocacy demonstrations (*demo*) on a broad range of issues such as a rise in the price of milk, the building of a noisy bowling alley in a residential neighborhood, air and water pollution, U.S. involvement in Vietnam, expansion of Narita International Airport (Tokyo), dated university policies, increased military spending, the "pollution" of U.S. urban

military overflights, and courthouse group support for activists on trial.
The annual "spring struggles" (*shunto*) have been a kind of festival march of
workers calling for ever better wages and working conditions. Colorful
demonstrations have been a major feature of Japan's political culture. Usually, they have been peaceful, but violence erupted occasionally between
1950 and 1971. A few major examples follow.

The May Day Incident, 1952–1979

Japan's independence was restored on the effective date of the San
Francisco Peace Treaty ending World War II, April 28, 1952. On May
Day and other spring days destructive demonstrations took place in Tokyo and other cities, giving rise to court cases involving violence and freedom of assembly, the last of which were not decided until 1979. In the
May Day Incident in Tokyo, after a political rally at Meiji Park thousands
proceeded downtown to Hibiya Park (Japan's Hyde Park) and then to the
Imperial Palace Plaza nearby. Around 3,000 demonstrators methodically
broke the windshields of cars belonging to occupation personnel. Police
and military vehicles were overturned and burned; rocks were thrown.
The violence of Communist-led participants reduced public support for
the Japan Communist Party (JCP) for decades; in 2002 the JCP is peaceable and one of the most democratic of Japan's political parties.

Tear gas and guns were used by the police but not by demonstrators.
Two were killed by police gunfire. Over 2,300 people were injured. Remarkably, this was the last time police used firearms in Japan's last half
century of political demonstrations. Of the 1,232 arrested, 261 were indicted. Before decision days in early 1970, 1,792 court sessions were held,
16 defendants passed away, and a few others were excused to allow their
repatriation to North Korea. Most criminal cases are decided expedi-
tiously by Japan's justice system. The May Day cases dragged on because of the trials' political sensitivity even decades after the events and
because of the civil law practice of spreading out court sessions on a
case over time.

Between January 28 and February 14, 1970, the Tokyo District Court,
denying improper delay of justice, convicted 115 defendants and acquitted 119. The court meted out small fines or suspended jail sentences, and
the prosecutors chose not to appeal the acquittals, as they can do in Japan's
civil law system. In general, leniency is characteristic. On June 19, 1970,
most of the acquitted were granted per diem monetary compensation for
the days they were held in detention, ranging from 24 to 350 days. The
court found those convicted had obstructed officers in the performance of
their duties and had showed "joint unlawful intent" to engage in "crimes

of riot." The Tokyo High Court reversed 84 of the 101 convictions appealed on November 21, 1972.

Another key event in the history of freedom while these trials were going on was the 1958 failure of the ruling Liberal Democratic Party (LDP) to gain Diet approval of restrictive revisions of the Police Duties Execution Law. Vivid memories of pre–1945 police oppression fueled fistfights and obstructive violence within parliament and mass demonstrations outside, but moderates prevailed and the offensive provisions were never enacted into law.

The Security Treaty "Crisis," 1960

The year 1960 was a milestone for freedom of assembly and democratic politics in Japan. The protracted national debate from late 1959 through June 1960 focused on whether Japan should continue its uniquely important relationship with the United States under a new and more equal treaty than that in force since 1952 (which specified no time frame for abrogating the treaty and was open to notable infringement on Japan's sovereignty) or should change to another partner (favored by few) or to armed (not widely supported) or unarmed (seriously considered by some) neutrality. Months of large-scale civil disturbances led to cancellation of President Dwight Eisenhower's planned state visit. The U.S. mass media claimed anti-Americanism was rampant, but attitudes toward the United States were a distant third priority. The first concern of the majority of Japanese was the confirmation and defense of democracy against those who, it was thought, might lead Japan onto a "reverse course" back to militarist authoritarianism. Second came the treaty issue.

The author lived in central Tokyo at the time and witnessed daily the passionate debate and demonstrations on campuses, on the streets, and in the Diet. Leaflets were distributed by conflicting organizations at universities and train stations or were dropped from helicopters. On many days, hundreds of thousands massed around the Diet: students, white-collar workers, blue-collar citizens, men and women representing a wide range of political views. No postwar issue had been so long debated by parliament as the revision of the Security Treaty. At the height of tensions, one could see protestors weeping and bloodily pawing the barbed wire surrounding the parliament building. Inside, politicians opposing ratification of the Japan-U.S. Security Treaty attempted to block voting on the treaty and manhandled the House Speaker.

Injuries were incurred on the streets, many as a result of fights between left-wing student demonstrators (Zengakuren) and small rightist groups and some caused by clashes with police. And yet in contrast to other, much smaller mass political actions of much shorter duration around the world, in which numerous lives have been lost and many serious injuries suffered, there was a striking measure of collective self-restraint in Japan among the majority of demonstrators and police. Then as often later in Japan, more of the defensively equipped riot police (Kidotai) than protestors were injured. Despite provocations, relatively few demonstrators were mistreated by police, perhaps a few hundred out of millions of protestors. Rocks and sticks were often the weapons of the violent. No shots were fired by any participants, and no knives were used. For the first time since 1952, tear gas was used on rare occasions. Only one person died during the months of the "crisis." Kamba Michiko, a coed, was either trampled to death by fellow demonstrators or died from police brutality, depending on one's source.

Eventually, Prime Minister Kishi Nobusuke, a member of the wartime Tojo cabinet and a rehabilitated war crime suspect who symbolized the threat to democracy in many minds, resigned under pressure from his own party to take responsibility for the violence and the failure to win a consensus. In Japan's political culture the norm is consensus; majority rule is the fallback position if consensus cannot be achieved. Kishi's loss of support, symbolized by the millions who signed a petition against his leadership, resulted largely from his high-nosed (*hana no takai*), undemocratic arrogance in pushing through a tyrannical majority vote in the Diet to approve the new treaty before consensus was reached.

Only in mid-June did the influential national newspapers unanimously call for an end of violence; that statement and the humid summer heat encouraged moderation in the months that followed. At the time, many foreigners saw Japan as a democracy in crisis. The democratic rule of law was not in danger, however, but was confirmed. In time, popular support for the treaty firmed up, and after more than forty years it remains the foundation for Japan-U.S. relations and the cornerstone of Japan's diplomacy, along with the United Nations. (Japan was admitted into the United Nations in 1956.) After Kishi and the "crisis," Japan quietly prepared for the 1964 Tokyo Olympics under the low-posture leadership of Prime Minister Ikeda Hayato and moved swiftly forward toward becoming the world's second-most prosperous and powerful nation, except in military terms.

The Tokyo Ordinance Decision, 1960

The Security Treaty crisis in the first half of 1960 was followed on July 20 by the most important Supreme Court decision on freedom of assembly in Japan's history. Local public safety ordinances requiring permits or prior notification of local authorities were the most common forms of law regulating as many as 45,000 demonstrations a year in the unsettled 1950s. Additional thousands of demonstrations took place without thought of complying with ordinances or other law. A local public safety commission of civilians oversees the implementation of each ordinance.

Although some scholars argued at the time that a notification system was less restrictive than a permit system, in practice conditions can be placed on public gatherings equally under both systems, for example, to fit a demonstration into traffic flow or to avoid clashes between two conflicting groups planning to demonstrate at the same time and place. From 1964 through 1978 the Tokyo Public Safety Commission denied no permit requests in most years, and the number of requests declined to under 2,000 a year. The commission placed conditions on the time, place, and manner of a demonstration or parade about half the time. Some observers have suggested that the freedom to engage in demonstrations and advocacy is rather limited in Japan. Progressive constitutional lawyers who have served on that commission, however, such as Ukai Nobushige and Sato Isao, have strongly disagreed. No nation recognizes a right to riot, but perhaps Japan allows as much freedom of assembly as any country. Colorful and usually peaceful demonstrations remain a part of daily public life. With few exceptions, violations of related law have been treated leniently.

Many lower-court decisions have upheld the constitutionality of these ordinances, but a few courts, for example, Tokyo District Courts in 1958 and 1959, found an ordinance objectionable. In November 1959 another Tokyo court refused to allow police to detain students who had demonstrated without a permit; this and other ordinance cases went on accelerated appeal to the Supreme Court. In reversing, the highest tribunal, under Chief Justice Tanaka Kotaro, spelled out democratic principles for judging the constitutionality of public safety ordinances such as that of Tokyo as follows.

The constitutional guarantee of freedoms such as freedom of assembly "is the most important feature that distinguishes democracy from totalitarianism." As with other fundamental rights, citizens may not abuse expression rights and must exercise them responsibly "for the public welfare." The task of the courts is "to draw a proper boundary between freedom and the public welfare," to determine the minimum necessary restraints that may be placed on the freedom to hold "gatherings peacefully respecting order." The degree and kind of legal restriction that is appropriate depend on the nature of the "expression," a word that refers to varied activities. For example, "collective activities" such as political demonstrations differ from writing and may lead a crowd to become "a mob" acting illegally. "Unavoidably," local authorities adopt public safety ordinances setting forth "minimum measures necessary to maintain law and order." The duties of the Tokyo Public Safety Commission are to grant permits for public gatherings unless they "will directly endanger the maintenance of the public peace" and to show "maximum respect for freedom of expression." No important difference exists between a "notification" system and a "permit" system; under both, "strictly limited" restraints may be imposed, as for traffic control.

With later judicial refinements regarding the time, place, and manner of public gatherings, the Tokyo Ordinance Decision still provides authoritative guidelines for assessing demonstrations such as the judges had seen in the streets of the government district of Tokyo.

The University Crisis, 1968–1971

As in Europe and the United States, many universities in Japan went through upheaval from 1968 through 1970. Taking advantage of the universities' tradition of autonomy and exclusion of police from campuses, radical student groups such as Zenkyoto at Tokyo University and other influential schools occupied campus buildings for many months, ransacked classrooms and offices, bullied professors, and stole their books. Buildings were defaced, and political banners were everywhere. Even the sacrosanct university entrance examinations had to be canceled at over 100 schools in 1969.

The author was a guest of Tokyo University's Faculty of Law from 1969 to 1971. Both government and academic leaders were in shock over student violations of law and custom, which lasted many months. In contrast to the United States, the faculty controls university administration in Japan and was extremely reluctant to invite the riot police to restore order on campuses, even after students took over buildings. Until students engaged in significant collective violence, the professoriat was generally sympathetic to their causes, such as university reform and opposition to the U.S. involvement in Vietnam.

The police responded to rocks and Molotov cocktails with armored water-cannon vehicles and protective uniforms and shields. In the dramatic finale at Tokyo University police held back, allowing banner-waving students to sing the "Communist Internationale" before giving themselves up without a struggle. The public had been very tolerant of students' youthful exuberance and idealism since the occupation years, but repugnance over their violence during the "university crisis" drained—

perhaps permanently—the vibrance, legitimacy, and influence of the student movement (Zengakuren and its successors). What remained were small, tightly organized extremist groups—each with its distinctive helmet symbol; all with rigid, mutually intolerant ideologies—fighting each other more than the establishment and willing to kill each other on occasion.

MASS MEDIA FREEDOM

All sectors of Japan's massive media system enjoy considerable freedom and provide substantial coverage of issues in constitutional politics and law. As members of the private Japan Newspaper Publishers and Editors Association (Nihon Shimbun Kyokai; NSK), the print and broadcast media regulate themselves under "The Canon of Journalism," first adopted in 1946 and most recently revised on June 21, 2000. It reads in part:

> The people's right to know is a universal principle that sustains a democratic society. That right cannot be ensured without the existence of media, operating with the guarantee of freedom of speech and expression while being totally committed to a high moral standard and fully independent of all powers. Member newspapers resolve to retain their role as the fittest standard-bearer in this regard.
>
> In a modern society flooded with a vast range of information, the public is constantly required to make correct and swift decisions on what is true and which information to select. It is the responsibility of member newspapers to respond to such requirements and fulfill their public and cultural mission through accurate and fair reporting, and through responsible commentaries. . . .
>
> Freedom and Responsibility. Freedom of expression is a fundamental human right, and newspapers have that absolute freedom in both their news coverage and editorial comment. In exercising that freedom, however, member newspapers must be duly aware of their heavy responsibility and be constantly mindful not to impair public interests.
>
> Accuracy and Fairness. Newspapers are the first chroniclers of history, and the mission of reporters lies in the constant pursuit of truth. Reporting must be accurate and fair, and should never be swayed by the reporter's personal conviction or bias. Editorial comment should be an honest expression of the writer's belief, not to court popularity.
>
> Independence and Tolerance. Member newspapers uphold their independence in the interests of fair comment and free speech. They must reject interference by any outside forces, and resolve to remain vigilant against those who may wish to use the newspapers for their

own purposes. On the other hand, they should willingly give space to opinions that differ from their own, provided such opinions are accurate, fair, and responsible.

Respect for Human Rights. Member newspapers should pay utmost respect to the dignity of human beings, put a high value on individuals' honor, and give serious consideration to their right to privacy. They should also acknowledge errors and correct them promptly, and in cases when an individual or a group has been unjustly maligned, adequate steps should be taken to rectify the situation, including the provision of an opportunity to reply.

Decency and Moderation. In the performance of their public and cultural mission, member newspapers must be available for anyone to read anytime, anywhere. They should maintain decency both editorially and in the area of advertising, and in their circulation practices they should at all times exercise moderation and good sense.

Japanese are served by 108 daily newspapers, of which the 5 national dailies (publishing both morning and evening editions) are the most important: *Asahi Shimbun* (probably the most influential), *Yomiuri Shimbun* (with the largest morning circulation at over 10 million), *Mainichi Shimbun*, *Nihon Keizai Shimbun* (a counterpart to the *Wall Street Journal*), and *Sankei Shimbun*. With a diffusion rate of 576 copies per thousand population, Japan leads the world in newspapers by a large margin; the United Kingdom ranks second, with 314 per thousand; the United States distributes 209 papers per thousand people. In broadcasting, besides the publicly sponsored Japan Broadcasting Corporation (Nihon Hoso Kyokai; NHK), Japan has five commercial television networks, all based in Tokyo: TBS (27 local stations), Fuji Television (27), Nippon Television (25), Television Asahi (23), and Television Tokyo (5). In all, there are 129 television stations and 48 AM and 52 FM radio outlets. The use of satellite broadcasting is rapidly increasing.

NHK is well funded by monthly compulsory fees paid by television owners; it reaches about 20 million households throughout Japan. Almost half of NHK's programming is news, more in numbers of minutes and programs (excepting "all news" organizations) than any major broadcaster in the West, democratic Asia, or Oceana. About 50 percent of news reporting has focused on how the bureaucratic state deals with public problems and manages conflict. In contrast, 2 percent of the news in the United States deals with the bureaucracy, and much attention is given to the president, the cabinet, and conflicts. Ellis Krauss's work suggests that NHK's dominance of television news from the 1960s through the 1980s helps explain how Japan's democratic state became legitimized and thus stabilized after the instability and polarized politics of 1945 to 1960.

Since the LDP governed everything through this period, NHK may have developed a higher comfort level with the LDP than with other interests. Nevertheless, the public generally relies on the fairness and competence of news coverage by the television networks and national newspapers much more than it trusts the Diet, the bureaucracy, or any political party or politician.

In response to growing public awareness of human rights and increasing instances of alleged media violations of the individual's rights to personal dignity, reputation, and privacy, in June 1997 NHK and the National Association of Commercial Broadcasters established the Broadcast and Human Rights/Other Related Rights Organization (BRO). The purpose of BRO, as Japan's first third-party entity to deal with complaints against broadcasters, is to ensure free speech in broadcasting and the human rights of viewers and listeners. BRO's core group is the BR Committee (BRC), which considers complaints and presents its "views, opinions, or recommendations." BRC consists of up to eight members, which must include a human rights attorney, a former justice of the Supreme Court, a person with vast international experience, an expert on the Broadcasting Law, and others, but no one connected to a broadcaster. A council of up to five scholars and other prestigious members, none with ties to broadcasters, appoints the BRC members for three-year terms. The BRC chair in 2002 is the eminent media law scholar–lawyer Professor Shimizu Hideo; the other members are also persons with high credibility. The BRC is generally activated by an individual's complaint about a rights violation by a specific program, but the BRC may act on its own initiative when a serious infringement of rights seems to have occurred. Hundreds of complaints were soon forthcoming, with what result only time will tell.

In 2000 Japan published almost 3,000 periodicals, 87 of them weeklies. The *manga*, comic books and comic magazines for both children and adult audiences, are extremely popular, accounting for over 22 percent of sales. Even the constitution is the subject of *manga*! The United Kingdom leads in the number of book titles published each year with over 100,000, compared with 71,500 in Germany, 62,000 in the United States, and 56,000 (counting only first editions) in Japan.

The country's film industry peaked in 1960, when 547 feature films domestically produced were seen by over a billion theatergoers. In 2000 about 270 movies were produced in Japan, and 298 were imported for an audience of 145 million. Japanese society is rather tolerant of violence and erotica in print, pictures, and other media but is also keenly aware of the need to protect minors' development rights from violent and adult fare. All films are screened by the industry's self-regulatory organ, the Motion Picture Ethics Commission (Eirin). Imported movies are also monitored by the Customs Bureau in a process of widely questioned constitutionality.

Hundreds of "reporters clubs" (*kisha kurabu*), each containing representatives of major news organizations, are the main source of domestic political news for Japan's news media and have been referred to as an "information cartel." By custom, many of these institutions have their own offices at government ministries, the Diet, political party headquarters, the police department, economic organizations, the courts, the prime minister's office, and elsewhere.

These reporters cover a beat for only two or three years, and like U.S. reporters relying on anonymous authoritative sources, may not be immune to the spins of veteran government and business spokespersons. Reporters from different media companies sometimes form a consensus on what should be reported rather than competing. Deviation from the shared view may bring ostracism and reassignment. Nonmembers, domestic and foreign, have been excluded from the nation's main news-gathering process. In-group dependence may discourage independent investigative journalism.

The resultant restraints on access to information and opinions critical of the government and the establishment should not be exaggerated, however. Exposure of corruption is as commonplace as in many other democracies. Editorials and opinion columns are often unhesitatingly critical of the government. The so-called Chrysanthemum taboo against dealing critically with the emperor remains a problem in that reporters and public figures have occasionally been attacked by small right-wing extremist groups for allegedly making disrespectful comments about the emperor. In a particularly chilling but isolated event, a rightist group, Sekihotei, took uncorroborated responsibility for murdering one *Asahi Shimbun* reporter and wounding another on Constitution Day, May 3, 1987. This and seven related incidents are referred to as National Police Agency Case File No. 16. None of these cases has been solved.

Popular attitudes regarding Emperor Akihito and Empress Michiko are not commonly reverential but instead are mildly interested. An *Asahi Shimbun* poll in December 2001 indicated 64 percent of voters (73 percent of women) view the imperial family positively, and 28 percent see it negatively. In 2001 the pregnancy of Crown Princess Masako generated much excitement, in part because it raised the possibility of a female successor to the throne. Premodern Japan had empresses. The prewar constitution and Imperial House Law limited the throne to male heirs; that legal provision somehow remains on the books but is unconstitutionally discriminatory. Eighty-three percent of voters favor allowing a woman, perhaps Princess Aiko, on the throne.

With these qualifications, reporters clubs do an excellent and efficient job. To this writer Japan's newspaper coverage of foreign affairs seems superior to that of most U.S. newspapers, in part because of the vast resources generated by enormous circulation. *Asahi Shimbun* has been ranked among the twenty greatest newspapers in the world.

With its diverse newspapers, broadcasters, magazines, books, universities, and films, Japan is home to free expression of a great variety of views. The law of freedom is taken for granted as the ideal, but government openness has come only gradually. As Prime Minister Ohira Masayoshi said in a 1978 speech, "Japan is a free society, but not an open society." But that society has been changing toward greater openness.

Since around 1980, on the initiative of progressive activists in the freedom of information movement, all prefectures and major metropolitan governments have adopted information disclosure ordinances. In May 1999 the Diet passed an Information Disclosure Law, which became effective on April 1, 2001. On the first day of its effect, over 1,500 requests for information from the central government were filed at 1,800 locations. The applications came mainly from the media, nonprofit organizations, and citizens' groups. For example, the Freedom of Information Citizen Center in Tokyo asked for data on the entertainment expenses of cabinet ministers.

Thousands of formally documented requests will be made each year for information in files regarding public works, education, and consumer and environmental safety. The local and national mandatory disclosure systems also have encouraged hundreds of thousands of successful but undocumented informal requests for information annually. Public officials are more willing than in the past to disclose information to the media and the public in a positive manner and to respond more quickly to requests. This new openness is a major achievement in a government and a society with a penchant for secrecy.

Also contributing to greater government openness has been a network of private attorneys and activists referred to as the "citizen ombudsman movement." Since 1994 they have used local disclosure ordinances to audit local government accounts and have dramatically reduced corrupt practices such as systematic falsification of expense vouchers and excessive entertainment of national officials in pursuit of support for local government projects. The mass media has joined forces with such efforts by giving local and national government scandals abundant publicity and criticism. Like U.S. civil servants, Japan's may be among the world's most competent and dedicated, but not without occasional problems, as the cases that follow illustrate. The Supreme Court's opinions and reasoning in this case and in cases presented later may differ from those of the reader, as they sometimes do with those of fellow legal professionals and opinion makers in Japan. Bear in mind, however, that the highest tribunal is the most authoritative interpreter of the constitution in concrete cases and that the Supreme Court generally enjoys more popular respect and support than other government agencies or political parties.

The Nishiyama Official Secrets Case

In 1978 the Supreme Court first ruled on a journalist's news gathering and the preservation of state secrets. In a major peaceful transfer of territory hardly appreciated in the United States, Okinawa reverted to Japanese sovereignty in 1972. During the preparatory negotiations between Japan and the United States, Nishiyama Takichi, a reporter for the *Mainichi Shimbun* assigned to cover the Foreign Ministry, acquired related secret documents from a ministry secretary, Hasumi Kikuko, with whom he was having an affair. Both were married. He promised not to reveal his news source, but did; he also told a member of parliament. The affair ended when Nishiyama finished related news gathering. Shortly after the Okinawa Reversion Agreement was concluded in mid-1971, this opposition socialist revealed before the Diet that contrary to government assurances that no secret agreements would be made, Prime Minister Sato Eisaku had secretly agreed to pay Okinawans $5 million for land damage claims. The embarrassed Sato took responsibility but did not admit to improper suppression of information. Sato won the Nobel Peace Prize. Both Nishiyama and Hasumi were found out, arrested, and convicted. They left their places of employment.

Hasumi and Nishiyama had violated the National Public Employees Law (NPEL), she by leaking secrets she had learned in the course of fulfilling her official duties (Article 100, 1), he by inducing a public servant to commit a crime (Article 111). The maximum penalty for such an offense is a year in prison and a modest fine (Article 109, 12). Hasumi received a six-month sentence but with a one-year delay in its execution (that is, she would not go to prison if she behaved during that year). Nishiyama was acquitted in district court as having acted within the bounds of press freedom allowed by Article 21 of the constitution. He was convicted by the Tokyo High Court and Supreme Court on a prosecutorial appeal, however, and was sentenced to four months' confinement, delayed for a year. Such penalties would hardly deter an enterprising mole, and Japan has no antiespionage law. Attempts to pass a state secrets law since the 1980s have been vehemently and successfully opposed as contrary to the spirit of the constitution.

The Supreme Court held that (1) the courts have the authority to determine what constitutes a state secret under the NPEL and what is merely a political secret, (2) the government's secrecy in this case was appropriate, (3) the government's failure to bring all the facts to the Diet did not violate the constitutional order or constitute illegal secrecy, and (4) free news gathering and reporting are of critical importance to the people's right to know and to general freedom of expression, but in this case Nishiyama violated the legal prohibition against inducement in his ethically questionable relations with Hasumi. The Court stated:

> The defendant seriously infringed on the personal dignity of an individual, Hasumi, when she was the target of news-gathering activities. Such acts . . . are not acceptable at all from the standpoint of social ideas in light of the spirit of the whole legal order with respect to the ways and means of news gathering; he exceeded the boundary of legitimate news-gathering activities.

Scholarly comment on the case supported Nishiyama's claim that he was simply engaged in legitimate news gathering but criticized the ethics of his modus operandi.

The Hakata Station Film Case

Sometimes relationships among the media, the constitution, and politics have been complex. An example is the 1969 Hakata Station Film case, which led to a landmark Supreme Court decision on press freedom and freedom of information. Early in 1968 around 300 students of the Anti-Yoyogi Faction (the Yoyogi student arm of the Communist Party was considered traitorously moderate) arrived at the Hakata Train Station in southwest Japan on their way home from protesting a visit of the aircraft carrier USS *Enterprise*. When they stopped to visit nearby Kyushu University, their way was impeded by 870 riot police and railroad security personnel. Virtually no injuries occurred. Four students were arrested; only one was indicted, and he was acquitted on April 11, 1969.

Countercharges of police abuse of authority were lodged against the prefectural police commissioner and other police by twenty attorneys, thirty-six opposition members of parliament (Japan Socialist Party), and other supporters. At plaintiffs' request, the Fukuoka District Court asked four local television stations for their film of the incident. The companies demurred: "The use of this film as court evidence might render free and impartial news gathering and reporting impossible." On August 28 the court issued a formal Order to Submit (*teishutsu meirei*) all the Hakata film for use as evidence. The companies countered with separate appeals to the Fukuoka High Court and the Supreme Court in September. During months of heated debate, fourteen media companies in Fukuoka and the NSK endorsed the position of the television stations.

On November 26, 1969, the Supreme Court quashed the companies' appeal in a unanimous Grand Bench decision. The justices agreed with the appellants that Article 21 of the constitution guarantees not only the freedom to express ideas but also freedom in gathering news and reporting facts; these freedoms serve the people's right to know in a democracy and provide them with the material they need to form judgments on public affairs. This freedom, however, must be balanced on occasion against the constitutional right to a fair criminal trial. Negative impact on the media's service to freedom of information should be kept to the minimum necessary. In this case the media film at issue had already been used in broadcasts, so freedom of reporting was not at issue but rather the media's fear of imaginable future impediments to news gathering. The Supreme Court assumed that the film in question had great value as evidence for the lower court's deliberations.

On the day of the Supreme Court's seminal decision, a media representative telephoned Professor Ito Masami, who was chatting with the author, for advice on how to respond to the Court's judgment. As in the United States and other democracies, enforcement of a major Supreme Court decision is not always easy, but Professor (later Justice) Ito added significantly to the legitimacy of the decision by urging media compliance based on the Supreme Court's prerogative to have the final say in interpreting the constitution. Support for the television companies' position dwindled. The four companies continued to be intransigent, so the Court issued a seizure warrant for the film on March 4, 1970, the only legal option remaining since the police refused to cooperate. On August 26, 1970, the district court dismissed the students' case on grounds of insufficient evidence. Indeed, an abuse of police authority had occurred, but the police commissioner had refused to cooperate, and the identity of the guilty individual policemen could not be pinpointed on the videotapes.

The Hakata Station Incident resulted in a five-sided conflict involving the mass media, students, politicians, the police, and the courts. The controversy had activated and spread understanding of the rule of law, freedom, and criminal justice; and media freedom was not diminished.

The Sankei Political Advertisement Case

In late 1973 the ruling Liberal Democratic Party (LDP) took out advertising space in the *Sankei Shimbun* and another newspaper concerning the policies of the Japan Communist Party (JCP). The militant party program of the JCP in 1961 was placed alongside its moderate and democratic program in 1973. The advertisement asked: "Dear Mr. Japan Communist Party, please clarify" the contradictions. The JCP went to court demanding free and equal space in which to refute the allegedly defamatory advertisement, but the court dismissed the case (June 1974). The JCP then lodged another suit stressing the party's constitutional "right to respond" (rebut), unsuccessfully.

The Tokyo District Court—in a decision that led to clarification of the NSK's Newspaper Advertising Code of Ethics (May 19, 1976)—found no serious falsification of documents, the existence of others besides the defendants who had noticed contradictions, and the inevitability of harsh reciprocal criticisms between political parties in a democracy, with response always possible through some public forum. The court noted that the *Sankei Shimbun* had honored its own code of ethics and had no obligation to pay for a JCP advertisement responding to the LDP's paid advertisement. The JCP had negotiated at length with the newspaper and the LDP on points in the ad dealing with such issues as the Self-Defense Force and the emperor's status, to no avail.

The Repeta Note-Taking Case

In 1985 Lawrence Repeta, a U.S. attorney trained in Japanese law at the University of Washington, began attending trial sessions at the Tokyo District Court. Before each session, Repeta asked the presiding judge for permission to take research notes and was denied under a national judicial policy as an exercise of "courtroom police powers" (Article 17, Court Organization Law). Only members of the local reporters' club attached to a court were allowed to take notes while the court was in session.

Repeta sued the government, claiming a spectator's right to know under constitutional provisions for equal treatment under the law (Article 14), freedom of information and expression (Article 21), and public trial (Article 82). He also relied on Article 19 (freedom of expression) in both the UN Universal Declaration of Human Rights and the International Covenant on Civil and Political Rights. Repeta argued that a right to take notes in court or in any public place (*"memoken,"* a "memo right") is implied by the right of anyone to attend a trial under Article 82. "In reality," he said, "if people do not take notes, they cannot fully understand trials nor transmit knowledge concerning trials."

The Tokyo District Court and the Tokyo High Court disagreed, stressing a judge's authority to decide whether a particular activity might interfere with an orderly and fair trial. On March 8, 1989, the Supreme Court, in a complex opinion, upheld judicial prerogative and did not recognize a constitutionally protected right to observe a particular trial or to take notes in the courtroom. The justices changed policy, however, by holding that the trial judge's denial of permission was "an exercise of the courtroom police power poorly grounded in reason" and failed to appreciate the importance of courtroom note taking under Article 21 freedom of expression.

A survey of democracies by the Japan Federation of Bar Associations indicated that until this decision, Japan and South Korea were the only democracies that virtually banned note taking in court. Although the courts continue to show special respect for the public function of reporters' clubs, the Supreme Court's recognition of a virtual right to take notes has opened courtrooms to scholars, free-lance and magazine writers, and novelists, citizens, and foreigners hitherto denied that right. This seems a significant small step toward greater openness and internationalism.

"MY HOMEISM" AND SOCIAL RIGHTS

Japan emerged from the war poor but soon found the spirit to attack the rubble of war by constructing new streets, schools, housing, and other buildings. The passion of 1950s political life was matched by the equally organized energy with which Japan plunged into economic redevelopment. People had little, but those who could think beyond food and shelter needs saved religiously for their children's education and for better urban housing.

By 1970 "my homeism" was taking hold: preoccupation with private nuclear-family life; a keen interest in the newest consumer products and fashions rather than in what others did in, for, or against society; and a form of *non pori* (apolitical) individualism, widely practiced while often criticized. More families were gradually accumulating the standard home appliances of wealthier nations, designed to fit apartments and houses of modest size in Japan's economy of space.

By 1990 Japan was the world's second-ranking economic power, with standards of living as high as those of virtually any other country, and it remained so in 2002. Among all industrialized democracies, the narrowest gap between the richest 10 percent and the poorest 10 percent of citizens exists in Japan, whereas the widest gap is found in the United States.

Since 1990 Japan has accounted for around 17 percent of the world's annual economic product. The so-called bubble burst in the economy has had less negative impact on the average household than might be gathered from reports preoccupied with stocks, finance, and "restructuring" the administrative system. On the positive side, astronomical urban land prices have fallen precipitously over the past decade, to middle-class benefit and the dismay of speculators.

Employment is both a duty and a right under the constitution (Article 27). The 5 percent unemployment rate during the worst economic slump since the 1940s was Japan's most noteworthy problem in 2002. This was an intolerably high figure to a people accustomed to a 2 percent unemployment rate and a labor shortage in some sectors. From 1953 until 1995 the unemployment rate never exceeded 3 percent. In 1996 it reached 4 percent and in 1999, 4.9 percent, but in 2001 it fell to 4.7 percent before rising again. These figures are well below the 10 percent and higher rates of many countries in Europe and elsewhere.

Japan's much-discussed "lifetime employment system" has applied to only 20 percent of the work force—mostly to employees of large companies—and that figure is decreasing. Traditionally, the strong expectation was that leaders of large firms would reward worker loyalty with job security and generous benefits. In hard times many assumed executives should be the first to take pay cuts. (The notion of some that a corporate executive should receive a large bonus for presiding over major layoffs is at odds with the moral sense of Japanese and many others.)

Although most companies have attempted to maintain a quasi-familial model of labor relations, employees of medium and small enterprises and millions of temporary workers have enjoyed fewer benefits. Small-business bankruptcies have soared to thousands a year, contributing to the nation's 20,000 homeless (almost all men, many over fifty) in large cities, about 70 percent of whom are found in Tokyo and Osaka. The government accepts its constitutional responsibility to take remedial action in this area, but many officials also welcome recent bureaucracy-free private efforts on behalf of homeless and other disadvantaged people. For example, Social Security Services—an inventive nonprofit, nongovernmental organization—now assists about 10 percent of Tokyo's homeless with shelter, meals, and help in applying for welfare support. Beneficiaries must only comply with a few common-sense rules.

Welfare and Social Security

From the Meiji period until the postwar occupation, Japan's government provided little social welfare aid. The state allowed with some liberality, however, the volunteerism of businesspeople, corporations (for example, the Mitsui Group), and Christian organizations to serve the needy through hospitals, disaster relief, orphanages, settlement houses, and other programs. Article 34 of the 1898 Civil Code, on the German model, established the provision that still governs nonprofit organizations: "An association or foundation relating to worship, religion, charity, science, art or otherwise relating to public interests and not having for its objective the acquisition of gain may be made a juristic person subject to the permission of the competent authorities."

In the years after World War II as never before, the Japanese people greatly needed welfare assistance. Japan was a poor nation. Once mighty cities were prostrated and flattened by bombing. About 2 million Japanese died in the war, a third of them civilians. Over 6 million were repatriated from former colonies and war zones around Asia. More than 15 million found themselves homeless. Thousands of job seekers arrived weekly in Tokyo's train stations. Homeless and destitute migrants lying along the sidewalks were a common sight into the 1950s. And a new constitution and government were established.

As in many other democracies but not in the United States, law in Japan came to recognize as constitutional rights a number of rights affecting the quality of socioeconomic life. When asked in periodic opinion surveys to choose the most important of their constitutional rights, Japanese increasingly select the right to a decent life under Article 25 rather than freedom of expression or other rights they enjoy.

The most fundamental human right, based on respect for the dignity of each individual, is the right to live (*seizonken*) guaranteed by Article 25 of the constitution: "All people shall have the right to maintain minimum standards of wholesome and cultured living. 2. In all spheres of life, the State shall use its endeavors for the promotion and extension of social welfare and security, and of public health." Social rights (*shakaiken*) include rights to welfare assistance, health care, and education, as well as rights as workers, all of which are surveyed in this chapter. (The rights set forth in this and related provisions arose from Japanese sources, not from a SCAP proposal.)

Some might suspect that the abstractions of Article 25 merely state desirable national goals, not legally enforceable rights. True, among scholars numerous theories compete on the nature of the moral and legal rights of the individual and government obligations created by these constitutional provisions. The constitution, however, not only permits state intervention in socioeconomic processes; it obliges the state to assist all citizens, especially the disadvantaged, with appropriate laws and policies. Many constitutional lawyers advocate more use of the right to sue for remedial action and compensation, as in electoral district malapportionment cases, when social legislation or administrative policy falls short of fulfilling the government's obligations to the individual.

Under Article 89 of the constitution the post-1946 government has monopolized both provision of and control over social welfare programs. Allegedly, Article 89 has complicated the provision of welfare assistance by banning in most cases public expenditures for charitable works not under strict government control: "No public money or other property shall be expended or appropriated for the use, benefit, or maintenance of any religious institution or association, or for any charitable, educational, or benevolent enterprises not under the control of public authority."

With Articles 25 and 89, the government was required to take on direct constitutional responsibility for establishing a welfare state hardly imagined in Meiji times. For many years one side effect of these provisions seemed to be discouragement of volunteerism in Japan's civil society. The 1951 Social Services Law requires that all welfare programs are to be managed by national, prefectural, or city governments. Volunteer nonprofit organizations can be "registered" as "social welfare corporations," but only under strict government control can they provide services in line with government programs. Japan was a mature, if bureaucratic welfare state by 1970. Local governments have formed social welfare councils to assist local volunteers, sometimes with government financial aid since 1975.

Most grassroots volunteer organizations have been small and financially poor, without the wherewithal to scale the bureaucratic walls to official recognition as a legal person. Without legal-person status, such groups have lacked full social legitimacy, eligibility for some forms of official assistance, and the capacity to perform a wide range of legal acts— among them signing contracts, hiring staff, opening bank accounts, owning property, signing leases for office space and machinery, and joining in projects with international organizations and domestic government agencies. With legal and political changes in the 1990s, however, volunteer groups have become important in supporting human rights, serving the needs of foreign workers and the elderly, and furthering environmental causes. In 1980 the Japanese Council of Social Welfare reported 1.603 million active volunteers. By 1995 that figure had risen to 5.015 million, and in 1999 it was 6.958 million.

The Kobe earthquake (the Great Hanshin-Awaji earthquake) in January 1995 killed over 6,000, left 350,000 homeless, and destroyed infrastructure. The earthquake also revealed that volunteers could respond to disaster more quickly and impressively than the government. Necessary communications and authorizations among agencies and levels of government responsible for disaster response were in some instances painfully slow. This community experience of volunteer effectiveness and government shortcoming was a catalyst for national appreciation of the importance of citizen volunteerism in providing disaster assistance and meeting social needs without excessive bureaucratism. In 1998, based on virtually unprecedented collaborative dialogue among political parties, the government, and a federation of citizen lobbying groups (the Coalition for Legislation to Support Citizens' Organizations), the Diet passed the Law to Promote Specified Nonprofit Activities (the NPO Law). The NPO Law eased considerably the incorporation procedures for small organizations and encouraged volunteer activities; in so doing, the law has also enhanced enjoyment of the constitutional freedom of association among Japanese.

The Supreme Court has allowed the Diet broad discretion in deciding what levels of welfare support are appropriate but reserves to itself the right of final review should the Diet abuse its power by action or inaction. In the Asahi Tuberculosis case (1967), the Supreme Court held that welfare "benefits the needy person receives or is receiving under the provisions of the Livelihood Protection Law are not benefits given merely as a benefice of the State or as a reflection of social policy. It should be interpreted as a right under the law which may be termed the right to receive a livelihood . . . a personal right . . . not transferable or inheritable." Asahi Shigeru, a long-term tuberculosis patient at a public sanatorium, received a monthly allowance in addition to medical care and meals. When his brother supplemented this modest payment, the authorities reduced his allowance by the amount of his brother's contribution. Asahi sued for restoration of his usual allowance, pleading that the payment schedule was inadequate. Asahi died while the case was on appeal in 1964. The Court decided that death had ended the case, but the long national debate stirred up by the litigation further institutionalized social rights under the constitution and led to a rise in payments.

On occasion, the Diet or an administrative agency has changed relevant law or practice to resolve a dispute after a lower-court judgment but before the Supreme Court has reversed on appeal. For example, in a landmark case decided in 1982 by the highest court, Ms. Horiki, a blind woman living on disability payments, asked for further public assistance in 1970 to help her raise her son Mamoru. She had cared for him since his birth fifteen years earlier, abandoned by and without support from her husband. Hyogo Prefecture rejected her request on grounds that the Child Support Allowance Law forbade concurrent payment of child support to

International Comparison of Social Security Benefits and Medical Expenses, 1997

	Social Security Benefits Per Capita	*% of GNP*	*Medical Costs as % of GNP*
Japan	$4,000	12	7.3
France	$5,000	19	10.0
Italy	$4,000	20	7.6
Germany	$4,000	14	10.4
United States	$2,200	8	14.0
Great Britain	$1,150	6	6.7

Source: Foreign Press Center of Japan, *Facts and Figures of Japan, 2000 Edition* (Tokyo: Foreign Press Center of Japan, 2000), 77.

a disability pensioner. She filed a suit claiming the ban violated her constitutional right to a decent life and her right to equal treatment under the law (Article 14). She won in Kobe District Court (1972) but lost on appeal in the Osaka High Court and the Supreme Court. The Diet, however, eliminated the legal ban at issue with the Child Support Law of 1973 and raised the relatively low payment levels. In practice, justice was served, but only during a tortuous legal process.

Approximate figures for the late 1990s lend perspective on policy priorities and costs of social security benefits per capita, their percentage share of the gross national product (GNP), and medical expenditures.

Health Care

In 2000, in a survey of 191 nations, the World Health Organization (WHO) ranked Japan first in overall health system achievement based on five indicators: healthy life expectancy, system responsiveness in terms of patient satisfaction and human rights, fewest inequalities in responsiveness across the population, lowest rates of discrimination based on patient status (for example, gender, race), and fairness in financial contributions (WHO, "Health Systems: Improving Performance"). (The United States ranked only thirty-seventh because of very low scores on fairness of financial contributions and preventive medicine for adults). Like many other democratic capitalist countries, Japan provides a flexible mix of social and private medicine. Any legal resident of Japan can have easy access to quality health care at relatively low cost.

Since 1961, law has required every citizen to have health insurance. The state provides and manages a health insurance program that serves about 38 million small-business employees. Health insurance associations related to large companies cover over 33 million, and municipalities administer a national insurance program for over 40 million self-employed

The Constitution of Japan

individuals and others. Typically, these programs pay 80 percent of medical costs.

Local governments are responsible for any medical attention provided to the uninsured and the many illegal foreigners, particularly emergency care. In some metropolitan areas, however, private clinics and associations have proven more helpful. For example, in 1993 the International Legal Labor Union Bright was formed in Tokyo to help illegal foreigners by negotiating worker compensation payments (for which illegal workers are eligible) and by paying 70 percent of medical expenses for a monthly fee of 5,000 yen (about $50). The union serves thousands of foreign members. In Yokohama the Minatomachi Medical Center provides medical services and a mutual-aid insurance program (called "MF-MASH") for a monthly fee of 2,000 yen to over 7,000 illegals from seventy-six countries. Year by year, nongovernmental initiatives, under new enabling legislation, have become a much more visible and important part of Japan's capacity to assist the most vulnerable.

The Old-Age Welfare Law of 1963 established nursing homes, free annual physical examinations, a home helpers system, and local welfare centers for the elderly. In 1973 the government added free medical care for everyone over age seventy. In 2002 a major concern was provision of adequate care for Japan's older citizens, the fastest-growing elder population in the world. The tradition of family bedside participation in the care of hospital patients continues. On the other hand, the proportion of elders well cared for in their later years by their families has declined. In response, a new long-term nursing care system paying 90 percent of costs was put in place in 2000. Municipalities operate the program, supported by premiums paid by those over forty years old.

At the other end of the age spectrum an increase in *ijime*, group bullying of a fellow student at school, and physical abuse of children in juvenile homes ("child protective institutions") led to calls for more rigorous oversight. Under the Child Welfare Law, 552 such facilities operate under prefectural governments, taking care of young orphans from early childhood through teenage years.

The medical profession was gratified by the WHO Report's appreciation of Japan's health care attainments, but it is also self-critical. For example, in a 2001 report (interim report, November 15, 2000) on the views of the 174,000 members of the Japan Federation of Medical Workers Unions, over 90 percent of nurses admitted to inadvertent involvement or near involvement in malpractice cases as a result, among other causes, of exhaustion caused by rotating shifts, staff shortages, or deficient technical experience. The union called for major systematic preventive measures.

For many years the mentally ill were poorly cared for, despite recurring complaints from doctors, lawyers, and journalists. Only with the Utsunomiya Incident in 1984 was Japan sufficiently aroused to pass remedial legislation; mental patients in a psychiatric hospital were detained under horrible conditions, and some had been beaten to death by staff. At the time, around 300,000 patients were in Japanese mental hospitals. Most had been confined involuntarily, two-thirds were under twenty-four-hour lockup, and their external communications were restricted. With exceptions, such hospitals are private and were only minimally monitored by the government.

Major improvements have been achieved thanks in part to a doggedly persistent attorney, Totsuka Etsuro, who rallied nongovernmental human rights organizations—domestic and international—and the United Nations to insist that Japan fulfill its obligations under international human rights law as a party to the UN International Covenant on Civil and Political Rights. Specifically, Article 9(1) of the covenant provides that "no one shall be subjected to arbitrary . . . detention," and Article 9(4) insists that "anyone who is deprived of his liberty by . . . detention shall be entitled to take proceedings before a court, in order that that court may decide without delay on the lawfulness of his detention." Japanese law in 1984 did not contain such guarantees; but by 2000, under the Law Relating to the Mental Health and Welfare of Mentally Disordered Persons passed in 1995, voluntary admission had become the rule.

Every candidate for involuntary admission must be medically examined by a designated physician. Such physicians must be certified under rigorous standards by the minister of health and welfare. Moreover, a patient may request release from a hospital through the governor and a Psychiatric Review Board (PRB) in each prefecture. The PRB is composed of three designated physicians, one lawyer, and one person with relevant knowledge and experience. It functions as an independent administrative tribunal. The law also requires that at time of admission the hospital director must inform each patient of his or her rights in writing, that limited restrictions can be imposed on a patient's activities, and that no restraints can be placed on sending and receiving mail. Without international pressure it is unlikely that such improved protection of patient rights would have been achieved at the time. It was Totsuka Etsuro and his colleagues, however, not the international community, who instigated the international movement to improve Japan's compliance with international human rights law and with rights under the Constitution of Japan.

Education

All citizens have a constitutional right to "receive an equal education correspondent to their ability"; parents and guardians have a duty to be sure their children receive the free compulsory education (Article 26). Nine years of schooling is compulsory, with no charge for tuition or textbooks. In fact, about 97 percent of youths graduate from senior high school in one of the world's outstanding precollegiate school systems. About 50 percent of both men and women go on to college, whereas 27 percent enter a technical training school. There are 585 junior colleges and 622 universities. Teachers at all levels are respected and well recompensed.

High and humane standards are set nationally, and public spending levels per student are approximately equal throughout Japan. This stress on equality contrasts with U.S. policies and constitutional law. Discrepancies in funding between American states and school districts are dramatic, based primarily on varying property tax revenues. Federal-state politics also impedes establishment of uniformly high standards and approximately equal funding per student.

In multinational studies, Japan has repeatedly ranked at or near the top in precollegiate science and mathematics education. For example, in the Organization for Economic Cooperation and Development international tests for fifteen-year-olds in thirty-two countries administered in July 2000, Japanese students ranked first in mathematics, second in science, and eighth in reading skills. Remarkably, this record is achieved in spite of the exceptional demands of learning their own written language (twice the time Americans spend learning English) and six years of English-language study in junior and senior high school. To upgrade Japan's national English competence, English instruction will soon begin in elementary school. Moreover, the government's Japan Exchange and Teaching Program brings thousands of college graduates each year from English-speaking countries to assist Japanese teachers of English. Contrary to a common misunderstanding, Japan's schools do not heavily favor memorization at the expense of thinking and creativity. The curriculum is well-balanced for the development of the individual, but the rigorously enforced minute rules of some schools have been criticized and have generated calls for reform.

All students study Japanese and Western music and the arts, as well as national and world history. Social skills are stressed. Students wear uniforms, which as in the United States and other nations seem to reinforce the egalitarianism of the constitution. In addition, they may enhance academic performance and diminish student competition based on fashion and family financial differences. Students and teachers do not go separate ways for lunch in large cafeterias. Rather, teachers and students often join to serve and eat lunch in classrooms. Students rotate lunch-time responsibilities as well as the task of cleaning the building after school. The traditional worldwide curricular wall between domestic arts for girls and industrial arts for boys is being breached in Japan, as in some other nations. Since the 1990s both boys and girls must take courses in wood-working, electricity, homemaking, and foods.

The most intractable problem of precollegiate education in Japan may be the "*juku*" (cram schools) and the "*kyoiku mama*" (education moth-ers) in Parent-Teacher Associations who are obsessed with their children's educational success, especially that of their sons, from preschool days until entrance into a good university. The stakes are high: such university en-trance is perceived as virtually guaranteeing career success. Few drop out or fail out of college. To gain an eventual advantage over others' children in the university entrance examinations, parents—with mothers shoulder-ing the primary responsibility—send their children to one of the 50,000 *juku*, private schools offering classes before and after the normal school day and on weekends. The *juku* have become an industry generating bil-lions in U.S. dollars and adding to the normal burdens of adolescence and an already demanding school system.

Complicating life for Japan's immense higher-education system is the continuing drop in the number of college-age youth and a related fear that this is leading to a decline in public school standards. Well-to-do parents may send their offspring to high-priced private schools whose rigor may give their sons and daughters a new advantage in preparing for entrance examinations. The sharp drop in potential students may endan-ger many junior colleges and less prestigious universities. In some, en-trance exams have become pro forma or have been replaced by a smoother road to admission (for example, giving more weight to high school records and letters of recommendation). Yet although their admission standards may go down as fewer students compete, the national and leading private universities will continue to prosper, drawing a good share of the serious among the brightest.

Workers' Rights

Workers' rights are set forth in Articles 27 and 28 of the constitution and in numerous pursuant laws on child exploitation, "wages, hours, rest, and other working conditions" (Article 27, 2). The basic Labor Union Law went into effect before the constitution, on March 1, 1946. Article 1 still sets the tone for democratic labor relations:

> The purposes of the present law are to elevate the status of workers by putting them on an equal footing in negotiations with their employers; to protect the practice on the part of workers of autonomous organization and association in labor unions, so that they may act collectively, as in the designation of representatives of their own choosing for negotiation of the terms and conditions of work; and to encourage the practice and procedures of collective bargaining resulting in labor agreements governing relations between employers and workers.

In fundamental orientation regarding the domestic and global economy, many Japanese would reject the assumption of U.S. neoclassical economics that labor is simply like other factors in production, such as land and machinery. They would instead tend to agree with Professor Joseph E. Stiglitz, Nobel laureate in economics and former chief economist for the World Bank:

> Labor is not like other factors. Workers have to be motivated to perform. While under some circumstances it may be difficult to coach a machine to behave in the way desired (for example, trying to get a computer not to crash), what is entailed in eliciting the desired behavior out of a person and out of a machine are, I would argue, fundamentally different. . . . [A] standard message [of neoclassical economists and policy makers] to increase "labor market flexibility" [has] the not-so-subtle subtext . . . to lower wages and lay off unneeded workers . . . [so that] even when labor market problems are not the core of the problem facing a country, all too often workers are asked to bear the brunt of the costs of adjustment. ("Democratic Development as the Fruits of Labor," American Economic Association, Boston, January 2000)

Unions, which in Japan include both blue-collar and white-collar employees, vigorously exercise the constitutional rights of workers to "organize and to bargain and act collectively." Thousands of public- and private-sector unions collaborate in debates and action on domestic and foreign policy under the umbrella of the Japan Trade Union Confederation (Rengo; 7.31 million members). On bread-and-butter issues, however, a union local generally identifies in a quasi-familial manner with a local enterprise rather than with a national union. In July 2000, 11.54 million, or 21.5 percent, of the work force was unionized; 54.2 percent of workers in firms with over 1,000 employees had unions, compared with 18.8 percent of employees in companies with between 100 and 999 employees and only 1.4 percent of workers in firms with fewer than 30 employees. Strikes are rare but colorful. For example, employees wear headbands in the workplace to show disappointment with unjust employers, or they picket, for example, to discourage the public from patronizing their bank or department store.

Under 2001 amendments to labor law, working parents are entitled to take leave or to use flextime or reduced working hours to care for their sick children three years old or younger. (Prior law required parents to use paid or unpaid holiday time to make up for time taken to care for sick children.) The number of days a father or mother may take for sick-child care annually is left open. Moreover, either parent may refuse to work overtime more than 150 hours in a year or more than 24 hours in a month. The amendments also prohibit discrimination against those who take child care leave in matters of promotion or internal job shifting and require that management take employees' family circumstances into account when deciding on domestic or international transfers. To those long familiar with employer disregard of these employee concerns and with the system's confinement of special provisions that support parents to mothers (excluding fathers), these changes represent noteworthy improvements in implementing the spirit of constitutional rights of workers.

As in some other democracies, civil servant participation in politics and strikes has been limited. The consensus among Japan's constitutional lawyers, however, is that some of the restraints on members of public-employee unions are unconstitutional. For example, in the Sarufutsu case, Mr. Osawa, a postal worker in the village of Sarufutsu in northern Japan, helped a Socialist candidate in his 1967 House of Representatives election campaign. Osawa put up six posters on a public bulletin board during off-duty hours and mailed the poster to friends for public posting. In 1974 the Supreme Court overturned acquittals in this and two related cases and convicted Osawa and others of violating the ban on all civil-servant political activities except voting. In the other cases, four women in the prime minister's office had passed out leaflets listing candidates for the Tokyo Assembly endorsed by their union, and in 1965 a postal worker had served as master of ceremonies at a rally for a Communist candidate for the Diet.

Earlier Supreme Court opinions had recognized the legitimacy of allowing more freedom of political expression to lower-level public employees—such as janitors, postal workers, and chauffeurs—than to higher civil servants with policy-related responsibilities, such as teachers and ministry officials. For example, in the Tokyo Central Post Office case, the Supreme Court held in 1966 that in general, public employees possess the ordinary rights of workers, as in this case; but the nature of one's official duties may dictate special restrictions. In 1958 union leaders had induced some postal workers to leave their work stations for a few hours to participate in a strike rally. With exceptions such as police, firemen, and SDF troops, national and local civil servants can form unions but can do little else. Private-sector labor unions have been allowed a broader range of political and labor dispute activities.

EQUALITY UNDER THE LAW

Over time, values have been modified, in the courts as in society. For example, in its 1973 Aizawa Patricide Decision, the Supreme Court changed a position it had adopted in 1950 favoring heavier penalties for killing a lineal ascendant than for ordinary homicide, based on a Confucian family ethic. With only one dissent, the Court held Article 200 of the Criminal Code in violation of the guarantee of equality under the law by providing only for life imprisonment or the death penalty for patricide rather than allowing much lighter punishment for manslaughter and other killing. From ages fourteen to twenty-nine the defendant had been repeatedly raped by her father and even bore children by him. When she told him she wanted to marry a fellow employee, she was physically abused. Finally, to end these problems, she strangled him and turned herself into the police. Article 200 was left on the books until a 1995 code amendment but was never again invoked by a prosecutor.

Minority Rights

Although careful recognition of each individual's place in the social hierarchy is a core element of Japan's social life, a sense of equal dignity and of a right to equally respectful treatment under the law is also strong. This rights consciousness contrasts with prewar patterns and results in part from living with the 1947 Constitution, but a noteworthy sense of ethnic nationality also remains. In the United States it may be better not to speak of minorities or minority groups because every American is equally and fully American, and no particular race or ethnicity has special constitutional standing, at least not formally. That may be behind the U.S. inclusionary universalism, the tendencies to imagine peoples abroad hunger to be like Americans and to downplay cultural differences while honoring individuality in the U.S. Constitution.

Whereas many Americans may assume foreign residents will want to become U.S. citizens, Japanese more often presume foreigners will have no particular interest in becoming Japanese citizens. Japan, with its relative homogeneity and defensive ethnic separatism, may be the opposite of the United States: it is prone to exaggerate its distinctiveness more than most and to assume only ethnic Japanese are likely to be part of the real

Japan. Japan recruited Japanese Brazilians during a labor shortage based on this ethnicist assumption; to its embarrassment, Japanese Brazilians proved to be Brazilians.

Japan has had minorities who have suffered legal and social discrimination, but by 2002 laws, policies, education, and media criticism of discrimination had greatly mitigated their pain. They total a few million out of a population of over 127 million; of these, 1.55 million were registered foreigners (Justice Ministry). This figure represents the largest voluntary influx of foreigners in over 1,000 years. It is also a noteworthy undercount of hundreds of thousands of illegal entrants.

The number of people affected is relatively small, but cases of illegal discrimination against foreigners have drawn domestic and international criticism. In a few places, signs have been posted outside public baths, eateries, or shops indicating foreigners are unwelcome. Some real estate agents find it distasteful to deal with foreigners seeking housing. Most businesses eagerly serve all who enter their premises, however, and show no inclination to discriminate. The principal categories of people subject to varying degrees of discrimination in the past and their current social status can be described only briefly here.

1. *Burakumin* (1.5–2.5 million, depending on one's source), descendants of those engaged in historically outcast occupations—such as executioners, butchers, and leathersmiths—have had formal legal equality as Japanese since the late nineteenth century. Improvements in their situation since around 1960 resulted from their vigorous, well-organized movement and from positive government and elite response to their demands. One knotty problem in the past was the hesitancy of local political leaders to accept help for urban *burakumin* areas under special law because that involves the embarrassing admission of the need for special assistance.

2. Over 1 million Okinawans rejoined fellow Japanese when the Ryukyu Islands reverted from U.S. control to Japanese sovereignty in 1972. Historically, the Okinawan kingship system and culture were notably different from those of Japan. Many on the main islands have never viewed the prefecture as a true part of Japan; rather, Okinawa has been "quasi-foreign," there to be exploited. This notion was inherited from the Satsuma region of the main islands, which controlled Okinawa from 1609 until 1868.

   No part of Japan suffered more during the Battle of Okinawa in 1945; 150,000 civilians died, one-third of the population. Since reversion, the Japanese government has made some effort to provide equal treatment under the law for Okinawans and to institute economic development for this poorest of prefectures. A residue of social prejudice against Okinawans remains, however.

Okinawa's perennial spokesman, Professor and former governor Ota Masahide, believes the inequality of treatment under the law represented by the presence of 75 percent (39) of U.S. military bases in Japan on Okinawa's 0.6 percent of Japan's land area is so extreme that it is unconstitutional. The bases have stunted, not helped, Okinawa's development in the view of many Okinawans, and they account for only 5 percent of the prefecture's gross product. The issue is less the presence or absence of U.S. forces in Okinawa than the wildly disproportionate presence of U.S. bases in Okinawa compared with the rest of Japan.

3. About 750,000 resident Koreans constitute a complex mix of ethnic Koreans, some Japanese citizens (over 150,000 naturalized Japanese), and others not citizens but permanent residents or offspring of such, most of whom are descended from those brought to Japan for wartime forced labor. Some support North Korea, others South Korea. For them, as for some other groups of foreign residents, the practice of compulsory periodic fingerprinting was long symbolic of discriminatory treatment under the law, but new law has ended that practice. Prejudicial treatment of permanent resident Koreans is not a daily occurrence and is not condoned. Most Japanese rarely meet an ethnic Korean and harbor no special feelings toward them, positive or negative, unless they use their Korean names rather than their Japanese names (which they had as prewar Japanese subjects). A 2001 survey conducted by the Korean Residents Union (Mindan) indicated that half of the 1,325 respondent Korean residents between ages thirteen and sixty-four identify themselves by their Japanese names most of the time. Only 13 percent use their ethnic names. Law allows either practice; the courts support the individual's right to name choice. A substantial proportion of Korean residents understandably hope society will become indifferent to which name they use.

Some of those who are not citizens hold positions in public schools, law, and the civil service. These Koreans and their Japanese neighbors are central to the recent movement of many local governments to allow foreigners to vote and hold office. To allow foreigners such privileges of citizenship is an extraordinary manifestation of democratic internationalism. Might many national governments welcome foreign residents to leadership positions in the twenty-first century?

Japan annexed Taiwan in 1895 and Korea in 1910, so all residents of those regions were Japanese citizens until after World War II. During the war, thousands were wounded in service to the state. A few sought disability pension payments from the government in 1991 and were turned down. They went to court, claiming a right to treatment equal to that afforded Japanese veterans under Article 14 of the constitution. The Supreme Court quashed their appeals in April 2001 because they were no longer Japanese citizens. The Court urged the Diet, however, to pass a law providing adequate relief for the plaintiffs. (In 2000 the legislature had passed a related law that granted ex-citizen soldiers pension payments much lower than those of Japanese disabled veterans.)

In a decision more favorable to a foreign atomic bomb victim once resident in Japan, on December 26, 2001, the Nagasaki District Court ordered the government under the Atom Bomb Victim Relief Law to pay a substantial health allowance to Lee Kang Young (age seventy-four), a resident of Pusan, South Korea, who lived in Nagasaki on August 9, 1945, but moved to Korea in December 1945. The government argued that only victims residing in Japan were eligible for such relief, but Lee successfully contended that the argument represented unconstitutional discrimination on the basis of place of residence.

Emperor Akihito lightened the horizon of sometimes troubled Japan-Korea relations in December 2001 during preparations for the two countries' joint sponsorship of World Cup soccer in 2002. He publicly stated his sense of "a certain kinship" with Koreans based on Korea's major contributions to Japan's development in ancient times and the intermarriages between their royal families in the eighth century.

4. A few thousand Ainu aboriginals are present whose heritage is being honored and preserved in their ancestral location of Hokkaido and among groups in Tokyo. Most intermarried with ethnic Japanese over past centuries.

5. Over 300,000 Chinese live mainly in large cities.

6. South Americans, mostly Japanese Brazilians (over 225,000) and Japanese Peruvians (over 40,000), are present. Some Japanese officials encouraging this influx have been surprised to learn they were not Japanese in culture.

7. Hundreds of thousands from Southeast Asia have entered Japan since 1980—legally and illegally—seeking employment in sectors with labor shortages. Of these, Filipinos, at over 115,000, are the most numerous. The estimated number of illegal entrants, principally from Asia, is around 300,000.

8. Mixed-blood children (*konketsuji*) of Japanese men and women who have married foreigners are also found. In the 1990s as many as

28,000 such marriages took place each year. Since passage of the 1985 Nationality Law, a child has Japanese nationality if either parent is a Japanese national. Previously, such children were Japanese citizens only if their fathers were Japanese, unless they were illegitimate.

9. Hundreds of thousands of Japanese—principally business, academic, and diplomatic families—have come to "reek of foreignness" (*gaijin kusai*) during substantial residence abroad, in the view of some in the homeland. Their children (*shikokushijo*) have required special educational programs to ease the great culture shock felt when they return to Japan. On balance, however, they usually reassimilate and contribute much to Japan's cultural globalization.

10. Atomic bomb victims (*hibakusha*) and their descendants' families still live in the Hiroshima and Nagasaki areas. Over 200,000 people have died as a result of the two bombs dropped in August 1945. (Too seldom noted are the 100,000 who died from the Tokyo fire-bomb raid in early March 1945.) Although they have drawn worldwide sympathy, the *hibakusha* have suffered much because of discrimination, as well as from their physical wounds. Sometimes premarital investigations by one or both families have tried to determine whether the prospective mate has been affected by atomic bombs that fell long ago. People from supposedly contaminated areas have not been deemed suitable marriage partners or desirable company. Should a nuclear, chemical, or biological war occur in the future, all affected societies seem likely to divide radically between the terrified "clean" and the victims of war pollution. Our only empirical reference point for grasping such a scenario is Japan's response to two relatively small atomic bombs.

Women's Rights

More significant than any of the previous groups and their rights, because they constitute half the population, has been the revolutionary expansion of the rights of Japanese women under the Constitution of Japan and the international law of human rights. The disproportionate Western attention to the fascinating geisha tradition may have deflected focus from the realities of daily life and law affecting most Japanese women since 1946.

Every woman has the same great inherent value and dignity as every man. No persuasive foundation in philosophy, science, or religion exists for thinking otherwise. Yet in most cultures recognition by both men and women that all humans have inherent rights and that women are entitled to the same human rights as men in constitutional, international, and other law has come only gradually and very recently—since World War II. Articles 14, 24, and 44 of the constitution and the Universal Declaration of Human Rights covenants and conventions of the UN have radically changed not only the legal status of Japanese women but the very nature of Japanese society.

Enhanced women's rights protection in the United States has been accompanied by instability in its nuclear-family system, whereas in Japan that system has never been stronger as the status of women has improved. Relatively few young adults now submit to parentally arranged marriages (*omiai*), and most are free to choose their marriage partner. Family, friends, and a "go-between" (*nakodo*) are commonly involved in facilitating wedding and family-bonding arrangements, however. Since marriages are now more often entered into for love and for life, wives are much less tolerant of infidelity than under the earlier regime. The divorce rate is rising, and divorce procedures can be simple; but divorce is still rare. The most common ground for divorce is female infidelity.

One indicator of the change is the demise of son preference in Japan. Throughout world history women in a great majority of cultures have been bedeviled by a dominant societal preference for boy babies over girl babies among parents, extended family, and society. Today, India and China illustrate the contemporary scope of the problem. Ubiquitous, low-cost ultrasound machines tell parents the sex of an unborn child. If the baby-to-be is female, that is often the signal in India to have an abortion; if the fetus is male, it is cause for rejoicing. China's policy of punishing families with more than one child has accentuated the problem of son preference in that country. Pre-1945 Japan shared this common human preference for sons, but it no longer does. Survey research has confirmed that over five decades, parental preference for sons over daughters has gradually disappeared. Another notable shift in attitude is illustrated by the greatly increased number of both men and women who disagree with the proposition "man is the breadwinner and woman the homemaker." Approximately 60 percent (66 percent of men, 56 percent of women) still agreed with this philosophy in 2001, but 90 percent had agreed in 1950. Most important, the social roles of parent and homemaker are not accorded less respect and dignity than monetarily gainful employment.

A few other improvements in the status of women since 1945 include the right to vote and to run for elective office; the end of the patriarchal *ie* (house) extended-family system; the end of primogeniture; equal rights in marriage; inheritance rights for widows (half the estate) and children; capacity to carry out legal acts autonomously; the right to a national pension separate from the husband's pension; poverty relief payments equal to those received by men (women received 85 percent of what men received before 1985); capacity to handle household financial matters (now wives generally handle the family's daily financial affairs, with many husbands receiving a periodic allowance); repeal of the crime of adultery, which had punished only unfaithful wives; equal educational rights; and rights to equal treatment as civil servants in national and local government. Unfortunately, the equality provision (Article 14) was long held to apply only to employees in the public sector, not to those in private businesses.

From the 1960s on, women have challenged discriminatory treatment in court and more often than not have won, although the costs in time and resources have been prohibitive for many aggrieved employees. Examples of practices the courts have held to be illegal include compulsory retirement after giving birth, forced retirement at age thirty (a girl should be married by then!), forced retirement at an age lower than the male retirement age (for example, fifty versus fifty-five), discriminatory layoffs of married women, and different promotion standards for men and women. Many company men have preferred that regardless of qualifications, women should be "office flowers" who are present to pretty up the working environment and serve tea, but attitudes have gradually changed.

Major improvements came with Japan's response to the 1979 passage of the UN Convention on the Elimination of All Forms of Discrimination Against Women, an important achievement of the UN Decade for Women (1976–1985). To comply with legal requirements of the convention prior to ratification in 1985, after many years of debate involving Japan's government, business, and labor interests, scholars, and many women's organizations, labor law was amended by the Equal Employment Opportunity Law (EEOL), also in 1985. The law was the first statute to require equal treatment of women in the private sector with regard to "wages, working hours, and other working conditions" (Articles 3 and 4). The law prohibits discrimination against women with respect to training, fringe benefits, retirement age, and dismissal but requires only that employers "endeavor" to treat men and women equally regarding recruitment, hiring, job assignment, and promotion.

As is true so often in various subject areas, rather than specify penalties for violations of the law, Japan's government relied on administrative guidance and persuasion to gain voluntary compliance with the law. In spite of deficient sanction provisions, many companies have complied without compulsion, to a degree that would surprise most Americans. Needed amendments in 1997 (in effect from 1999) clearly prohibit discrimination with no qualifying reference to "endeavor." Although many companies have complied, many still prefer to hire men rather than women university graduates for management-track positions. Legislation in 1995 expanded child care leave (eight weeks at 25 percent of salary) and family care leave (for example, to care for an elderly sick parent) for both men and women employees.

As in the United States, sexual harassment (*seku hara*) is a perennial problem in Japan, and one wife in twenty complains of being physically abused by her husband. Under the 2001 Law on the Prevention of Spousal Violence and the Protection of Victims, anyone found guilty may receive a sentence of up to one year in prison and a fine of 1 million yen. Psychological violence is not covered by the statute, however. A 2000 statute against stalking imposes on those convicted up to six months in prison or a fine of up to 500,000 yen. With a rise in public consciousness, the EEOL, and convention ratification in 1985, women have become less compliant when employers refuse to take action against workplace harassment. In 1999 women brought ten times more complaints to government counselors than they had six years earlier, and 35 percent more cases were brought that year than in 1998. One small remedial step suggested to raise women's comfort level has been to designate certain subway and train cars "for women only."

The case of Governor Yokoyama Nokku of Osaka capsulizes the mood on related issues in 2002. Yokoyama took liberties with a coed volunteer during an election campaign. When she complained he denied his activity, trivialized the issue, and accused the media of harassment. In the process, however, he also drew police attention, became an object of national opprobrium and ridicule, lost his job, and was given an eighteen-month suspended sentence.

Symptomatic of the continuing revolution regarding women's rights are recent public-sector victories: constitutional law professor Doi Takako leads the Democratic Socialist Party and served as the first woman speaker of the House of Representatives; in 1994 Takahashi Hisako, head of the Women's and Minors' Bureau of the Labor Ministry, became the first woman appointed justice of the Supreme Court; the second is Yoko Kazuko (age sixty), former ambassador to Ireland and senior pension administrator. Ota Fusae of Osaka was the first woman elected governor; Shiotani Yoshiko of Kumamoto Prefecture became Japan's second woman governor in 2000; and in 2001 Domoto Akiko (age sixty-eight), an independent in Chiba Prefecture, was the third woman to be elected governor. In some municipal assemblies women hold as many as 40 percent of seats. In addition, a few women have been elected mayor, and a woman has been appointed local police chief. At the national level Ogi Chikage is head of the

New Conservative Party and minister of transport, Kawaguchi Yuriko was
the first minister of the new Environment Ministry and in 2002 succeeded
Tanaka Makiko as foreign minister, and Professor Ogata Sadako of Sophia
University represented Japan for ten years as the UN high commissioner
for refugees and in 2002 was Japan's lead representative in aiding Afghanistan.

In the House of Representatives election in June 2000, 202 of 1,404
candidates were women. Thirty-five—the most ever—won seats, and combined with women in the House of Councillors, seventy-eight women
now serve in the Diet. In 2001 Prime Minister Koizumi Junichiro appointed a record five women to his seventeen-member cabinet. In 2000
the government's Council for Gender Equality adopted a five-year agenda
for expanding women's participation in policy making, examining discriminatory customs, establishing battered women's shelters, passing legislation against physical abuse by men, and making public the names of
discriminatory firms.

In December 2001 the birth of Princess Aiko (also known as
Toshi-no-miya) raised the possibility of coronating another Japanese empress. As noted earlier, Japan's premodern tradition of leaving the throne
open to both male and female occupants was changed by the 1889 Meiji
Constitution, which limited the position to "male descendants." Early in
the occupation period, in disregard of the 1947 Constitution's equality
provisions, the Japanese government established an Imperial House Law
that similarly restricts the throne to "male offspring." This provision,
however, is widely considered unconstitutional. Princess Aiko appears to
have a presumptive right of succession to the throne as the firstborn of the
imperial couple.

CRIME AND SUSPENDED PUNISHMENT

A prime test of the effectiveness of a constitution in the daily life of a
nation is the state of its criminal justice system. Crime rates in Japan are
low compared with many other countries and have dropped further since
around 1950. Although 99.9 percent of those formally indicted are convicted and a much higher percentage of perpetrators is arrested in Japan
than in the United States, only about 45 persons per 100,000 are incarcer-
ated in Japan compared with 426 per 100,000 in the United States (Texas
has the highest rate of any state, at 1,035 per 100,000). Few Japanese ever
experience a day in jail, whereas millions of Americans have been in confinement. With 5 percent of the global population, the United States
accounts for 25 percent of the world's prisoners, more than any other
country. The imprisonment rate for convicted felons in Japan is one-fifth

that in the United States, but the difference is not great with respect to the most serious crimes.

Articles 31–40 guarantee many procedural rights. In summary: "No person shall be deprived of life or liberty, nor shall any other criminal penalty be imposed except according to procedure established by law" (Article 31). All citizens have access to the courts (Article 32), "the right to a speedy and public trial by an impartial tribunal," and the right to call witnesses at public expense (Article 37). Arrest (Article 33) and search and seizure (Article 35) are permissible only by judicial warrant, except when a person is caught in a criminal act. If arrested, a person "must be at once informed of the charges" and has "the immediate privilege of counsel" (Article 34). The state will provide "competent counsel" if anyone accused cannot afford a lawyer (Article 37). Torture and cruel punishment "are absolutely forbidden" (Article 36). "No person shall be compelled to testify against himself," nor may anyone be convicted solely on the basis of his or her confession (Article 38). No one may be held liable for an act that was not unlawful at the time it was committed (Article 39). If acquitted, one "may sue the State for redress" (Article 40). These are the constitutional standards, and improvements in honoring them have come over time.

Prosecutors exercise considerable quasi-judicial discretion. They are career civil servants, not politicians eager for convictions. They often decide not to bring to trial obviously indictable offenses, and sometimes they delay indictment (*kiso yuyo*) to see if the suspect shows remorse and intent to reform. Ninety-five percent of suspects confess (compared with 85 percent in the United States), but confession cannot be the sole basis for conviction under Article 38 of the constitution. In important cases many U.S. district attorneys must consider the impact of their conviction rates on their prospects in the next election. Japan's prosecutors, like those in other systems with career prosecutors, are in general under no such public pressure to prosecute and win convictions. Lest prosecutors be too lenient, 207 Prosecution Review Commissions (Kensatsu Shinsakai) of local voters randomly selected for six-month terms carefully review serious cases not sent to trial.

Police sometimes use technicalities and their own discretion to free suspects, with no more than a periodic summary report of such cases sent to a prosecutor's office. Similar police leniency is not unknown in other systems. They also at times ask a person to "voluntarily accompany" them to a police station to discuss a crime that has occurred. In this way they can investigate without imposing the severe stigma of "arrest," which could also lead to lengthy confinement and interrogation. Law establishes a presumption of innocence, but society and the media may treat arrest as implying guilt, as in the United States and other countries.

In handing down sentences, judges are often very lenient. The execution of a sentence, which may be a fine or a prison sentence or both, is sometimes delayed (*shikko yuyo*). If the criminal is well behaved during a probationary period, the sentence may be set aside. Judges understand that punishment is of limited use as a deterrent to crime. Why bother sending a person to a prosecutor, to trial, or to prison unnecessarily? Japan's criminal justice system is driven less by politics, resources for prison construction, vengeance, and punishment than by "benevolent paternalism," as Daniel Foote calls it. The goal is to generate shame and repentance and, when feasible, to reintegrate the lawbreaker into the community ("reintegrative shaming").

Violent crime is rare. It is safe to walk through virtually any urban neighborhood in Japan at any time. A few comparative statistics reported by David H. Bayley (1995) may enhance perspective. The United States has 146 times as many robberies as Japan and 86 times more aggravated assault cases. Of eighteen developed democratic countries surveyed, Japan had the lowest victimization rate for robbery, burglary, car theft, and robbery of items in cars and was close to the lowest in all other adult crime categories. (The U.S. robbery rate was over twice that of the next highest industrial democracy.) Illegal drugs have been a negligible problem. Graffiti and vandalism are rare. A few high-ranking public- and private-sector officials are occasionally caught in high-profile white-collar corruption and are usually brought to justice without preferential treatment.

Few gun deaths occur, and most are the result of feuds between factions in the organized-crime world (*yakuza*). Gun ownership and use are rigorously controlled by law. Registration is required for all firearms, swords, and knives over six centimeters long. Importantly, except for members of an international shooting team, no private person can have a handgun. Over 575,000 crimes involving firearms have occurred within a year in the United States, compared with only 150 in Japan.

Whatever the type of crime, the special circumstances of the individual suspect are taken into account. Similar offenses committed in different parts of the country are treated similarly. With so little crime, police spend less time on law enforcement than on training, preventive measures, and citizen education. Local police stationed in hundreds of small neighborhood police boxes (*koban*) know their territories intimately and are a key part of the infrastructure of the nation's community policing. In contrast to their prewar image, the police constitute an unthreatening, friendly, and helpful presence—most visible perhaps in helping people from outside the neighborhood look for an address in the intricate urban labyrinth of narrow winding streets and alleyways.

Japan may seem a veritable paradise for police and prosecutors, but heaven is not for the living. In some, not most, cases they have used technicalities to extend a suspect's preindictment confinement and interrogation for as long as twenty-three days without providing easy access to an attorney. The suspect rarely faces physical abuse, but considerable interrogation pressure to confess can be applied. Once indicted, the accused has a right to and usually receives a "speedy and public trial." Only 20 percent of suspects retain counsel before indictment. A few politically charged cases, such as those arising from the 1952 May Day Incidents and the 1960 Security Treaty Crisis introduced earlier, have lasted many years, but that situation is very rare.

The government has not recognized a duty to provide state-appointed counsel until after formal indictment. Scholars and defense attorneys claim such counsel should be available to all suspects and accused under international human rights law and Article 37 as a check against hasty confession under long interrogation. Membership in a bar association is compulsory for all lawyers. In the 1990s the Japan Federation of Bar Associations (JFBA; Nichibenren) instituted a "duty-attorney" system under which a suspect in custody can contact the local bar association, and an attorney on call will go immediately to the police station and provide an hour of free initial consultation. The Code of Criminal Procedure (Articles 76, 77, 203, 204) requires police, prosecutors, and judges to inform suspects and defendants that they may appoint counsel, but they have not been obliged to inform interested parties of the duty-attorney system. The JFBA has said "it should be compulsory for investigators to inform a suspect" of the duty-attorney option. Officials seem to be responding positively.

For many years prosecutors severely restricted the frequency and length of attorney visits with inmate clients, but few restraints remain. The daily regime of prison life for those convicted in court is strict and austere but is much safer for inmates than is the case in many U.S. facilities. Conditions are particularly hard for foreigners who do not speak Japanese and can thus inadvertently break one of the complex prison rules. (In 1999, 2,970 foreigners were in confinement, few compared with the United States but ten times the number in 1990.) Visits and communications with anyone but a relative require special permission. All correspondence, including that with one's attorney, is subject to censorship, in violation of Japan's obligations under the Law of the International Covenant on Civil and Political Rights. Japan's Prison Law and unpublished detailed internal rules have not been substantially revised since 1908. For some years the government's own Corrections Bureau has called in vain for new legislation. Improvements seem probable with more transparency and loosening of unnecessary rigors. Whatever changes may come, very few Japanese spend any time in government custody, and few of those who do serve long sentences.

The most drastic exercise of state power over a citizen is the death penalty. For good reasons, many nations have abolished capital punishment. The preponderance of criminological evidence indicates that the death penalty does not deter crime. In this writer's view, it is also cruel punishment. Numerous innocent people have been executed. However understandable the rage of those affected by a murder, vengeance killing is neither moral nor socially constructive. Healing and closure on hatred are not achieved by taking an additional human life. According to Amnesty International, seventy-five countries have abolished the death penalty for all crimes, and fourteen other nations limit capital punishment to a few serious crimes, whereas the laws of eighty-six other countries allow a death sentence.

Since the 1870s Japan has imposed the death penalty by hanging. Except in the 1950s (254 cases), relatively few executions have taken place under the 1947 Constitution: from 1982 through 1990, thirteen; 1990 through 1992, none; 1993 and 1994, seven executions. In the 1970s and 1980s a movement to abolish capital punishment was encouraged by acquittals in four death penalty retrial cases after the Supreme Court eased conditions for granting a retrial in 1975. All four cases involved murder, as long ago as 1948; and all the convictions resulted from faulty police work, overreliance on early and later repudiated confessions, and a rush to judgment by prosecutors and judges. The innocent convicts had spent from twenty-nine to thirty-five years each in prison before being freed under Article 435(6) of the Code of Criminal Procedure, which requires a "declaration of innocence" if clear new evidence has been found. A 1987 study by the Sentencing Project indicated that in the United States, 350 innocent defendants were convicted of capital crimes between 1900 and 1985. Although recognition of error and apology for mistakenly sentencing a person to execution or imprisonment provide small comfort to victims and their families, it seems essential to a democratic criminal justice system that the state provide by law, as in Japan, substantial compensation to victims and their survivors for such state mistakes (Article 40).

The leadership of eminent criminal law scholar Justice Dando Shigemitsu and these late acquittals raised public support for abolition of the death penalty. In the 1990s, however, the indiscriminate subway murders with the use of sarin gas by members of the Aum Shinrikyo cult unfortunately revived public support for capital punishment, which stood at 77 percent in 2001. Nevertheless, that same year a nonpartisan group of seventy-six Diet members, headed by the powerful former police official and policy chief of the LDP, Shizuka Kamei, called for abolishing the death penalty. The long-term effect was not clear at this writing in 2002, but high-level abolitionist movements in Japan and South Korea have offered mutual support.

In the United States the lack of national consistency is striking and a scandal. Some states allow capital punishment but never carry it out, other states do not allow the death penalty, and still others regularly use execution as a tool of criminal justice. Whether one is executed for a particular crime may depend largely on where one lives, one's race, and one's socio-economic status. Between 1977 and 1989 eleven southern states (led by Texas with 53) executed 104 persons, whereas the remaining thirty-nine states combined imposed the death penalty only 10 times. Of 85 executions in 2000, 40 took place in Texas and 11 in Oklahoma. As of 2002 the annual execution rate was dropping, but thirty-seven states and the federal government held 3,539 men and 54 women on death row.

Why is Japan's crime rate so low? Why are so few in prison? Why is such emphasis placed on confession, shame, and repentance? Some Japanese and foreign observers claim cultural homogeneity is a key factor in explaining Japan's success in this and other areas. The alleged collective sameness of homogeneity, however, does not in itself imply the presence of a particular set of cultural characteristics that discourage crime. That said, certain cultural traits may indeed affect criminal behavior patterns, as suggested later.

Does population density affect patterns of criminal behavior? Crowdedness has increased in Japan's urban areas year by year as more low buildings have been replaced by ever taller and larger structures as living standards have risen, but crime has not increased significantly. In the 1990s New York City, with about 11,500 people per square mile, had a much higher crime rate than the Tokyo-Yokohama megalopolis, with over 25,000 people per square mile.

Criminologists commonly relate crime rate differentials to such structural factors as poverty, unemployment, income disparity, gun laws, certainty of punishment, and the stability of family and other institutions. They have tended to downplay the relevance of social culture. And yet to answer the questions of "why" posed two paragraphs earlier, it seems reasonable to take into account what Japanese generally consider normal thought and behavior patterns in ordinary daily life apart from the realm of officially noted crime. To some extent, criminal behavior and criminal justice mirror social culture. David Bayley (1995) has argued that "an international theory of crime must see structural factors as operating within cultural envelopes." Without denying the importance of other factors, he posits three characterizations that may help explain Japanese criminal justice: "propriety, presumption, and pride."

Propriety is taken to mean that Japanese are "rule-bound" by "standards of appropriateness . . . etiquette, civility, morality and law [that] blend together in a seamless web of discipline and conformity." Presumption points to the essential importance most Japanese place on belonging to a tight-knit in-group that exercises informal social control over members while enabling personal fulfillment. "Fitting into groups" and conforming to group purposes "becomes the ultimate discipline," but those purposes must reflect the consensus of the group after taking seriously each member's views. "Enormous pride is taken . . . in performing the roles demanded of them" with alacrity in fulfilling obligations, whatever one's occupation or social status. Great coherence in performing group tasks may be a key reason for Japan's modern successes. Although such groupism may be loosening, it remains relevant to an understanding of Japanese behavior. Few Japanese have been motivated to commit crime, and most of those who do are encouraged to feel shame, to reform, and to reintegrate with the community. The response of some of Japan's leaders to collective World War II crimes has been quite different.

EDUCATION, SHINTO, AND NATIONALISM

During Japan's "dark valley" war years of 1930 to August 1945, elementary and high school education and state textbooks were permeated by an unscientific, undemocratic, and bellicose nationalism. Unlimited individual self-sacrifice for the emperor-state was the heroic ideal during the war. The 1947 Constitution cast bright light across that dark valley and inspired an educational system dedicated to democracy, freedom, and peace. That spirit still dominates Japan's educational ethos, but it has been challenged repeatedly by the aggressive Shinto nationalism of a small minority who enjoy full democratic freedom. How political leaders and history textbooks represent Japan's wartime behavior and how law should deal with Shinto shrines and ceremonies have been central to the battles for Japanese minds.

Ritual is one way human groups—whether a nation or a private organization like the Free Masons, the Boy Scouts of America, or college fraternities—express and confirm their communities. Ritual commonly includes such elements of law as regularity, predictability, and order, as well as clarity and firmness about behavior. The Shinto ceremonies related to Emperor Akihito's accession in 1989 showed Japanese ritual in a grand manner, but some questioned whether they were constitutional. Similarly questioned, as violating the separation of religion and the state, have been the ritual visits (official or private) of political leaders to Yasukuni Shrine (Tokyo). Although most attention here is given to issues involving Shinto, Japan is religiously complex, with over 2,000 new religions established since 1945 added to the many other religions of East and West on the scene much longer.

The courts have found the use of public moneys for the care and ceremonies of Shinto shrines to constitute illegal support of a religion. Every country needs a way to remember and mourn its war dead with solemnity, but in Japan governmental remembrance of millions of casualties at Shinto shrines is not politically neutral but inflammatory. The problem is not that Yasukuni Shrine is the central memorial where families pay their private respects to loved ones lost in the war. The problem is that political visits to Shinto shrines for the war dead by government leaders imply to many in Japan and abroad a unity of Shinto and the state and implicit government approval of what Japan's government did long ago during the militarist period.

In 2001 Prime Minister Koizumi Junichiro's cabinet seriously discussed forming an impartial panel to make recommendations on how to permanently defuse the Yasukuni issue. The advisory body might consider, among other alternatives, establishing a national memorial or national cemetery, with no political or religious taint, to honor not only Japan's war dead but the deceased of the former enemy. How to distinguish, if at all, between the treatment of deceased ordinary soldiers and the public remembrance of convicted war criminals may remain controversial.

A nation must learn to live with its past wars, whether won or lost, and all wars bring loss to almost all involved. All peoples have a duty to pass on the truth about their wars to their young and to succeeding generations. Some in Japan, however, still find it hard to accept the country's record of aggression in World War II. Japanese, like others, have downplayed the costs to other countries of their wars. We tend to mourn our own losses but not those of others. (For example, the United States takes its loss of 60,000 in the Vietnam War more seriously than it remembers the 2 million or more Vietnamese lives lost.) Nevertheless, especially noteworthy atrocities in Japan's record book have made nationalistic denial particularly repugnant to many Japanese and others.

Mao Zedong and other modern Chinese leaders have been responsible for more Chinese deaths than the Japanese have, but Japanese troops committed the Nanjing Massacre in 1937. Hundreds of thousands may have died, although precisely how many is still debated. In some cases the modes of killing were sickening. Moreover, the proportion of prisoners of war (POWs) who died or were tortured in Japanese camps was extremely high compared with the fate of POWs under other governments. In addition, the officially sanctioned system of "comfort stations" with "military comfort women" to provide sexual services to frontline troops enslaved many thousands of Japanese, Chinese, Korean, and other women, mostly Asian. Sadly, that operation was small compared to the present world traffic in sex slaves, with government connivance in some areas.

In weaponry of mass destruction, the work of Japan's Unit 731 in North China was potentially as horrific in its effect as atomic weapons. Confirming other sources, in November 2000 a member of Japan's Unit 731 first testified in a Japanese court about that unit's projects. In 1941 Unit 731 was formed to expand on research conducted in Manchuria since 1932. Leading Japanese biochemists, pathologists, and epidemiologists were brought together to develop new disease weapons to offset the numerical superiority of China, the USSR, and the United States. In related experiments to mass-produce such disease weapons as anthrax, botulism, cholera, smallpox, and typhus, over 3,000 Chinese, White Russians, and Allied POWs died.

Unit 731 thought big. For example, when the war ended in August 1945, Japan was preparing to deploy in September 8 million plague-infested rats in an offensive against Russia. Such weapons were used with effect on a smaller scale in campaigns against the USSR (for example, Nomonhan, 1939) and China. Moreover, during the bitterly fought Battle of Saipan, a ship bringing bacteriological weapons to Saipan was sunk by a U.S. submarine. Japan hoped eventually to be able to dump disease on the United States and Canada from balloons. After the war the USSR sentenced captured members of Unit 731 to prison terms as war criminals, but the U.S. government granted all members of Unit 731 immunity from prosecution as war criminals in exchange for cooperation, findings, and records.

Regardless of whether the U.S. bombing of Hiroshima and Nagasaki in August 1945 was unethical on other grounds, the resort to atomic bombing probably reduced the human losses of World War II. In the 1940s Japan's atomic weapons program lacked the resources and success of the U.S. program. Had Japan developed such weapons in time, no evidence indicates it would not have used them. The emperor is credited with the decision to surrender, but the military historian Edward Drea suggests that if he and his staff had not interpreted the Potsdam Declaration as assuring the survival of the emperor institution, the emperor was prepared to suffer unlimited losses in a last-ditch defense of the throne.

Since 1945, Japan has consistently opposed nuclear weaponry. As nations have developed ever more efficient nuclear, biological, and chemical weapons of mass destruction, ever more insistent voices have called for a ban on their use. By 1998 the world debate on nuclear weapons had advanced to the point where some members of the International Court of Justice held that any threat or use of nuclear weapons is contrary to humanitarian international law. Perhaps the bombing of the World Trade Center and the Pentagon on September 11, 2001, will nudge hesitant politicians toward more serious action against weapons of mass destruction.

During the militarist period, Japan brought thousands of Koreans and Chinese to Japan for forced labor. In 2001 survivors and relatives of deceased workers, like some comfort women and their families, were still in court involved in around sixty cases demanding apologies and compensation from the government or from the companies for which they worked over half a century ago. These suits have generally been unsuccessful, often on understandable legal grounds. High politics, domestic and international, has also been at work, however.

The Supreme Court first presided over a compromise agreement between Korean workers and a machine toolmaker in July 2000, in a case brought in 1992. The first court settlement involving Chinese laborers and a Japanese company was reached in the Tokyo High Court in November 2000 by the Kajima Company (construction) and worker plaintiffs. Of the 986 Chinese brought to work in mines at Odate, Akita Prefecture, in 1944 and 1945, 418 died—113 as a result of an unsuccessful uprising (Hanaoka Incident). In 1989 Kajima had offered a public apology, taking full responsibility, but agreement on compensation came only in 2000: 500 million yen to establish a "fund for peace and friendship" to be managed and distributed by the Japan Red Cross.

The importance of public apology, especially in East Asia, should not be underrated. Apology, in public as in private life, is enormously important in Japan for mending and smoothing the social fabric. The alleged refusal of the Japanese government to present an unambiguous acknowledgment of and official apology for its wartime behavior in East Asia has continued to bother neighboring nations. Unless such is forthcoming, reconciliation will be incomplete. Exceptions in the 1990s were Prime Ministers Murayama Tomiichi and Hosokawa Morihiro, who acknowledged that Japan's war was aggressive and mourned the war dead of Japan and other countries. In 2001 Prime Minister Koizumi clearly apologized for Japan's past behavior. If good-faith apology and compensation lead victims to forgive the perpetrators and achieve reconciliation, they would seem morally and politically useful. Otherwise, they seem diplomatically useless.

The gaffes of conservative politicians in the 1980s and 1990s illustrate a problem of defensive nationalism. A justice minister was forced to resign for calling the Nanjing Massacre a "hoax." In May 2000 Prime Minister Mori Yoshiro stated before a gathering of legislators and Shinto leaders, "We hope the Japanese people acknowledge that Japan is a divine land centering on the Emperor." A shock wave went through Japan and neighboring countries. In the face of outrage, Mori apologized but claimed his words had been taken out of context, which only generated an aftershock. "Utter nonsense," said a representative embarrassed politician.

In 1998 another leader expressed doubt that the government had used force on the comfort women, as many survivors have contended in recent litigation. Such views have manifested not only a persistent unhealthy nationalism but also a defensive discomfort with history. The views of Mori and some in his cabinet were so far from mainstream public opinion that their approval rating fell to 9 percent in 2001, before Mori's early departure from office. Perhaps Mori's unprecedented unpopularity explains in part the great popularity of the cabinet of his successor, Prime Minister Koizumi Junichiro. Unregenerate Shinto nationalists appear at odds with Emperor Akihito, whom they claim to honor. He has publicly welcomed criticism of the emperor institution and even of his father, Hirohito, as an exercise of constitutionally guaranteed free speech.

A few court cases may add insight into Japan's related constitutional debates: the Ienaga Textbook Review cases (1982, 1989), the Nakaya Serviceman Enshrinement case (1988), the Shinto Groundbreaking Ceremony case (1977), and disputes about public funding of Yasukuni Shrine in honor of the war dead in Tokyo and of other shrines.

The Ienaga Textbook Review Cases (1982, 1989)

Government certification of textbooks used during years of compulsory education—nine years of elementary and junior high school in Japan—is common among democracies and other countries. Sterilizing history textbooks for the young is also common. For example, as Frances Fitzgerald (1980) and James Loewen (1995) have documented, U.S. textbooks sometimes cover up ugly and embarrassing history. Texts have also encouraged stereotypes of Asians. (In the case of U.S.-Japan perceptions, scholars and teachers in both countries have worked together systematically for decades to achieve balanced textbook representations.) Legitimation of error and slanted perspective in textbooks remains an issue of free speech and children's educational rights well worth arguing about in any country.

In Japan, the Ministry of Education relies on a generally nonpartisan Textbook Authorization Research Council of appointed teachers and scholars to recommend approval, rejection, or revision of draft textbooks for national use. Junior high school history texts are produced by competing commercial publishers following ministry curriculum guidelines such as balanced content, appropriate vocabulary, more emphasis on individual thinking and less on memorization of facts, and the nurture of adults "who will build a democratic and peaceful nation." (The ministry has no interest in regulating other books.)

Text drafts are submitted for ministry approval every four years. In April 2001 the ministry approved eight history textbooks from eight publishers for use beginning in April 2002. Even after revisions, most of the eight revised history texts are seen by some at home and throughout East Asia as less clear about Japan's wartime behavior than texts currently used. Prefectural and municipal boards of education have chosen which of the approved texts their schools will use after receiving recommendations of teacher groups, but the role of teachers is being diminished in many prefectures, in part because of political pressure from the right.

Two books were found particularly offensive for their narrow nationalism: the history and civics texts compiled by the Japan Society for History Textbook Reform (Atarashii Rekishi Kyokasho wo Tsukuru Kai). This rightist organization was formed in 1997, in essence to exonerate Japan of blame for its wartime activities and to promote a fervent emperor-centered nationalism among the young by presenting an alternative to what it sees as "masochistic" texts that "cost Japan its pride." As a condition for approval, the Textbook Council required revisions of 137 sections of the draft history text. A few matters dealt with in offending passages are the Nanjing Massacre, the forcible annexation of Korea (1910), the military comfort women, the imperial myths, and the mob killing of Koreans and Chinese after the Great Earthquake in 1923. The influential *Asahi Shimbun* remarked that the society's "offerings lack balance. We consider them unfit for classroom use." China and South Korea officially protested.

Education Minister Toyama Atsuko assured the South Korean and Chinese governments that their objections would be studied from an objective, academic perspective and that recommendations for change would be sent to publishers as needed. In October 2001, when during a visit to Seoul Prime Minister Koizumi expressed Japan's remorse for Korean suffering under Japan's colonialism, the great Korean president Kim Dae-jung welcomed it in a spirit of reconciliation but noted that the textbook issue is the only unresolved problem in Japan–South Korea relations. Perhaps more powerfully diffusing the controversy is the fact that all but a few schools have chosen not to adopt the most offensive textbooks.

In 2002, for the first time in Japan's postwar history, in the most recent revisions all texts were required to mention the national flag and anthem ("Kimigayo"), which became official under a 1999 law. To some, the flag and anthem are still linked with the emperor system and militarism. To many Japanese the lyrics of the anthem are more odd than subversive. Some, however, see enforcement of the law as a violation of the constitutional freedoms of thought and conscience (Article 19).

From the 1960s until recent years, national debate on textbooks centered around the distinguished historian Ienaga Saburo, author of a widely adopted high school textbook on Japanese history. In 1965, 1967, and 1984 he sued the Ministry of Education for unconstitutional tampering with the content of his book in its system of certifying precollegiate texts. In court proceedings extending over decades with mixed results, Ienaga alleged violation of his freedom of expression, academic freedom, and freedom of thought.

Single words in a textbook may carry a heavy burden of political sensitivity. The ministry objected to such representations of the past as the following: "All" (*subete*) of Japan's Shinto mythological writings were allegedly a means of legitimizing the emperor's government. Workers and farmers were presented as more important makers of history than better-known leaders. Ienaga claimed the wartime neutrality pact with the Soviet Union was based on Japanese initiative.

In a 1989 Tokyo District Court decision on the 1984 case, Ienaga was awarded compensation for ministry abuse of authority on one point, but on other points he lost. For example, his mention of Unit 731's experiments on Chinese was deleted. In out-of-court discussions, however, the ministry yielded to Ienaga's position in calling Japan's incursions into China an invasion rather than an "advance" and in attributing the Nanjing Massacre not to "chaos" but to "the Imperial Japanese Army." For students, textbooks have great power in representing what their elders say they should believe is true.

The Nakaya Serviceman Enshrinement Case (1988)

Nakaya Takafumi, a member of the SDF killed in a traffic accident, was given Shinto enshrinement (*goshi*) in 1972 at the request of the Self-Defense Forces Friendship Association (SDF Friends) and with the support of the SDF's Regional Liaison Office. In 1973 his wife, Yasuko, a

Christian (he and his family were not Christian), claimed in court that the SDF Friends, as an auxiliary of the SDF, had violated the separation of religion and the state. She asked for a retraction of the enshrinement and for damages to be paid by the state and the SDF Friends for infringement of her personal religious rights. The lower courts awarded her damages, but they, like the Supreme Court in 1988, did not require that the enshrinement be cancelled. Dissenting, Justice Ito Masami said:

> I am of the opinion that in modern society the interest of not being disturbed in one's mind by unwanted stimuli from others, that is, the interest of peace of mind, can be a legal interest under tort law. When this interest is acknowledged with respect to religion, we might call it the personal right of religion or of religious privacy; the terminology can be worked out. It might be based on Article 13 of the Constitution.... The act of applying for an enshrinement at *Gokoku* [guardian of the state] Shrine, according to Shintoism and not other religions, in its effect gives special treatment to and favors Shintoism, and can be considered [unconstitutional] aid and promotion of Shintoism. [Article 13. All of the people shall be respected as individuals. Their right to life, liberty, and the pursuit of happiness shall, to the extent that it does not interfere with the public welfare, be the supreme consideration in legislation and in other governmental affairs.] (Beer and Itoh, 1996, 509–511)

Considerable insensitivity to the widow's wishes had been shown. The offending relationships among Shinto, the SDF Liaison Offices, and SDF Friends were subsequently modified throughout Japan to avoid such problems in the future.

The Shinto Groundbreaking Ceremony Case (1977)

In a third case, the Supreme Court held that a Shinto groundbreaking ceremony did not violate the constitutional separation of religion and the state because it was not religious but merely custom and secular in nature (Beer and Itoh, 1996, 478). Under the Meiji Constitution subjects were given religious freedom but not freedom from adhering to State Shinto, defined as not a "religion." In the case at hand, it is the customs of Shinto that are given state legitimation. Prior to commencing construction of a city gymnasium in 1965, Tsu City had four Shinto priests conduct a groundbreaking ceremony (*jichinsai*), receiving stipends paid out of city funds. The plaintiff, a city assemblyman who attended the ceremony at the mayor's invitation, sued for return of the funds to public coffers and for compensation for mental suffering caused by his coerced attendance.

The district court dismissed his case, claiming the ceremony was merely secular custom that only appeared to be religious. The Nagoya High Court reversed, holding that Shinto is indeed a religion as understood in the constitution and that the ceremony closely adhered to Home Ministry directives of 1907, in force all during the prewar period of compulsory organic integration of Shinto, the state, and extreme nationalism. With five justices strenuously dissenting, the Supreme Court gave Shinto new public life by reducing it to state secular custom. In an analogous but less politically charged custom, members of the clergy commonly open U.S. legislative sessions with prayer.

Shinto festivals, weddings, groundbreaking, and other ceremonies are generally a delightful and deeply embedded part of Japan's culture. In the realm of constitutional law and politics, however, Shinto has been made the repository for a divisive latent nationalism. The premodern emperors were generally not revered or even much noticed by Japanese commoners; but by the prewar era of Emperor Hirohito, the sacralized imperial institution, the military, and suppression of civil liberties were integrated in Japan's constitutional imagery. The schools taught that to be Japanese was to be a loyal State Shintoist.

Postwar calls to revive any one of the three elements were often taken to mean change in the other two: enhancing the emperor's position meant undesirable rearmament and danger for human rights; rearmament put revival of suppression and reverence for the emperor on the horizon; and suppression of rights implied a threat of return to emperor-centered militarist politics, both domestic and international. The potential for nationalist exploitation of the imperial institution has diminished substantially since around 1950. The strength of Japan's system of human rights constitutionalism, however, may still depend in important part on maintaining international pacifism.

BIBLIOGRAPHICAL NOTE

Works have been chosen that convey both the factual background and the sociopolitical context within which problems of constitutional law and human rights law occur. Where a source has not been given in the text, it is a Japanese newspaper, most often *Asahi Shimbun*. Items that harken back to the wartime period are listed because they shed light on current constitutional debates.

David H. Bayley, *Forces of Order: Police Behavior in Japan and the United States* (Berkeley: University of California Press, 1976). Excellent; influential in the community policing movement.

————, "Modern Public Safety: Can East Meet West?" unpublished paper, School of Criminal Justice, SUNY Albany, May 1995.

————, *Police for the Future* (New York: Oxford University Press, 1996).

Lawrence W. Beer, *Freedom of Expression in Japan: A Study in Comparative Law, Politics, and Society* (Tokyo: Kodansha International, 1984). A comprehensive study.

John Braithwaite, *Crime, Shame, and Reintegration* (Cambridge: Cambridge University Press, 1989). General theory drawing on Japan's criminological experience.

John Creighton Campbell and Naoki Ikegami, *The Art of Balance in Health Policy: Maintaining Japan's Low-Cost Egalitarian System* (Cambridge: Cambridge University Press, 1998).

William K. Cummings, *Education and Equality in Japan* (Princeton: Princeton University Press, 1980).

Edward J. Drea, *In the Service of the Emperor: Essays on the Imperial Japanese Army* (Lincoln: University of Nebraska Press, 1998).

Eric Feldman, *The Ritual of Rights in Japanese Law, Society, and Health Policy* (Cambridge: Cambridge University Press, 2000).

Frances Fitzgerald, *America Revised: History Schoolbooks in the Twentieth Century* (New York: Vintage, 1980).

Daniel Foote, "The Benevolent Paternalism of Japanese Criminal Justice," *California Law Review* 80, no. 2 (1992): 317–390.

Foreign Press Center, Japan, *Facts and Figures of Japan, 2000 Edition* (Tokyo: Foreign Press Center, 2000).

V. Lee Hamilton and Joseph Sanders, *Everyday Justice: Responsibility and the Individual in Japan and the United States* (New Haven: Yale University Press, 1992).

Laura Hein and Mark Selden (eds.), *Censoring History: Citizenship and Memory in Japan, Germany, and the United States* (Armonk, N.Y.: M. E. Sharpe, 2000).

Higuchi Yoichi (ed.), *Five Decades of Constitutionalism in Japanese Society* (Tokyo: University of Tokyo Press, 2001).

Nobutaka Inoue, *Contemporary Japanese Religion*, About Japan Series, no. 25 (Tokyo: Foreign Press Center, 2000).

Honda Katsuchi, *The Nanjing Massacre: A Japanese Journalist Confronts Japan's National Shame*, Frank Gibney (ed.), Karen Sandness (trans.), (Armonk, N.Y.: M. E. Sharpe, 1999).

Ienaga Saburo, *Japan's Past, Japan's Future*, Richard H. Minear (trans.), (Boulder: Rowman and Littlefield, 2001).

Sumiko Iwao, *The Japanese Woman: Traditional Image and Changing Realities* (Cambridge: Harvard University Press, 1993).

Yuji Iwasawa, *International Law, Human Rights, and Japanese Law* (Oxford: Clarendon, 1998). Discusses the impact of international human rights law on Japan's internal law.

Japan Institute for Social and Economic Affairs, *Japan 2001: An International Comparison* (Tokyo: Keizai Koho Center, December 2000).

David T. Johnson, *Prosecuting Crime in Japan* (Oxford: Oxford University Press, 2001).

Ellis Krauss, *Broadcasting Politics in Japan* (Ithaca: Cornell University Press, 2000).

Robert Leesma and Herbert Walberg (eds.), *Japanese Educational Productivity* (Ann Arbor: Center for Japanese Studies, University of Michigan, 1992).

Mark A. Levin, "Essential Commodities and Racial Justice: Using Constitutional Protection of Japan's Indigenous Ainu People to Inform Understandings of the United States and Japan," *New York University Journal of International Law and Politics* 33, no. 2 (2001): 410.

James W. Loewen, *Lies My Teacher Told Me* (New York: Touchstone, 1995).

Susan O. Long (ed.), *Caring for the Elderly in Japan and the U.S.: Practices and Policies* (London: Routledge, 2000).

Miyazawa Toshiyoshi, *Nihon Koku Kempo* (the Constitution of Japan) (Tokyo: Nihon Hyoron Shinsha, 1963).

John K. Nelson, *Enduring Identities: The Guise of Shinto in Contemporary Japan* (Honolulu: University of Hawai'i Press, 2001).

Nihon Shimbun Kyokai (ed.), *The Japanese Press* (Tokyo: Japan Newspaper Publishers and Editors Association, 2002 edition).

David M. O'Brien and Yasuo Ohkoshi, *To Dream of Dreams: Religious Freedom and Constitutional Politics in Postwar Japan* (Honolulu: University of Hawaii Press, 1996).

Keinosuke Ohki, "Broadcast and Human Rights/Other Related Rights Organization (BRO) Founded in Japan," *NHK Broadcasting Culture and Research*, no. 3 (1998): 19.

Susan J. Pharr and Ellis S. Krauss (eds.), *Media and Politics in Japan* (Honolulu: University of Hawaii Press, 1996).

Edwin O. Reischauer and Marius Jansen, *The Japanese Today* (Cambridge: Harvard University Press, 1995).

Lawrence Repeta, *Local Government Disclosure Systems in Japan* (Seattle: National Bureau of Asian Research, 1999).

Joseph E. Stiglitz, "Democratic Development as the Fruits of Labor," Boston, American Economic Association, January 2000.

Kazuo Sugeno, *Japanese Labor Law*, Leo Kanowitz (trans.), (Seattle: University of Washington Press, 1992).

Noel Williams, *The Right to Life in Japan* (New York: Routledge, 1997).

World Health Organization, "Health Systems: Improving Performance," a report (Washington, D.C.: WHO, 2001).

Yamazaki Masakazu, *Individualism and the Japanese: An Alternative Approach to Cultural Comparison*, Barbara Sugihara (trans.), (Tokyo: Japan Echo, 1994).

Yoshimi Yoshiaki, *Comfort Women: Sexual Slavery in the Japanese Military During World War II*, Suzanne O'Brien (trans.), (New York: Columbia University Press, 2000).

8
From Imperial Myth to Constitutional Democracy

After centuries of isolation and feudal federalism under the "living constitution" of the Tokugawa family, Japan was forced to open to a military and cultural challenge from Western nation-states in the 1850s. By 1889 Japan's government had devised a constitutional system that centered around a newly sacralized emperor institution and accorded great power to Japan's modern military from 1894 until 1945. In the later years under the Meiji Constitution, Japan reached barbarism in the use of war as an instrument of divinized foreign policy. Since 1945, with the people as sovereign, the nation has pursued and achieved peace, civility, and prosperity. Japan has experienced itself as two fairly different modern nation-states in the past 130 years.

The oligarchs of the Meiji period, most notably Ito Hirobumi, actively investigated foreign constitutional ideas before finalizing the Meiji Constitution in 1889. In 1946, when Americans and Japanese shared in the creation of the 1947 Showa Constitution, the Japanese founders of the current constitutional regime were more familiar than the occupation personnel with the rich diversity of modern European constitutional thought and practice. Although the constitution was not "imposed" on Japan, it is unlikely that Japan would have soon had a revolutionary democratic constitution had it not been for the defeat and occupation. That reality is widely acknowledged in Japan, usually with gratitude.

Under the Meiji Constitution, the individual subject's rights were not human rights but legally limited gifts of a kindly sovereign emperor. In 1947 the roles were reversed. Now, the imperial family institution exists at the sufferance of the sovereign people. Each citizen possesses many rights simply by virtue of being a human being. This rights revolution and the radical change from militarism to international pacifism altered the foundations of government, law, politics, and society.

Buttressed by other factors, the Constitution of Japan has made a difference over a long period in many concrete ways. A few of these areas are exceptionally peaceable international relations; ever more social openness, however slowly achieved; richly diverse views in the political party system and in many other spheres of cultural and social endeavor; much more active local government; more gender equality; more official and social attention to minority problems; a strong, confident, and independent court system; more freedom of speech, press, and mass media in general; more freedom of religion; more separation of religion and the state; academic freedom; better and more widely available health care and educational opportunities; much improved working conditions; unprecedented prosperity; a higher consciousness of individual rights and an increased willingness to assert those rights and one's personal interests; and an unbroken succession of democratic elections to choose representative governments without bloodshed.

All this is not meant to suggest a belief that constitutional democracy—in Japan, the United States, or other countries—is destined to be perfectly achieved or to continue indefinitely. Japanese stories often have sad endings, but recent history gives solid reason for hope unless the constitution is unwisely changed, East Asian international relations destabilize, or an economic disaster occurs.

COMMISSIONS ON THE CONSTITUTION, 1957–2002

Since the Constitution of Japan came into force on May 3, 1947, conservative political parties have sought its amendment or revision, off and on, as "occupation imposed." Under Article 96 of the constitution, amendment requires approval by a two-thirds majority of the members of each house of the Diet and by a majority of those voting in a subsequent special or regular election. No political party has had the necessary majorities in the Diet or enjoyed wide public support. Oddly perhaps, the ruling party has been elected for decades in spite of, not because of, the desire of some of its members to change the constitution. Opposition parties generally have been against revision but have lacked voter appeal on other policy grounds. Attempts to change the constitution have consistently failed.

In June 1956 the ruling Liberal Democratic Party (LDP) won passage of a law to establish the Kempo Chosakai (literally, the Commission to Investigate the Constitution), officially the Commission on the Constitution. The law provided for a membership of fifty: twenty members of the House of Representatives, ten from the smaller House of Councillors, and twenty persons of "learning and experience." It was chaired by the eminent specialist in Anglo-American law, Professor Takayanagi Kenzo of Tokyo University. Some constitutional scholars, such as members of the private Committee to Study Constitutional Issues (Kempo Mondai Kenkyukai), refused to cooperate. Minority parties such as the Japan Socialist Party and the Japan Communist Party refused to fill their allotted seats on grounds that the commission's mission was revision.

The law provided, however, that the duties of the commission were to study, investigate, and deliberate on the constitution and related problems and to "report the results to the Cabinet and through the Cabinet to the Diet." Between 1957 and 1964 the commission carried out a massive investigation of every aspect of the constitution, including the controversial issue of its drafting and promulgation under the occupation. It prepared hundreds of reports on its meetings and deliberations, which were published for public sale at low prices by the government's printing office. All meetings except those of its executive committee were open to the public.

Individual citizens and representatives of organizations expressed their views and told of their experiences under the constitution in nationwide public hearings. The process constituted a kind of Japanese "constitutional convention," building consensus through unhurried, exhaustive discussion. The freely expressed will of the people about their form of government was revealed. Perhaps the commission's work rendered moot and unpersuasive the claims of revisionists that Japan's constitution is rooted not in Japan but in a long-past Allied Occupation.

The media provided extensive coverage, and scholarly journals carried substantive analyses. Massive consultations took place between constitutional lawyers and government officials whose duties involved constitution-related issues; expert foreign opinion was sought on both Japanese and general constitutional problems.

The commission's final report, written by Professor Sato Isao—a participant on both the commission and the academics' committee of dissent—included 1,161 pages: 882 pages of main text and 279 pages of appended tables and valuable factual material. The report was submitted to Prime Minister Ikeda Hayato on August 13, 1964, as Japan was preoccupied with the Tokyo Olympics and the miracle of its surging economy.

Professor Takayanagi, who chaired the commission brilliantly for seven years, concluded that the constitution is not an imposed document but a product of collaboration between occupation personnel and Japanese founders and that it is "a living constitution," alive and well and in need of no revision or amendment. The commission made no recommendation to revise because, Takayanagi later said, any such recommendation would have been a policy matter beyond the commission's authority. He also pointed out that at an early meeting the commission decided that "in the absence of unanimity after due deliberation, the Commission was not to resort to majority rule." A large majority of those participating were revisionists (because many antirevisionists refused to join the commission), but both revisionist and antirevisionist views appeared in the final report.

The commission's work made clear there was support for a variety of revisions, but there was virtually unanimous support for the basic principles of renunciation of war, popular sovereignty, and the guarantee of fundamental human rights. No strong resentment was shown toward the occupation regime and its actions in relation to the constitution. Investigations unearthed no serious defects or omissions in the constitution, as might have been expected had the constitution been imposed in a high-handed manner by a victorious occupation. By extension, this finding supports the view set forth in this book that the constitution was the result of a creatively cooperative effort on the part of both the defeated and the victors. Professor Takayanagi strongly supported this collaboration theory.

The revision movement faded, but many (by no means all) in the LDP continued to favor Japan's rearmament, enhancement of the emperor's position, and strengthening of the old family system. Revision remained a dormant political issue for about thirty-five years. In 1999 the LDP and three minor parties amended the Diet Law to provide for the establishment of Diet research committees. Two Kenpo Chosakai (Committees to Investigate the Constitution, or Commissions on the Constitution) were established. The House of Representatives commission has fifty members, and the House of Councillors committee has forty-five, taking into account the difference in total membership of the two houses. The commissions are authorized to carry out "broad and comprehensive" research and to recommend, but not submit, bills to the Diet. They are required to present separate reports to the speaker of each house, who then presents the reports to the full house for debate and possible action. These commissions differ from the earlier Commission on the Constitution in that they are not connected to the cabinet and include no independent "persons of learning and experience."

Beginning in 2000 the commissions held hearings to which they had invited (at the time of this writing in 2002) only a limited range of interested parties to present their views. The earlier commission found virtually unanimous support for popular sovereignty and fundamental human rights. A problem for the present commissions is to detect some hitherto undiscovered flaws, omissions, or possible corrections regarding these principles. Most controversy centers on whether, and if so how, to modify the peace provisions of Article 9, as discussed in Chapter 6.

Perhaps the work of the commissions and the Diet will extend over a period of years and will issue in some historic development, but in 2002 many of Japan's most respected constitutional lawyers remained skeptical regarding the need or usefulness of this legislative exercise. In any case, Japan's political, social, and economic life today—at home and abroad—bears little resemblance to that in the 1957–1964 period of deeply polarized politics and rather fresh memories of the war and the occupation. In the private sector, competing national newspapers and magazines put forth proposals during the 1990s for and against some change in the constitution. Important examples are those of the somewhat conservative *Yomiuri Shimbun* (November 3, 1994) and the progressive *Asahi Shimbun* (May 3, 1995). Some modification of the text, although by no means certain in 2002, was no longer as politically unthinkable to many Japanese as in the past. New issues had arisen.

CONSTITUTIONAL DISCOURSE IN THE TWENTY-FIRST CENTURY

The constitution has set the parameters of continuing public debate. Among the issues widely discussed in 2002 are the following: Under Article 9 to what extent, if at all, may Japan arm for purposes of self-defense in collaboration with the United States or for increased participation in UN peace-keeping or even peace-making operations? Should Article 9 be amended? Should it contain a provision rejecting the production, importation, and use of nuclear, chemical, and biological weapons of mass destruction? Should the constitution explicitly recognize a right to privacy or environmental rights and duties or other rights? What improvements in the position of women should the Council on Gender Equality recommend after its five-year study (mentioned in Chapter 7)?

In light of the new information technology, with respect to what content and activities should law and society regulate expression or access to information regarding government or the individual citizen? Should the constitution establish any new organs of government? (For example, an independent Human Rights Protection Agency is likely to be established by law in 2002.) Should the prime minister be directly elected by the voters? If so, how would that fit with the cabinet and Diet systems? Should most or all such matters be left to judicial decision or legislative developments? With respect to the legal reforms explained in Chapter 5, for the fair functioning of the constitution, how substantially should the number of attorneys, prosecutors, and judges be increased; how quickly; and by what educational path?

When will the voting rights of the hundreds of thousands of Japanese living abroad be effectively honored? Should long-term foreign residents in Japan be granted the rights to vote and to stand for office in local elections throughout the country? (In January 2002 the municipal assembly of Maihara, Shiga Prefecture, voted to allow foreign residents to participate in a plebiscite on proposals to merge with neighboring cities, the first instance of bestowal of a limited voting right on foreigners.) In national elections? Should these foreigners be eligible for hire on a merit basis for positions as civil servants, even as government administrators? (An increasing number of prefectures and cities have eliminated the nationality requirement for such positions established in 1953.) How should unpleasant wartime history be treated in textbooks and in domestic and international government policy statements? How should the war dead of modern Japan be remembered in a politically neutral manner? All these questions are the stuff of daily Japanese constitutional discourse.

As Japan entered the twenty-first century, its people could look back on more than half a century of solid economic accomplishments and also of contribution to the most basic of human tasks: the advancement of civility throughout the world and the restraint of barbarism under the rule of law and constitutionalism. Echoing the pride felt by many Japanese, female politician Owaki Masako could say, "This Constitution has effectively become Japan's identity. It should be heralded to the world as a constitution that will shine in the 21st century."

Japan's people, statehood, democratic constitutionalism, and pacific renunciation of war and of the use or threat of force in settling international disputes are intertwined in the nation's constitution. Its escape from its violent and militaristic past makes it a useful and realistic model for some nations as a peaceful and responsible member of the human community.

Appendix: Documents

THE CONSTITUTION OF THE EMPIRE OF JAPAN (*DAI NIPPON TEIKOKU KEMPO*), 1889

Preamble (*Joyu*)

Having, by virtue of the glories of Our ancestors, ascended the Throne of a lineal succession unbroken for ages eternal; desiring to promote the welfare of, and to give development to the moral and intellectual faculties of Our beloved subjects, the very same that have been favored with the benevolent care and affectionate vigilance of Our ancestors; and hoping to maintain the prosperity of the State, in concert with Our people and with their support, We hereby promulgate, in pursuance of Our Imperial Rescript of the 12th day of the 10th month of the 14th year of Meiji, a fundamental law of the State, to exhibit the principles, by which We are guided in Our conduct, and to point out to what Our descendants and Our subjects and their descendants are forever to affirm.

The rights of sovereignty of the State, We have inherited from Our Ancestors, and We shall bequeath them to Our descendants. Neither We nor they shall in the future fail to wield them, in accordance with the provisions of the Constitution hereby granted.

We now declare to respect and protect the security of the rights and of the property of the people, and to secure to them the common enjoyment of the same, within the extent of the provisions of the present Constitution and of the law.

The Imperial Diet shall first be convoked for the 23rd year of Meiji and the time of its opening shall be the date, when the present Constitution comes into force.

When in the future it may become necessary to amend any of the provisions of the present Constitution, We or Our successors shall assume the initiative right, and submit a project for the same to the Imperial Diet. The Imperial Diet shall pass its vote upon it, according to the conditions imposed by the present Constitution, and in no otherwise shall Our descendants or Our subjects be permitted to attempt any alteration thereof.

Our Ministers of State, on Our behalf, shall be held responsible for the carrying out of the present Constitution, and Our present and future subjects shall forever assume the duty of allegiance to the present Constitution.

Chapter I. The Emperor

ARTICLE 1. The Empire of Japan shall be reigned over and governed by a line of Emperors unbroken for ages eternal.

ARTICLE 2. The Imperial Throne shall be succeeded to by Imperial male descendants, according to the provisions of the Imperial House Law.

ARTICLE 3. The Emperor is sacred and inviolable.

ARTICLE 4. The Emperor is the head of the Empire, combining in Himself the rights of sovereignty, and exercises them, according to the provisions of the present Constitution.

ARTICLE 5. The Emperor exercises the legislative power with the consent of the Imperial Diet.

ARTICLE 6. The Emperor gives sanction to laws, and orders them to be promulgated and executed.

ARTICLE 7. The Emperor convokes the Imperial Diet, opens, closes, and prorogues it, and dissolves the House of Representatives.

ARTICLE 8. The Emperor, in consequence of an urgent necessity to maintain public safety or to avert public calamities, issues, when the Imperial Diet is not sitting, Imperial Ordinances in the place of law.

(2) Such Imperial Ordinances are to be laid before the Imperial Diet at its next session, and when the Diet does not approve the said Ordinances, the Government shall declare them to be invalid for the future.

ARTICLE 9. The Emperor issues or causes to be issued the Ordinances necessary for the carrying out of the laws, or for the maintenance of the public peace and order, and for the promotion of the welfare of the subjects. But no Ordinance shall in any way alter any of the existing laws.

ARTICLE 10. The Emperor determines the organization of the different branches of the administration, and salaries of all civil and military officers, and appoints and dismisses the same. Exceptions especially provided for in the present Constitution or in other laws, shall be in accordance with the respective provisions [bearing thereon].

ARTICLE 11. The Emperor has the supreme command of the Army and Navy.

ARTICLE 12. The Emperor determines the organization and peace standing of the Army and Navy.

ARTICLE 13. The Emperor declares war, makes peace, and concludes treaties.

ARTICLE 14. The Emperor declares a state of siege.

(2) The conditions and effects of a state of siege shall be determined by law.

ARTICLE 15. The Emperor confers titles of nobility, rank, orders, and other marks of honor.

ARTICLE 16. The Emperor orders amnesty, pardon, and commutation of punishments and rehabilitation.

ARTICLE 17. A Regency shall be instituted in conformity with the provisions of the Imperial House Law.

(2) The Regent shall exercise the powers appertaining to the Emperor in His name.

Chapter II. Rights and Duties of Subjects

ARTICLE 18. The conditions necessary for being a Japanese subject shall be determined by law.

ARTICLE 19. Japanese subjects may, according to qualifications determined by laws or ordinances, be appointed to civil or military or any other public offices equally.

ARTICLE 20. Japanese subjects are amenable to service in the Army and Navy, according to the provisions of law.

ARTICLE 21. Japanese subjects are amenable to the duty of paying taxes, according to the provisions of law.

ARTICLE 22. Japanese subjects shall have the liberty of abode and of changing the same within the limits of the law.

ARTICLE 23. No Japanese subjects shall be arrested, detained, tried, or punished, unless according to law.

ARTICLE 24. No Japanese subject shall be deprived of his right of being tried by the judges determined by law.

ARTICLE 25. Except in the cases provided for in the law, the house of no Japanese subject shall be entered or searched without his consent.

ARTICLE 26. Except in cases mentioned in the law, the secrecy of the letters of every Japanese subject shall remain inviolate.

ARTICLE 27. The right of property of every Japanese subject shall remain inviolate.

(2) Measures necessary to be taken for the public benefit shall be provided for by law.

ARTICLE 28. Japanese subjects shall, within limits not prejudicial to peace and order, and not antagonistic to their duties as subjects, enjoy freedom of religious belief.

ARTICLE 29. Japanese subjects shall, within the limits of law, enjoy the liberty of speech, writing, publication, public meetings, and associations.

ARTICLE 30. Japanese subjects may present petitions, by observing the proper forms of respect, and by complying with the rules specially provided for the same.

ARTICLE 31. The provisions contained in the present Chapter shall not affect the exercise of the powers appertaining to the Emperor, in times of war or in cases of a national emergency.

ARTICLE 32. Each and every one of the provisions contained in the preceding Articles of the present Chapter, that are not in conflict with the laws or the rules of discipline of the Army and Navy, shall apply to the officers and men of the Army and of the Navy.

Chapter III. The Imperial Diet

ARTICLE 33. The Imperial Diet shall consist of two Houses, a House of Peers and a House of Representatives.

ARTICLE 34. The House of Peers shall, in accordance with the Ordinance concerning the House of Peers, be composed of the members of the Imperial Family, of the orders of nobility, and of those who have been nominated thereto by the Emperor.

ARTICLE 35. The House of Representatives shall be composed of Members elected by the people, according to the provisions of the Law of Election.

ARTICLE 36. No one can at one and the same time be a Member of both Houses.

ARTICLE 37. Every law requires the consent of the Imperial Diet.

ARTICLE 38. Both Houses shall vote upon projects of law submitted to it by the Government, and may respectively initiate projects of law.

ARTICLE 39. A Bill, which has been rejected by either the one or the other of the two Houses, shall not be brought in again during the same session.

ARTICLE 40. Both Houses can make representations to the Government, as to laws or upon any other subject. When, however, such representations are not accepted, they cannot be made a second time during the same session.

ARTICLE 41. The Imperial Diet shall be convoked every year.

ARTICLE 42. A session of the Imperial Diet shall last during three months. In case of necessity, the duration of a session may be prolonged by the Imperial Order.

ARTICLE 43. When urgent necessity arises, an extraordinary session may be convoked in addition to the ordinary one.

(2) The duration of an extraordinary session shall be determined by Imperial Order.

ARTICLE 44. The opening, closing, prolongation of session, and prorogation of the Imperial Diet, shall be effected simultaneously for both Houses.

(2) In case the House of Representatives has been ordered to dissolve, the House of Peers shall at the same time be prorogued.

ARTICLE 45. When the House of Representatives has been ordered to dissolve, Members shall be caused by Imperial Order to be newly elected, and the new House shall be convoked within five months from the day of dissolution.

ARTICLE 46. No debate can be opened and no vote can be taken in either House of the Imperial Diet, unless not less than one-third of the whole number of Members thereof is present.

ARTICLE 47. Votes shall be taken in both Houses by absolute majority. In the case of a tie vote, the President shall have the casting vote.

ARTICLE 48. The deliberations of both Houses shall be held in public. The deliberations may, however, upon demand of the Government or by resolution of the House be held in secret setting.

ARTICLE 49. Both Houses of the Imperial Diet may respectively present addresses to the Emperor.

ARTICLE 50. Both Houses may receive petitions presented by subjects.

ARTICLE 51. Both Houses may enact, besides what is provided for in the present Constitution and in the Law of the Houses, rules necessary for the management of their internal affairs.

ARTICLE 52. No member of either House shall be held responsible outside the respective Houses, for any opinion uttered or for any vote given in the House. When, however, a Member himself has given publicity to his opinions by public speech, by documents in print or in writing, or by any other similar means, he shall, in the matter, be amenable to the general law.

ARTICLE 53. The Members of both Houses shall, during the session, be free from arrest, unless with the consent of the House, except in cases of flagrant delicts, or of offences connected with a state of internal commotion or with a foreign trouble.

ARTICLE 54. The Ministers of State and the Delegates of the Government may, at any time, take seats and speak in either House.

Chapter IV. The Ministers of State and the Privy Council

ARTICLE 55. The respective Ministers of State shall give their advice to the Emperor, and be responsible for it.

(2) All Laws, Imperial Ordinances, and Imperial Rescripts of whatever kind, that relate to the affairs of the State, require the countersignature of a Minister of State.

ARTICLE 56. The Privy Councillors shall, in accordance with the provisions for the organization of the Privy Council, deliberate upon important matters of State, when they have been consulted by the Emperor.

Chapter V. The Judicature

ARTICLE 57. The judicature shall be exercised by the Courts of Law according to law, in the name of the Emperor.

(2) The organization of the Courts of Law shall be determined by the law.

ARTICLE 58. The judges shall be appointed from among those who possess proper qualifications according to law.

(2) No judge shall be deprived of his position, unless by way of criminal sentence or disciplinary punishment.

(3) Rules for disciplinary punishment shall be determined by law.

ARTICLE 59. Trials and judgments of a Court shall be conducted publicly. When, however, there exists any fear, that such publicity may be prejudicial to peace and order, or to the maintenance of public morality, the public trial may be suspended by provisions of law or by the decision of the Court of Law.

ARTICLE 60. All matters, that fall within the competency of a special Court, shall be specially provided for by law.

ARTICLE 61. No suit at law, which relates to rights alleged to have been infringed by the illegal measures of the administrative authorities, and which shall come within the competency of the Court of Administrative Litigation specially established by law, shall be taken cognizance of by a Court of Law.

Chapter VI. Finance

ARTICLE 62. The imposition of a new tax or the modification of the rates (of an existing one) shall be determined by law.

(2) However, all such administrative fees or other revenue having the nature of compensation shall not fall within the category of the above clause.

(3) The raising of national loans and the contracting of other liabilities to the charge of the National Treasury, except those that are provided in the Budget, shall require the consent of the Imperial Diet.

ARTICLE 63. The taxes levied at present shall, in so far as they are not remodelled by a new law, be collected according to the old system.

ARTICLE 64. The expenditure and revenue of the State require the consent of the Imperial Diet by means of an annual Budget.

(2) Any and all expenditures overpassing the appropriation set forth in the Titles and Paragraphs of the Budget, shall subsequently require the approbation of the Imperial Diet.

ARTICLE 65. The Budget shall be first laid before the House of Representatives.

ARTICLE 66. The expenditures of the Imperial House shall be defrayed every year out of the National Treasury, according to the present fixed amount for the same, and shall not require the consent thereto of the Imperial Diet, except in case an increase thereof is found necessary.

ARTICLE 67. Those already fixed expenditures based by the Constitution upon the powers appertaining to the Emperor, and such expenditures as may have arisen by the effect of law, or that appertain to the legal obligations of the Government, shall be neither rejected nor reduced by the Imperial Diet, without the concurrence of the Government.

ARTICLE 68. In order to meet special requirements, the Government may ask the consent of the Imperial Diet to a certain amount as a Continuing Expenditure Fund, for a previously fixed number of years.

ARTICLE 69. In order to supply deficiencies, which are unavoidable, in the Budget, and to meet requirements unprovided for in the same, a Reserve Fund shall be provided in the Budget.

ARTICLE 70. When the Imperial Diet cannot be convoked, owing to the external or internal condition of the country, in case of urgent need for the maintenance of public safety, the Government may take all necessary financial measures, by means of an Imperial Ordinance.

(2) In the case mentioned in the preceding clause, the matter shall be submitted to the Imperial Diet at its next session, and its approbation shall be obtained thereto.

ARTICLE 71. When the Imperial Diet has not voted on the Budget, or when the Budget has not been brought into actual existence, the Government shall carry out the Budget of the preceding year.

ARTICLE 72. The final account of the expenditures and revenues of the State shall be verified and confirmed by the Board of Audit, and it shall be submitted by the Government to the Imperial Diet, together with the report of verification of the said Board.

(2) The organization and competency of the Board of Audit shall be determined by law separately.

Chapter VII. Supplementary Rules

ARTICLE 73. When it has become necessary in future to amend the provisions of the present Constitution, a project to the effect shall be submitted to the Imperial Diet by Imperial Order.

(2) In the above case, neither House can open the debate, unless not less than two-thirds of the whole number of Members are present, and no amendment can be passed, unless a majority of not less than two-thirds of the Members present is obtained.

ARTICLE 74. No modification of the Imperial House Law shall be required to be submitted to the deliberation of the Imperial Diet.

(2) No provision of the present Constitution can be modified by the Imperial House Law.

ARTICLE 75. No modification can be introduced into the Constitution, or into the Imperial House Law, during the time of a Regency.

ARTICLE 76. Existing legal enactments, such as laws, regulations, Ordinances, or by whatever names they may be called, shall, so far as they do not conflict with the present Constitution, continue in force.

(2) All existing contracts or orders, that entail obligations upon the Government and that are connected with expenditure, shall come within the scope of Article 67.

This is the semiofficial translation, which appeared in Hirobumi Ito, *Commentaries on the Constitution of the Empire of Japan*, M. Ito (trans.), (Tokyo: Igirisu-Horitsu Gakko, 1890).

THE CONSTITUTION OF JAPAN (*NIHONKOKU KEMPO*), 1947

We, the Japanese people, acting through our duly elected representatives in the National Diet, determined that we shall secure for ourselves and our posterity the fruits of peaceful cooperation with all nations and the blessings of liberty throughout this land, and resolved that never again shall we be visited with the horrors of war through the action of government, do proclaim that sovereign power resides with the people and do firmly establish this Constitution. Government is a sacred trust of the people, the authority for which is derived from the people, the powers of which are exercised by the representatives of the people, and the benefits of which are enjoyed by the people. This is a universal principle of mankind upon which this Constitution is founded. We reject and revoke all constitutions, laws, ordinances, and rescripts in conflict herewith.

We, the Japanese people, desire peace for all time and are deeply conscious of the high ideals controlling human relationship, and we have determined to preserve our security and existence, trusting in the justice and faith of the peace-loving peoples of the world. We desire to occupy an honored place in an international society striving for the preservation of peace, and the banishment of tyranny and slavery, oppression and intolerance for all time from the earth. We recognize that all the peoples of the world have the right to live in peace, free from fear and want.

We believe that no nation is responsible to itself alone, but that laws of political morality are universal; and that obedience to such laws is incumbent upon all nations who would sustain their own sovereignty and justify their sovereign relationship with other nations.

We, the Japanese people, pledge our national honor to accomplish these high ideals and purposes with all our resources.

Chapter I. The Emperor

ARTICLE 1. The Emperor shall be the symbol of the State and of the unity of the people, deriving his position from the will of the people with whom resides sovereign power.

ARTICLE 2. The Imperial Throne shall be dynastic and succeeded to in accordance with the Imperial House Law passed by the Diet.

ARTICLE 3. The advice and approval of the Cabinet shall be required for all acts of the Emperor in matters of state, and the Cabinet shall be responsible therefor.

ARTICLE 4. The Emperor shall perform only such acts in matters of state as are provided for in this Constitution, and he shall not have powers related to government.

(2) The Emperor may delegate the performance of his acts in matters of state as provided by law.

Article 5. When, in accordance with the Imperial House Law, a Regency is established, the Regent shall perform his acts in matters of state in the Emperor's name. In this case, paragraph one of the preceding article will be applicable.

Article 6. The Emperor shall appoint the Prime Minister as designated by the Diet.

(2) The Emperor shall appoint the Chief Judge of the Supreme Court as designated by the Cabinet.

Article 7. The Emperor, with the advice and approval of the Cabinet, shall perform the following acts in matters of state on behalf of the people:

(i) Promulgation of amendments of the constitution, laws, cabinet orders, and treaties;

(ii) Convocation of the Diet;

(iii) Dissolution of the House of Representatives;

(iv) Proclamation of general election of members of the Diet;

(v) Attestation of the appointment and dismissal of Ministers of State and other officials as provided for by law, and of full powers and credentials of Ambassadors and Ministers;

(vi) Attestation of general and special amnesty, commutation of punishment, reprieve, and restoration of rights;

(vii) Awarding of honors;

(viii) Attestation of instruments of ratification and other diplomatic documents as provided for by law;

(ix) Receiving foreign ambassadors and ministers;

(x) Performance of ceremonial functions.

Article 8. No property can be given to, or received by, the Imperial House, nor can any gifts be made therefrom, without the authorization of the Diet.

Chapter II. Renunciation of War

Article 9. Aspiring sincerely to an international peace based on justice and order, the Japanese people forever renounce war as a sovereign right of the nation and the threat or use of force as a means of settling international disputes.

(2) In order to accomplish the aim of the preceding paragraph, land, sea, and air forces, as well as other war potential, will never be maintained. The right of belligerency of the state will not be recognized.

Chapter III. Rights and Duties of the People

ARTICLE 10. The conditions necessary for being a Japanese national shall be determined by law.

ARTICLE 11. The people shall not be prevented from enjoying any of the fundamental human rights. These fundamental human rights guaranteed to the people by this Constitution shall be conferred upon the people of this and future generations as eternal and inviolate rights.

ARTICLE 12. The freedoms and rights guaranteed to the people by this Constitution shall be maintained by the constant endeavor of the people, who shall refrain from any abuse of these freedoms and rights and shall always be responsible for utilizing them for the public welfare.

ARTICLE 13. All of the people shall be respected as individuals. Their right to life, liberty, and the pursuit of happiness shall, to the extent that it does not interfere with the public welfare, be the supreme consideration in legislation and in other governmental affairs.

ARTICLE 14. All of the people are equal under the law and there shall be no discrimination in political, economic, or social relations because of race, creed, sex, social status, or family origin.

(2) Peers and peerage shall not be recognized.

(3) No privilege shall accompany any award of honor, decoration, or any distinction, nor shall any such award be valid beyond the lifetime of the individual who now holds or hereafter may receive it.

ARTICLE 15. The people have the inalienable right to choose their public officials and to dismiss them.

(2) All public officials are servants of the whole community and not of any group thereof.

(3) Universal adult suffrage is guaranteed with regard to the election of public officials.

(4) In all elections, secrecy of the ballot shall not be violated. A voter shall not be answerable, publicly or privately, for the choice he has made.

ARTICLE 16. Every person shall have the right of peaceful petition for the redress of damage, for the removal of public officials, for the enactment, repeal or amendment of laws, ordinances or regulations, and for other matters, nor shall any person be in any way discriminated against for sponsoring such a petition.

ARTICLE 17. Every person may sue for redress as provided by law from the State or a public entity, in case he has suffered damage through illegal act of any public official.

ARTICLE 18. No person shall be held in bondage of any kind. Involuntary servitude, except as punishment for crime, is prohibited.

ARTICLE 19. Freedom of thought and conscience shall not be violated.

ARTICLE 20. Freedom of religion is guaranteed to all. No religious organization shall receive any privileges from the State nor exercise any political authority.

(2) No person shall be compelled to take part in any religious act, celebration, rite, or practice.

(3) The State and its organs shall refrain from religious education or any other religious activity.

ARTICLE 21. Freedom of assembly and association as well as speech, press, and all other forms of expression are guaranteed.

(2) No censorship shall be maintained, nor shall the secrecy of any means of communication be violated.

ARTICLE 22. Every person shall have freedom to choose his occupation to the extent that it does not interfere with the public welfare.

(2) Freedom of all persons to move to a foreign country and to divest themselves of their nationality shall be inviolate.

ARTICLE 23. Academic freedom is guaranteed.

ARTICLE 24. Marriage shall be based only on the mutual consent of both sexes, and it shall be maintained through mutual cooperation with the equal rights of husband and wife as a basis.

(2) With regard to choice of spouse, property rights, inheritance, choice of domicile, divorce, and other matters pertaining to marriage and the family, laws shall be enacted from the standpoint of individual dignity and the essential equality of the sexes.

ARTICLE 25. All people shall have the right to maintain the minimum standards of wholesome and cultured living.

(2) In all spheres of life, the State shall use its endeavors for the promotion and extension of social welfare and security, and of public health.

ARTICLE 26. All people shall have the right to receive an equal education corresponding to their ability, as provided by law.

(2) All people shall be obliged to have all boys and girls under their protection receive ordinary education as provided for by law. Such compulsory education shall be free.

ARTICLE 27. All people shall have the right and the obligation to work.

(2) Standards for wages, hours, rest, and other working conditions shall be fixed by law.

(3) Children shall not be exploited.

ARTICLE 28. The right of workers to organize and to bargain and act collectively is guaranteed.

ARTICLE 29. The right to own or to hold property is inviolable.

(2) Property rights shall be defined by law, in conformity with the public welfare.

(3) Private property may be taken for public use upon just compensation therefor.

ARTICLE 30. The people shall be liable to taxation as provided by law.

ARTICLE 31. No person shall be deprived of life or liberty, nor shall any other criminal penalty be imposed, except according to procedure established by law.

ARTICLE 32. No person shall be denied the right of access to the courts.

ARTICLE 33. No person shall be apprehended except upon warrant issued by a competent judicial officer which specifies the offense with which the person is charged, unless he is apprehended, the offense being committed.

ARTICLE 34. No person shall be arrested or detained without being at once informed of the charges against him or without the immediate privilege of counsel; nor shall he be detained without adequate cause; and upon demand of any person such cause must be immediately shown in open court in his presence and the presence of his counsel.

ARTICLE 35. The right of all persons to be secure in their homes, papers, and effects against entries, searches, and seizures shall not be impaired except upon warrant issued for adequate cause and particularly describing the place to be searched and things to be seized, or except as provided by Article 33.

(2) Each search or seizure shall be made upon separate warrant issued by a competent judicial officer.

ARTICLE 36. The infliction of torture by any public officer and cruel punishment are absolutely forbidden.

ARTICLE 37. In all criminal cases the accused shall enjoy the right to a speedy and public trial by an impartial tribunal.

(2) He shall be permitted full opportunity to examine all witnesses, and he shall have the right of compulsory process for obtaining witnesses on his behalf at public expense.

(3) At all times the accused shall have the assistance of competent counsel who shall, if the accused is unable to secure the same by his own efforts, be assigned to his use by the State.

ARTICLE 38. No person shall be compelled to testify against himself.

(2) Confession made under compulsion, torture, or threat, or after prolonged arrest or detention shall not be admitted in evidence.

(3) No person shall be convicted or punished in cases where the only proof against him is his own confession.

ARTICLE 39. No person shall be held criminally liable for an act which was lawful at the time it was committed, or of which he has been acquitted, nor shall he be placed in double jeopardy.

ARTICLE 40. Any person, in case he is acquitted after he has been arrested or detained, may sue the State for redress as provided by law.

Chapter IV. The Diet

ARTICLE 41. The Diet shall be the highest organ of state power, and shall be the sole law-making organ of the State.

ARTICLE 42. The Diet shall consist of two Houses, namely the House of Representatives and the House of Councillors.

ARTICLE 43. Both Houses shall consist of elected members, representative of all the people.

(2) The number of members of each House shall be fixed by law.

ARTICLE 44. The qualifications of members of both Houses and their electors shall be fixed by law. However, there shall be no discrimination because of race, creed, sex, social status, family origin, education, property, or income.

ARTICLE 45. The term of office of members of the House of Representatives shall be four years. However, the term shall be terminated before the full term is up in case the House of Representatives is dissolved.

ARTICLE 46. The term of office of members of the House of Councillors shall be six years, and election for half the members shall take place every three years.

ARTICLE 47. Electoral districts, methods of voting, and other matters pertaining to the method of election of each House shall be fixed by law.

ARTICLE 48. No person shall be permitted to be a member of both Houses simultaneously.

ARTICLE 49. Members of both Houses shall receive appropriate annual payment from the national treasury in accordance with law.

ARTICLE 50. Except in cases provided by law, members of both Houses shall be exempt from apprehension while the Diet is in session, and any members apprehended before the opening of the session shall be freed during the term of the session upon demand of the House.

ARTICLE 51. Members of both Houses shall not be held liable outside the House for speeches, debates, or votes cast inside the House.

ARTICLE 52. An ordinary session of the Diet shall be convoked once per year.

ARTICLE 53. The Cabinet may determine to convoke extraordinary sessions of the Diet. When a quarter or more of the total members of either House makes the demand, the Cabinet must determine on such convocation.

ARTICLE 54. When the House of Representatives is dissolved, there must be a general election of members of the House of Representatives within forty (40) days from the date of dissolution, and the Diet must be convoked within thirty (30) days from the date of election.

(2) When the House of Representatives is dissolved, the House of Councillors is closed at the same time. However, the Cabinet may in time of national emergency convoke the House of Councillors in emergency session.

(3) Measures taken at such session as mentioned in the proviso of the preceding paragraph shall be provisional and shall become null and void unless agreed to by the House of Representatives within a period of ten (10) days after the opening of the next session of the Diet.

ARTICLE 55. Each House shall judge disputes related to qualifications of its members. However, in order to deny a seat to any member, it is necessary to pass a resolution by a majority vote of two-thirds or more of the members present.

ARTICLE 56. Business cannot be transacted in either House unless one-third or more of total membership is present.

(2) All matters shall be decided, in each House, by a majority of those present, except as elsewhere provided in the Constitution, and in case of a tie, the presiding officer shall decide the issue.

ARTICLE 57. Deliberation in each House shall be public. However, a secret meeting may be held where a majority of two-thirds or more of those members present passes a resolution therefor.

(2) Each House shall keep a record of proceedings. This record shall be published and given general circulation, excepting such parts of proceedings of secret session as may be deemed to require secrecy.

(3) Upon demand of one-fifth or more of members present, votes of the members on any matter shall be recorded in the minutes.

ARTICLE 58. Each House shall select its own president and other officials.

(2) Each House shall establish its rules pertaining to meetings, proceedings, and internal discipline, and may punish members for disorderly conduct. However, in order to expel a member, a majority of two-thirds or more of those members present must pass a resolution thereon.

ARTICLE 59. A bill becomes a law on passage by both Houses, except as otherwise provided by the Constitution.

(2) A bill which is passed by the House of Representatives, and upon which the House of Councillors makes a decision different from that of

the House of Representatives, becomes a law when passed a second time by the House of Representatives by a majority of two-thirds or more of the members present.

(3) The provision of the preceding paragraph does not preclude the House of Representatives from calling for the meeting of a joint committee of both Houses, provided for by law.

(4) Failure of the House of Councillors to take final action within sixty (60) days after receipt of a bill passed by the House of Representatives, time in recess excepted, may be determined by the House of Representatives to constitute a rejection of the said bill by the House of Councillors.

ARTICLE 60. The Budget must first be submitted to the House of Representatives.

(2) Upon consideration of the budget, when the House of Councillors makes a decision different from that of the House of Representatives, and when no agreement can be reached even through a joint committee of both Houses, provided for by law, or in the case of failure by the House of Councillors to take final action within thirty (30) days, the period of recess excluded, after the receipt of the budget passed by the House of Representatives, the decision of the House of Representatives shall be the decision of the Diet.

ARTICLE 61. The second paragraph of the preceding article applies also to the Diet approval required for the conclusion of treaties.

ARTICLE 62. Each House may conduct investigations in relation to government, and may demand the presence and testimony of witnesses, and the production of records.

ARTICLE 63. The Prime Minister and other Ministers of State may, at any time, appear in either House for the purpose of speaking on bills, regardless of whether they are members of the House or not. They must appear when their presence is required in order to give answers or explanations.

ARTICLE 64. The Diet shall set up an impeachment court from among the members of both Houses for the purpose of trying those judges against whom removal proceedings have been instituted.

(2) Matters relating to impeachment shall be provided by law.

Chapter V. The Cabinet

ARTICLE 65. Executive power shall be vested in the Cabinet.

ARTICLE 66. The Cabinet shall consist of the Prime Minister, who shall be its head, and other Ministers of State, as provided for by law.

(2) The Prime Minister and other Ministers of State must be civilians.

(3) The Cabinet, in the exercise of executive power, shall be collectively responsible to the Diet.

ARTICLE 67. The Prime Minister shall be designated from among the members of the Diet by a resolution of the Diet. This designation shall precede all other business.

(2) If the House of Representatives and the House of Councillors disagree and if no agreement can be reached even through a joint committee of both Houses, provided for by law, or the House of Councillors fails to make designation within ten (10) days, exclusive of the period of recess, after the House of Representatives has made designation, the decision of the House of Representatives shall be the decision of the Diet.

ARTICLE 68. The Prime Minister shall appoint the Ministers of State. However, a majority of their number must be chosen from among the members of the Diet.

(2) The Prime Minister may remove the Ministers of State as he chooses.

ARTICLE 69. If the House of Representatives passes a non-confidence resolution, or rejects a confidence resolution, the Cabinet shall resign en masse, unless the House of Representatives is dissolved within ten (10) days.

ARTICLE 70. When there is a vacancy in the post of Prime Minister, or upon the first convocation of the Diet after a general election of members of the House of Representatives, the Cabinet shall resign en masse.

ARTICLE 71. In the cases mentioned in the two preceding articles, the Cabinet shall continue its functions until the time when a new Prime Minister is appointed.

ARTICLE 72. The Prime Minister, representing the Cabinet, submits bills, reports on general national affairs and foreign relations to the Diet, and exercises control and supervision over various administrative branches.

ARTICLE 73. The Cabinet, in addition to other general administrative functions, shall perform the following functions:

(i) Administer the law faithfully; conduct affairs of state;

(ii) Manage foreign affairs;

(iii) Conclude treaties. However, it shall obtain prior or, depending on the circumstances, subsequent approval of the Diet;

(iv) Administer the civil service, in accordance with standards established by law;

(v) Prepare the budget, and present it to the Diet;

(vi) Enact cabinet orders in order to execute the provisions of this Constitution and of the law. However, it cannot include penal provisions in such cabinet orders unless authorized by such law;

(vii) Decide on general amnesty, special amnesty, commutation of punishment, reprieve, and restoration of rights.

ARTICLE 74. All laws and cabinet orders shall be signed by the competent Minister of State and countersigned by the Prime Minister.

ARTICLE 75. The Ministers of State, during their tenure of office, shall not be subject to legal action without the consent of the Prime Minister. However, the right to take that action is not impaired hereby.

Chapter VI. Judiciary

ARTICLE 76. The whole judicial power is vested in a Supreme Court and in such inferior courts as are established by law.

(2) No extraordinary tribunal shall be established, nor shall any organ or agency of the Executive be given final judicial power.

(3) All judges shall be independent in the exercise of their conscience and shall be bound only by this Constitution and the laws.

ARTICLE 77. The Supreme Court is vested with the rule-making power under which it determines the rules of procedure and of practice, and of matters relating to attorneys, the internal discipline of the courts, and the administration of judicial affairs.

(2) Public procurators shall be subject to the rule-making power of the Supreme Court.

(3) The Supreme Court may delegate the power to make rules for inferior courts to such courts.

ARTICLE 78. Judges shall not be removed except by public impeachment unless judicially declared mentally or physically incompetent to perform official duties. No disciplinary action against judges shall be administered by any executive organ or agency.

ARTICLE 79. The Supreme Court shall consist of a Chief Judge and such number of judges as may be determined by law; all such judges excepting the Chief Judge shall be appointed by the Cabinet.

(2) The appointment of the judges of the Supreme Court shall be reviewed by the people at the first general election of members of the House of Representatives following their appointment, and shall be reviewed again at the first general election of members of the House of Representatives after a lapse of ten (10) years, and in the same manner thereafter.

(3) In cases mentioned in the foregoing paragraph, when the majority of voters favor the dismissal of a judge, he shall be dismissed.

(4) Matters pertaining to review shall be prescribed by law.

(5) The judges of the Supreme Court shall be retired upon the attainment of the age as fixed by law.

(6) All such judges shall receive, at regular stated intervals, adequate compensation which shall not be decreased during their terms of office.

ARTICLE 80. The judges of the inferior courts shall be appointed by the Cabinet from a list of persons nominated by the Supreme Court. All such judges shall hold office for a term of ten (10) years with privilege of reappointment, provided that they shall be retired upon the attainment of the age fixed by law.

(2) The judges of the inferior courts shall receive, at regular stated intervals, adequate compensation which shall not be decreased during their terms of office.

ARTICLE 81. The Supreme Court is the court of last resort with power to determine the constitutionality of any law, order, regulation, or official act.

ARTICLE 82. Trials shall be conducted and judgment declared publicly.

(2) Where a court unanimously determines publicity to be dangerous to public order or morals, a trial may be conducted privately, but trials of political offenses, offenses involving the press, or cases wherein the rights of people as guaranteed in Chapter III of this Constitution are in question shall always be conducted publicly

Chapter VII. Finance

ARTICLE 83. The power to administer national finances shall be exercised as the Diet shall determine.

ARTICLE 84. No new taxes shall be imposed or existing ones modified except by law or under such conditions as law may prescribe.

ARTICLE 85. No money shall be expended, nor shall the State obligate itself, except as authorized by the Diet.

ARTICLE 86. The Cabinet shall prepare and submit to the Diet for its consideration and decision a budget for each fiscal year.

ARTICLE 87. In order to provide for unforeseen deficiencies in the budget, a reserve fund may be authorized by the Diet to be expended upon the responsibility of the Cabinet.

(2) The Cabinet must get subsequent approval of the Diet for all payments from the reserve fund.

ARTICLE 88. All property of the Imperial Household shall belong to the State. All expenses of the Imperial Household shall be appropriated by the Diet in the budget.

ARTICLE 89. No public money or other property shall be expended or appropriated for the use, benefit, or maintenance of any religious institution or association, or for any charitable, educational, or benevolent enterprises not under the control of public authority.

ARTICLE 90. Final accounts of the expenditures and revenues of the State shall be audited annually by a Board of Audit and submitted by the Cabinet to the Diet, together with the statement of audit, during the fiscal year immediately following the period covered.

(2) The organization and competency of the Board of Audit shall be determined by law.

ARTICLE 91. At regular intervals and at least annually the Cabinet shall report to the Diet and the people on the state of national finances.

Chapter VIII. Local Self-Government

ARTICLE 92. Regulations concerning organization and operations of local public entities shall be fixed by law in accordance with the principle of local autonomy.

ARTICLE 93. The local public entities shall establish assemblies as their deliberative organs, in accordance with law.

(2) The chief executive officers of all local public entities, the members of their assemblies, and such other local officials as may be determined by law shall be elected by direct popular vote within their several communities.

ARTICLE 94. Local public entities shall have the right to manage their property, affairs, and administration and to enact their own regulations within law.

ARTICLE 95. A special law, applicable only to one local public entity, cannot be enacted by the Diet without the consent of the majority of the voters of the local public entity concerned, obtained in accordance with law.

Chapter IX. Amendments

ARTICLE 96. Amendments to this Constitution shall be initiated by the Diet, through a concurring vote of two-thirds or more of all the members of each House and shall thereupon be submitted to the people for ratification, which shall require the affirmative vote of a majority of all votes cast thereon, at a special referendum or at such election as the Diet shall specify.

(2) Amendments when so ratified shall immediately be promulgated by the Emperor in the name of the people, as an integral part of the Constitution.

Chapter X. Supreme Law

ARTICLE 97. The fundamental human rights by this Constitution guaranteed to the people of Japan are the fruits of the age-old struggle of man to be free; they have survived the many exacting tests for durability and are conferred upon this and future generations in trust, to be held for all time inviolate.

ARTICLE 98. The Constitution shall be the supreme law of the nation and no law, ordinance, imperial rescript, or other act of government, or part thereof, contrary to the provisions hereof, shall have legal force or validity.

(2) The treaties concluded by Japan and established laws of nations shall be faithfully observed.

ARTICLE 99. The Emperor or the Regent as well as Ministers of State, members of the Diet, judges, and all other public officials have the obligation to respect and uphold this Constitution.

Chapter XI. Supplementary Provisions

ARTICLE 100. This Constitution shall be enforced as from the day when the period of six months will have elapsed counting from the day of its promulgation.

(2) The enactment of laws necessary for the enforcement of this Constitution, the election of members of the House of Councillors, and the procedure for the convocation of the Diet and other preparatory procedures for the enforcement of this Constitution may be executed before the day prescribed in the preceding paragraph.

ARTICLE 101. If the House of Councillors is not constituted before the effective date of this Constitution, the House of Representatives shall function as the Diet until such time as the House of Councillors shall be constituted.

ARTICLE 102. The term of office for half of the members of the House of Councillors serving in the first term under this Constitution shall be three years. Members falling under this category shall be determined in accordance with law.

ARTICLE 103. The Ministers of State, members of the House of Representatives, and judges in office on the effective date of this Constitution, and all other public officials, who occupy positions corresponding to such positions as are recognized by this Constitution shall not forfeit their positions automatically on account of the enforcement of this Constitution unless otherwise specified by law. When, however, successors are elected or appointed under the provisions of this Constitution, they shall forfeit their positions as a matter of course.

THE POTSDAM DECLARATION, JULY 26, 1945

Proclamation by the Heads of Governments, United States, China, and the United Kingdom. *Department of State Bulletin* 13, no. 307 (July 29, 1945): 137–138.

(1) We, the President of the United States, the President of the National Republic of China, and the Prime Minister of Great Britain, representing the hundreds of millions of our countrymen, have conferred and agree that Japan shall be given an opportunity to end this war.

(2) The prodigious land, sea, and air forces of the United States, the British Empire, and of China, many times reinforced by their armies and air fleets from the west are poised to strike the final blows upon Japan. This military power is sustained and inspired by the determination of all the Allied Nations to prosecute the war against Japan until she ceases to resist.

(3) The result of the futile and senseless German resistance to the might of the aroused free peoples of the world stands forth in awful clarity as an example to the people of Japan. The might that now converges on Japan is immeasurably greater than that which, when applied to the resisting Nazis, necessarily laid waste to the lands, the industry, and the method of life of the whole German people. The full application of our military power, backed by our resolve, will mean the inevitable and complete destruction of the Japanese armed forces and just as inevitably the utter devastation of the Japanese homeland.

(4) The time has come for Japan to decide whether she will continue to be controlled by those self-willed militaristic advisers whose unintelligent calculations have brought the Empire of Japan to the threshold of annihilation, or whether she will follow the path of reason.

(5) Following are our terms. We will not deviate from them. There are no alternatives. We shall brook no delay.

(6) There must be eliminated for all time the authority and influence of those who have deceived and misled the people of Japan into embarking on world conquest, for we insist that a new order of peace, security, and justice will be impossible until irresponsible militarism is driven from the world.

(7) Until such a new order is established and until there is convincing proof that Japan's war-making power is destroyed, points in Japanese territory to be designated by the Allies shall be occupied to secure the achievement of the basic objectives we are herewith setting forth.

(8) The terms of the Cairo Declaration shall be carried out and Japanese sovereignty shall be limited to the islands of Honshu, Hokkaido, Kyushu, Shikoku, and such minor islands as we determine.

(9) The Japanese military forces, after being completely disarmed, shall be permitted to return to their homes with the opportunity to lead peaceful and productive lives.

(10) We do not intend that the Japanese shall be enslaved as a race or destroyed as a nation, but stern justice shall be meted out to all war criminals, including those who have visited cruelties upon our prisoners. The Japanese government shall remove all obstacles to the revival and strengthening of democratic tendencies among the Japanese people. Freedom of speech, of religion, and of thought, as well as respect for fundamental human rights shall be established.

(11) Japan shall be permitted to maintain such industries as will sustain her economy and permit the exaction of just reparations in kind, but not those industries which would enable her to re-arm for war. To this end, access to, as distinguished from control of raw materials shall be permitted. Eventual Japanese participation in world trade relations shall be permitted.

(12) The occupying forces of the Allies shall be withdrawn from Japan as soon as these objectives have been accomplished and there has been established in accordance with the freely expressed will of the Japanese people a peacefully inclined and responsible government.

(13) We call upon the Government of Japan to proclaim now the unconditional surrender of all the Japanese armed forces, and to provide proper and adequate assurances of their good faith in such action. The alternative for Japan is prompt and utter destruction.

HARRY S. TRUMAN, WINSTON CHURCHILL, CHIANG K'AI-SHEK

UNITED STATES INITIAL POST-SURRENDER POLICY
FOR JAPAN, 1945

Purpose of This Document

This document is a statement of general initial policy relating to Japan after surrender. It has been approved by the President and distributed to the Supreme Commander for the Allied Powers and the appropriate U.S. departments and agencies for their guidance. It does not deal with all matters relating to the occupation of Japan requiring policy determinations. Such matters as are not included or are not fully covered herein have been or will be dealt with separately.

Part I. Ultimate Objectives

The ultimate objectives of the United States in regard to Japan, to which policies in the initial period must conform are:

(a) To insure that Japan will not again become a menace to the United States or to the peace and security of the world.

(b) To bring about the eventual establishment of a peaceful and responsible government which will respect the rights of other states and will support the objectives of the United States as reflected in the ideals and principles of the Charter of the United Nations. The United States desires that this government should conform as closely as may be to principles of democratic self-government, but it is not the responsibility of the Allied Powers to impose upon Japan any form of government not supported by the freely expressed will of the people.

These objectives will be achieved by the following means:

(a) Japan's sovereignty will be limited to the islands of Honshu, Hokkaido, Kyushu, Shikoku, and such minor outlying islands as may be determined, in accordance with the Cairo Declaration and other agreements to which the United States is or may be a party.

(b) Japan will be completely disarmed and demilitarized. The authority of the militarists and the influence of militarism will be totally eliminated from her political, economic, and social life. Institutions expressive of the spirit of militarism and aggression will be vigorously suppressed.

(c) The Japanese people shall be encouraged to develop a desire for individual liberties and respect for fundamental human rights, particularly the freedom of religion, assembly, speech, and the press. They shall be encouraged to form democratic and representative organizations.

(d) The Japanese people shall be afforded opportunity to develop for themselves an economy which will permit the peacetime requirements of the population to be met.

Part II. Allied Authority

1. MILITARY OCCUPATION

There will be a military occupation of the Japanese home islands to carry into effect the surrender terms and further the achievement of the ultimate objectives stated above. The occupation shall have the character of an operation in behalf of the principal Allied Powers acting in the interests of the United Nations at war with Japan. For that reason, participation of the forces of other nations that have taken a leading part in the war against Japan will be welcome and expected. The occupation forces will be under the command of a Supreme Commander designated by the United States.

Although every effort will be made, by consultation and by constitution of appropriate advisory bodies, to establish policies for the conduct of the occupation and control of Japan which will satisfy the principal Allied Powers, in the event of any differences of opinion among them the policies of the United States will govern.

2. RELATIONSHIP TO JAPANESE GOVERNMENT

The authority of the Emperor and the Japanese Government will be subject to the Supreme Commander, who will possess all powers necessary to effectuate the surrender terms and to carry out the policies established for the conduct of the occupation and the control of Japan.

In view of the present character of Japanese society and the desire of the United States to attain its objectives with a minimum commitment of its forces and resources, the Supreme Commander will exercise his authority through Japanese governmental machinery and agencies, including the Emperor, to the extent that this satisfactorily furthers United States objectives. The Japanese Government will be permitted, under his instructions, to exercise the normal powers of government in matters of domestic administration. This policy, however, will be subject to the right and duty of the Supreme Commander to require changes in governmental machinery or personnel or to act directly if the Emperor or other Japanese authority does not satisfactorily meet the requirements of the Supreme Commander in effectuating the surrender terms.

This policy, moreover, does not commit the Supreme Commander to support the Emperor or any other governmental authority in opposition to evolutionary changes looking toward the attainment of United States objectives. The policy is to use the existing form of Government in Japan, not to support it. Changes in the form of Japanese Government initiated by the Japanese people or government in the direction of modifying its feudal and authoritarian tendencies are to be permitted and favored. In the event that the effectuation of such changes involves the use of force by the Japanese people or government against persons opposed thereto, the Supreme Commander should intervene only where necessary to ensure the security of his forces and the attainment of all other objectives of the occupation.

3. PUBLICITY AS TO POLICIES

The Japanese people, and the world at large, shall be kept fully informed of the objectives and policies of the occupation, and of progress made in their fulfillment.

Part III. Political

1. DISARMAMENT AND DEMILITARIZATION

Disarmament and demilitarization are the primary tasks of the military occupation and shall be carried out promptly and with determination. Every effort shall be made to bring home to the Japanese people the part played by the military and naval leaders, and those who collaborated with them, in bringing about the existing and future distress of the people.

Japan is not to have an army, navy, air force, secret police organization, or any civil aviation. Japan's ground, air, and naval forces shall be disarmed and disbanded and the Japanese Imperial General Headquarters, the General Staff, and all secret police organizations shall be dissolved. Military and naval material, military, naval, and civilian aircraft shall be surrendered and shall be disposed of as required by the Supreme Commander.

High officials of the Japanese Imperial General Headquarters, and General Staff, other high military and naval officials of the Japanese Government, leaders of ultra-nationalist and militaristic organizations, and other important exponents of militarism and aggression will be taken into custody and held for future disposition. Persons who have been active exponents of militarism and militant nationalism will be removed and excluded from public office and from any other positions of public or substantial private responsibility. Ultra-nationalistic or militaristic social, political, professional, and commercial societies and institutions will be dissolved and prohibited.

Militarism and ultra-nationalism, in doctrine and practice, including para-military training, shall be eliminated from the educational system. Former career military and naval officers, both commissioned and non-commissioned, and all other exponents of militarism and ultra-nationalism shall be excluded from supervisory and teaching positions.

2. WAR CRIMINALS

Persons charged by the Supreme Commander or appropriate United Nations Agencies with being war criminals, including those charged with having visited cruelties upon United Nations prisoners or other nationals, shall be arrested, tried, and, if convicted, punished. Those wanted by another of the United Nations for offense against its nationals shall, if not wanted for trial or as witnesses or otherwise by the Supreme Commander, be turned over to the custody of such other nation.

3. ENCOURAGEMENT OF DESIRE FOR INDIVIDUAL LIBERTIES AND DEMOCRATIC PROCESSES

Freedom of religious worship shall be proclaimed promptly on occupation. At the same time it should be made plain to the Japanese that ultra-nationalistic and militaristic organizations and movements will not be permitted to hide behind the cloak of religion.

The Japanese people shall be afforded opportunity and encouraged to become familiar with the history, institutions, culture, and the accomplishments of the United States and other democracies. Association of personnel of the occupation forces with the Japanese people should be controlled, only to the extent necessary, to further the policies and objectives of the occupation.

Democratic political parties, with rights of assembly and public discussion, shall be encouraged, subject to the necessity for maintaining the security of the occupying forces.

Laws, decrees, and regulations which establish discriminations on the grounds of race, nationality, creed, or political opinion shall be abrogated; those which conflict with the objectives and policies outlined in this document shall be repealed, suspended, or amended as required; and agencies charged specifically with their enforcement shall be abolished or appropriately modified. Persons unjustly confined by Japanese authorities on political grounds shall be released. The judicial, legal, and police systems shall be reformed as soon as practicable to conform with the policies set forth in Articles 1 and 3 of this Part III and thereafter shall be progressively influenced, to protect individual liberties and human rights.

Part IV. Economic (excerpts only)

1. ECONOMIC DEMILITARIZATION

The existing economic basis of Japanese military strength must be destroyed and not be permitted to revive. . . .

2. PROMOTION OF DEMOCRATIC FORCES

Encouragement shall be given and favor shown to the development of organizations in labor, industry, and agriculture, organized on a democratic basis. Policies shall be favored which permit a wide distribution of incomes and of the ownership of the means of production and trade. . . .

3. RESUMPTION OF PEACEFUL ECONOMIC ACTIVITY

The policies of Japan have brought down upon the people great economic destruction and confronted them with the prospect of economic difficulty and suffering. The plight of Japan is the direct outcome of its own behavior, and the Allies will not undertake the burden of repairing the damage. It can be repaired only if the Japanese people renounce all military aims and apply themselves diligently and with single purpose to the ways of peaceful living. It will be necessary for them to undertake physical reconstruction, deeply to reform the nature and direction of their economic activities and institutions, and to find useful employment for their people along lines adapted to and devoted to peace. The Allies have no intention of imposing conditions which would prevent the accomplishment of these tasks in due time. . . .

(The remaining six sections, which deal with narrowly economic issues, are omitted.)

Source: Department of State Bulletin 13, no. 326 (September 23, 1945).

THE DECLARATION OF IMPERIAL HUMANITY (*NINGEN SENGEN*), JANUARY 1, 1946

Today we greet the New Year. My thought goes back to the beginning of the Meiji Era when Emperor Meiji proclaimed the Five Clauses of the Charter-Oath as the basis of our national policy. It reads:

1. Deliberative assemblies on a wide scope shall be convened, and all matters of government decided by public opinion.
2. Both the high and the low shall with a unity of purpose vigorously engage in the conduct of public affairs.
3. All the common people, no less than the servants of the state, civil and military, shall be enabled to fulfill each his just aspirations, lest discontent should infect their minds.
4. All the evil practices of the past shall be eliminated, and the nation shall abide by the universal rules of justice and equity.
5. Wisdom and knowledge shall be sought throughout the world to promote the prosperity of the Empire.

What more need be added to these open and lofty precepts? By reaffirming the Oath, I desire to direct the future course of our national fortunes. It is my wish that on the lines so indicated, old abuses shall be discarded, full play be allowed to popular will, all officials and people be wholeheartedly given to the pursuit of peace, and enriched culture and learning be attained, and the standards of living of the people be elevated. Thus shall a new Japan be constructed.

Devastations wrought by the war upon our cities and towns, the miseries of its victims, the stagnation of industries, the shortages of food, and the great and growing numbers of the unemployed are sorely heartrending. But as long as the nation faces indomitably the present ordeal, remains firm in its determination to seek civilization consistently in peace, and preserves the perfect accord to the end, there is no doubt but that a glorious prospect will be revealed not only for our country, but for the whole humanity.

Love of the family and love of the country are particularly strong in our land. With no less devotion should we extend this spirit, and dedicate ourselves to the love of mankind.

The protracted war having ended in defeat, our people are liable to become restive or to fall into utter despondency. The extremist tendencies appear to be gradually spreading, and the sense of morality is markedly losing its hold on the people. In effect, there are signs of confusion of thought, and the existing situation causes me deep concern.

I stand by my people. I am ever ready to share in their joys and sorrows. The ties between me and my people have always been formed by mutual trust and affection. They do not depend upon mere legends or myths. Nor are they predicated on the false conception that the Emperor is divine, and that the Japanese are superior to other races and destined to rule the world.

My government will leave no stone unturned to alleviate the trials and tribulations of the people. At the same time, I trust that my people will rise to the occasion, and strive courageously for the development of industry and culture as well as for the solution of their more immediate problems. If in their civic life my people maintain solidarity, practice mutual aid and assistance, and foster the spirit of broad tolerance, they will prove themselves worthy of their best traditions. In this manner, our nation will undoubtedly render a signal contribution toward the welfare and advancement of mankind.

The planning for the year is made at its commencement. I confidently hope that my beloved people will unite with me in my present resolve, and that they will dauntlessly and unflinchingly march onward for the accomplishment of the great undertaking which now confronts the nation.

Source: Foreign Relations of the United States 8 (1946): 134–135, the official translation.

Index

About the Authors

Lawrence Ward Beer was born in Portland, Oregon, on May 11, 1932, the second of four children of Norman H. Beer, an exporter of the rare figured woods of the Northwest, and Lucile H. Hodges Beer, managing secretary for a national lumber company. From 1950 until 1961 Beer was a student Jesuit. As such he received an A.B. degree in English literature and philosophy (1956), studied the Greek and Roman classics, and earned an M.A. in philosophy (1957) from Gonzaga University. After taking courses on Japanese economics and anthropology at Fordham University in summer of 1957, he went to Japan for four years where he completed an intensive two-year study of Japan's language and culture. He also taught English as a foreign language and philosophy at Sophia University in Tokyo. In 1960 he was a close observer of the so-called Security Treaty Crisis, a massive democratic movement. That direct experience of Japan's politics, along with the inspiration the Kennedy presidential campaign generated among minority Americans, marked the beginning of Beer's interest in government and politics.

While in Tokyo he introduced the credit union movement into Japan as a modest means of alleviating poverty among ragpickers. That involvement with credit unions, three summers during high school working on a railroad gang, and a year as a training director for the California Credit

Union League in 1961–1962 confirmed Beer's lasting special interest in socioeconomic human rights. His first book, co-edited with Colin Chilton, was *Credit Union Family Financial Counseling* (Oakland: California Credit Union League, and Madison: Credit Union National Association, 1962).

In 1961 Beer married Keiko Harada. Their four children have both Japanese and Anglo-American names; half of Beer's relatives are Japanese. Although they have represented a wide range of occupations and viewpoints, they have enjoyably taught him much about Japan. The main house of the samurai Harada family has been in the Nagano mountains since 1585, to which they escaped after losing the feudal wars.

In 1962, with the guidance of John M. Maki and Dan Fenno Henderson at the University of Washington—leading scholars of Japan's law and constitution—Beer decided to specialize in Japan's constitutional law. He received a Ph.D. in political science in 1966.

Beer has spent over ten years in Japan, teaching, lecturing, and conducting research at various schools—mainly at the Faculty of Law of the University of Tokyo. Beginning with Professors Ito Masami and Sato Isao, he has been generously helped by Japanese constitutional lawyers, judges, and attorneys. His approach to research has been governed by the simple guideline that one should learn, through writings in the vernacular and in person, from those who know most about Japan's constitutional law. His goal has been to communicate cross-culturally about Japan's (and Asia's) constitutional law and constitutionalism for readers of English, not just Americans. Part of this project has been to publish English-language translations of authoritative Japanese judicial decisions, as John Maki and a few others have done. The result has been two books with Hiroshi Itoh and other colleagues, *The Constitutional Case Law of Japan: Selected Supreme Court Decisions, 1961–70* (1978) and *The Constitutional Case Law of Japan, 1970 Through 1990* (1996), both from the University of Washington Press in Seattle.

But cases, however important, are only part of constitutional law and constitutionalism, and both need to be seen in a comparative and interdisciplinary context. To illustrate, Beer wrote the comprehensive volume *Freedom of Expression in Japan: A Study in Comparative Law, Politics and Society* (Tokyo: Kodansha International, 1984). To further comparative understanding of constitutionalism in Asia and in commemoration of the bicentennials of the U.S. Declaration of Independence, Constitution, and Bill of Rights, Beer published *Constitutionalism in Asia: Asian Views of the American Influence* (Berkeley: University of California Press, 1979; published in Japanese with the help of Sato Isao) and *Constitutional Systems in Late Twentieth Century Asia* (Seattle: University of Washington Press, 1992).

Central to Beer's continuing research have been introductions to leading jurists by many Japanese friends and continuing consultation with
Japanese constitutional lawyers who are deeply knowledgeable regarding
both the law and the context of Japan's living constitution.

John McGilvrey Maki was born November 19, 1909, in Tacoma, Washington. According to his birth certificate, acquired some years later, his
birth name was Hiroo Sugiyama, reflecting the fact that his parents were
Japanese immigrants. From a few weeks of age he was cared for and later
adopted by an American family, the McGilvreys. As a result he was completely Euro-American in cultural terms and knew virtually nothing of
the land of his parents.

He received his B.A. in English from the University of Washington in
1932. After completing the requirements for an M.A. in English at the
same institution, his interest shifted to Japanese literature, and he received
a Japanese government fellowship to study the Japanese language (to which
he had received an introduction as an undergraduate), literature, and history in Tokyo. The two and a half years (late 1936 to early 1939) provided
him with the basic skill to read the language, literature, and history—the
foundation for an academic career. But it also gave him the opportunity
to live under and observe a militaristic and authoritarian Japan under the
strain of the early years of its war with China. This experience gave him
unplanned and unknowing preparation for his wartime job in Washington, D.C.

After Pearl Harbor he continued to teach at the University of Washington until May 15, 1942, when he, his wife, Mary, and the rest of the
Seattle Japanese community were sent to the Western Washington State
Fairgrounds, the "assembly center." A month later they were released so
he could accept a position with the Foreign Broadcast Intelligence Service
of the Federal Communications Commission. His initial job in Washington was to analyze Tokyo's foreign and domestic radio broadcasts. In
1943 he transferred to the Office of War Information, where he became
involved in psychological warfare against Japan.

During the war he wrote his first book, *Japanese Militarism: Its Cause
and Cure* (New York: Alfred A. Knopf, 1945). The "cause" involved a historical analysis of the roots of militarism, and the "cure" was what the war
victors would have to do to eliminate the causes. That book is the foundation for the treatment of the Meiji Constitution and its ending in this book.

In February 1946 Maki arrived in Tokyo for six months of service as a
civilian assigned to the Government Section, General Headquarters,

Supreme Commander for the Allied Powers. His main tasks were to investigate the authoritarian ministries of Home Affairs and Education, along with other agencies, and to recommend changes in the government structure that would block the rebirth of the authoritarian militarist system dismantled during the occupation. Some of his recommendations were eventually put into effect.

Maki returned to the United States, where he received a Ph.D. in political science from Harvard University (his wartime work had shifted his interest from Japanese literature to its government and politics). He then returned to the University of Washington to resume his academic career.

His 1958–1959 sabbatical leave on a Fulbright fellowship in Tokyo focused his research interest on Japan's constitution. His project was to translate Japanese Supreme Court decisions on constitutional issues. With the collaboration of an American professor and two young scholars—one Australian and one Japanese—he published *Court and Constitution in Japan* (Seattle: University of Washington Press, 1962).

He also learned that in 1957 the Diet had created the Commission on the Constitution, charged with conducting and reporting on a massive investigation of the present constitution. He followed its work closely, and when it issued its lengthy final report in 1964, he resolved to translate it. Eventually, the translation was published under the title *Japan's Commission on the Constitution: The Final Report* (Seattle: University of Washington Press, 1980).

Some years after his retirement he decided to set down his thoughts about both the old and the new constitutions. The result was an essay of awkward length, too long to be a journal article and too short to be a book. A longtime friend of both present authors reacted favorably to the essay, and Maki was struck by a happy thought: Why not ask Beer, his student thirty-five years ago who had become a foremost authority on Japan's constitution, to collaborate on a book? Beer, recently retired and still not completely recovered from producing several massive books over the years, agreed on condition that it be a short book. This is it.